VISIONARIES

of the 20th Century

Visionaries

of the 20th Century

A Resurgence Anthology

Edited by Satish Kumar and Freddie Whitefield

GREEN BOOKS

First published in 2006
by Green Books Ltd
Foxhole, Dartington
Totnes, Devon TQ9 6EB
www.greenbooks.co.uk

Most photographs have been provided by the authors, or by the visionaries themselves
or their organisations, with the following exceptions: Peter Brook by Martine Francke,
courtesy of Magnum Photos; Joseph Campbell, courtesy of the Joseph Campbell
Foundation; Rachel Carson, courtesy of Erich Hartmann/Magnum; G. K. Chesterton,
courtesy of Howard Costner/National Portrait Gallery; Jacques Cousteau by Elliott Erwitt,
courtesy of Magnum Photos; Buckminster Fuller, courtesy of the Estate of R. Buckminster
Fuller; Edward Goldsmith, courtesy of Anne-Katrin Purkiss; Mary Harris ('Mother Jones')
photograph courtesy of Terence Vincent Powderly Photographs, The American Catholic
History Research Center and University Archives at The Catholic University of America;
Robert Hart, courtesy of Fransje de Waard; Ted Hughes, courtesy of Allen & Unwin
Publishers; J. M. Keynes, courtesy Dr Milo Keynes; Martin Luther King, photograph by
Isador Knox; Jiddu Krishnamurti, courtesy of Mark Edwards; Kumarappa, drawing by
K. M. Natarajan; D. H. Lawrence, photograph by Ernesto Guardia; José Lutzenberger,
courtesy of Susan Cunningham; Joanna Macy, courtesy of Hanna Morjan; Jerry Mander,
courtesy of Mikkel Aaland; Lynn Margulis, courtesy of Louis Rico; Peter Matthiessen,
courtesy of Vintage Books USA; Thomas Merton, photograph by Sibylle Akers, used with
permission of the Merton Legacy Trust and the Thomas Merton Center, Bellarmine
University; Raimon Panikkar, courtesy of Raimon Strahlender; Carlo Petrini, courtesy of
Foto Alberto Peroli; R. D. Laing, courtesy of Dorothee von Greiff; Theodore Roszak,
photograph by Gilles Mingasson for Figaro Magazine; Aruna Roy, courtesy of First City;
Arundhati Roy, courtesy of Pradip Krishen; Viktor Schauberger, copyright PKS;
E. F. Schumacher, courtesy of Sophie Baker; Aung San Suu Kyi, courtesy of Alison Wright
Photography; Thich Nhat Hanh, courtesy of Nang Sao; Thomas Merton, Merton Centre;
John & Nancy Todd, Kate Mount; Terry Tempest Williams, courtesy of Mark Babushkin;
Frank Lloyd Wright, courtesy of the Frank Lloyd Wright Foundation.

Design by Rick Lawrence, Samskara Design

Printed by MPG Books, Bodmin, Cornwall, UK
on Revive Matt paper (75% recycled)

British Library Cataloguing in Publication Data
available on request

ISBN-10: 1 903998 86 7
ISBN-13: 978 1 903998 86 1

CONTENTS

ECOLOGICAL VISIONARIES

SOCIAL VISIONARIES

CONTENTS

SOCIAL VISIONARIES (continued)

SPIRITUAL VISIONARIES

INTRODUCTION

The twentieth century was a century of wars: wars within human societies as well as a war on nature. These two kinds of war are not unrelated. The mindset of conquering, controlling, dominating and subjugating others for one's own narrow self-interest leads to wars. Millions of human beings were killed in these wars; and human beings have also wrought havoc on the natural world, causing the extinction of species, the destruction of biodiversity, the depletion of natural capital and the diminishment of atmospheric sustainability, leading to climate change and global warming.

Of course the power of money, the media and the military has been directed to wage and sustain these two kinds of war. Yet throughout the twentieth century there were individuals who saw the folly of such human arrogance. These visionaries raised their voices, often at great personal cost to themselves. They were often ignored, and worst of all, suppressed, imprisoned and tortured. But nevertheless they were the salt of the earth: they kept the torch of humanity burning, they gave hope to millions, and they restored confidence in the enduring human qualities of compassion, generosity, harmony, reverence and peace. They also achieved concrete results, such as the end of colonialism and the development of sustainable lifestyles. It is thanks to them that now we have a thriving social justice and earth justice movement around the world.

Towards the second half of the twentieth century *Resurgence* magazine was launched to give voice to these visionaries, and remind people that small inner voices have more power than might first appear. *Resurgence* presented a vision of society articulated by these great thinkers and activists who believed that all wars on humans and on nature are ultimately futile. *Resurgence* advocated that another world—a world of mutuality, reciprocity and solidarity—is possible; and that a world of sustainability, spirituality and frugality is more joyful than the world of consumerism, materialism and militarism.

Out of a long list of strong contenders, we have selected one hundred visionaries for this book who have made the greatest impact in creating and projecting a holistic world-view, where creativity, imagination and human well-being should be the basis of social, political and economic activities. The list is naturally subjective—there are many other visionaries who could have been included in this book. It is a list of those who have influenced the ethos of *Resurgence*, have been featured in its pages, and have made a profound impression on the magazine.

We offer this anthology to the world in the hope that the twenty-first century could be different. It could be the century of peace and ecology, a century of co-operation rather than conflict, a century of mutual respect rather than condemnation, and a century of living in harmony with the natural world rather than the endless exploitation of the earth.

We would like to give our special thanks to Kate Hartgroves for her help in researching, preparing and co-ordinating this book.

Satish Kumar
Freddie Whitefield
Hartland, September 2006

ECOLOGICAL VISIONARIES

"Evolution is a tightly coupled dance, with life and the material environment as partners. From the dance emerges the entity Gaia."

—James Lovelock

RACHEL CARSON
Earth Scientist

"The 'control of nature' is a phrase conceived in arrogance, born of the Neanderthal age of biology and the convenience of man."

"We stand now where two roads diverge. But unlike the roads in Robert Frost's familiar poem, they are not equally fair. The road we have long been travelling is deceptively easy, a smooth superhighway on which we progress with great speed, but at its end lies disaster. The other fork of the road—the one less travelled by—offers our last, our only chance to reach a destination that assures the preservation of the earth."

I N 1962, A POWERFUL GROUP of chemical industry representatives, government officials and salaried 'experts' on the environment set out to prevent the publication of the book of a much-loved naturalist. The naturalist in question was Rachel Carson; the book, *Silent Spring*. Carson placed herself—her reputation, her failing health—in the path of the juggernaut that, at the time, everyone still blithely referred to

as 'progress'—and she slowed it a little.

The narrowest of the book's objectives—a review of the aerial spraying of DDT over American towns, farmlands and forests—was achieved, and government policy on pesticides was significantly altered. Its wider objective—to radicalise our thinking about our relationship with the natural world—was barely recognised. At the same time, the storm of controversy and argument it provoked set the tone for our environmental debates for much of the forty-three years since its publication: debates that rarely address the most fundamental principles of Carson's thinking.

For Carson, what the twentieth century demanded was a new way of thinking about the world. She demanded not just an end to indiscriminate pesticide use, but a new science, a new philosophy. "The 'control of nature' is a phrase conceived in arrogance," she said at the conclusion of *Silent Spring*, "born of the Neanderthal age of biology and philosophy, when it was supposed that nature exists for the convenience of man."

Carson did not want to write *Silent Spring*. True, she was painfully aware of the indiscriminate use of pesticides, and had proposed articles on the problem to the magazines that she was writing for, as far back as the late 1940s, but *Silent Spring* was in many ways not her kind of project. In her great sea trilogy, *Under the Sea Wind*, *The Sea Around Us* and *The Edge of the Sea*, a singular voice emerges, at once rigorous and lyrical, a voice she had come to know as her own. It was not, in so many ways, the right voice for a 'crusading' book on DDT.

Silent Spring was published in September 1962. It would be a mistake to see it simply as a book about pesticides, though that was how it was quickly characterised by its opponents, who wanted to portray Carson as anti-chemicals and hence anti-progress.

In fact, some of Carson's best writing goes into the book, as she carries her readers along with the argument. Most of all, she wanted people to see the background to the problem with DDT. Carson is a careful guide through the complex web of political and fiscal shenanigans, explaining to a public that would have known almost nothing about biological as opposed to chemical pest control, exactly how government and other bodies manipulated the figures to make the biological option always seem 'too expensive'.

This alone makes *Silent Spring* a towering achievement. Carson makes the necessary case against DDT, but on the way she exposes the entire system. As Paul Brookes notes, in his excellent study of her work, *The House of Life*, "She was questioning not only the indiscriminate use of poisons but the basic irresponsibility of an industrialised, technological society toward the natural world."

The response from that society was not long in coming. Soon the men in grey were creeping out from behind their reports and balance sheets, ready to attack. Every effort was made to suppress or vilify the book, not only by chemical companies such as Monsanto and the National Agricultural Chemicals Association, but also by government departments, the Nutrition Foundation and even baby-food producers.

It made no difference. Carson was well prepared for the attacks; and not only would she not be intimidated, she even refused to go out of her way to defend her position, saying that the book could look after itself.

Meanwhile, the public, and most of the popular press, loved *Silent Spring*. It became a best-seller, a talking point in factories and drawing rooms, the subject of hundreds of newspaper articles, parodies, cartoons and debates. More importantly it reached the office of John F. Kennedy, who asked his scientific adviser to begin a study into the whole DDT question. A pesticides committee was set up, and it quickly produced a report criticising the chemical companies and endorsing Carson's views. Something had been achieved.

But only a little. Testifying to that same committee in June 1963, Carson took the opportunity to remind the world of the wider implications of her work: "We still talk in terms of conquest. We still haven't become mature enough to think of ourselves as only a tiny part of a vast and incredible universe. Man's attitude towards nature is today critically important simply because we have now acquired a fateful power to destroy nature. But man is part of nature and his war against nature is inevitably a war against himself."

It is over forty years since that statement. Spring has become a little more silent with each passing year. The skylarks and warblers that used to be so plentiful in our countryside are vanishing, especially on those big, 'profitable' farms the government seems to favour.

John Burnside

JAMES LOVELOCK
Gaian Scientist

*"Evolution is a tightly coupled dance, with life
and the material environment as partners.
From the dance emerges the entity Gaia."*

*"We have given Gaia a fever and soon her condition will
worsen to a state like a coma. She has been there before
and recovered, but it took more than 100,000 years.
We are responsible and will suffer the consequences."*

*"A billion could live off the earth; six billion living as we do
is far too many, and you run out of planet in no time."*

"An inefficient virus kills its host. A clever virus stays with it."

JAMES LOVELOCK INVENTED the electron capture detector. You may never have heard of it, but you know well the world it made. This subtle and immensely sensitive pollution sniffer, the size of a matchbox, allowed environmental scientists for the first time to spot tiny amounts of dangerous toxins.

Using his sniffer, Lovelock explored the world. He discovered the global spread of ozone-eating CFCs in the atmosphere. Others used it to track PCBs and pesticides in our food, in air and water and in living organisms worldwide. Lovelock's widget virtually launched modern environmental sciences.

But his greatest invention is intellectual—a brilliant, entirely original and immensely persuasive vision of the way our world works, known as Gaia.

Gaia is where cosmology and biology, palaeontology and computer sciences meet to address the question: why are we here? Why has life thrived on planet Earth? Why Earth and not Mars? How come this planet is just so damn nice?

But Lovelock seeks the answers not in the conventional scientific way, by breaking things down into little bits to see how they work. He says they don't work as little bits, but only as a grand whole—Gaia.

In the labs and senior common rooms you can hear them mutter: this isn't science, it's a New Age religion. Lovelock says the science establishment has lost the plot. They have forgotten that science is about seeing the whole, not peering down ever more powerful microscopes. In the jargon, he is holistic, while they are reductionist.

Old notions about life on Earth—implicit still in almost every school textbook—hold that living things evolved simply by adapting to their environment. But this was nonsense. Life fundamentally influenced its own environment. What is more, its influence seemed to be strong enough to maintain stable conditions over hundreds of millions of years, even though the chemistry of the atmosphere was itself very unstable.

It could even apparently respond to outside events. The atmosphere's temperature, for instance, had barely changed during a period when the Sun had grown 25 per cent hotter. If that extra heat had been transferred to the planet's surface without dampening, we would all long since have fried. A lucky chance? The more Lovelock thought, the more unlikely that seemed. We don't get that lucky—such constancy required the existence of an active control system. Life on Earth is controlling its environment for its own good. Crazy? Well, how else do you explain it?

The novelist William Golding soon afterwards coined for Lovelock the name Gaia, after the Greek Earth goddess. And a hypothesis was born, edging into the scientific literature through obscure journals. But making it from the scientific fringe to the top tables proved harder. For many years, journals such as *Nature* and *Science* refused Gaian papers. Even now, Gaia is the science that dare not speak its name. In the journals, it usually masquerades under the deadening title of 'geophysiology'.

But, inspired by the Gaian model of the world, scientists are seeking and finding some of the switches that may operate Gaian control systems such as the planetary thermostat. Here are two. We know that if it gets warmer, bacteria in soils work faster and speed up the weathering of rocks. That weathering absorbs carbon dioxide from the atmosphere, as the gas reacts with silicate rocks to produce carbonates. Carbon dioxide is a greenhouse gas. It helps keep the planet warm. So faster weathering reduces the amount of carbon dioxide in the atmosphere and lowers temperatures again. Greenhouse sceptics love this bit. See, they say, we don't have to worry about global warming. Nonsense, says Lovelock. These processes take too long to help us in slowing down global warming.

A second thermostat switch involves phytoplankton in the oceans. Over much of the planet, the sulphurous 'breath' of these marine plants is the main source of the condensation nuclei that allow clouds to form. Without the plankton, there would be many fewer clouds and the Earth's surface would be much warmer.

This entire line of research, with its most surprising discovery, was inspired by the Gaian idea. Whether or not Gaia is the literal truth, it is clearly a powerful way of looking at the world. By looking resolutely at the whole, it reveals things that you couldn't get from peering at the sum of the parts.

Fred Pearce

*The above extracts are reprinted
from an article in The Guardian.*

ARNE NAESS
Doyen of Deep Ecology

"Life is fundamentally one. . . . The deep ecology movement is the ecology movement which questions deeper. The adjective 'deep' stresses that we ask why and how, where others do not."

"The movement is not mainly one of professional philosophers and other academic specialists, but of a large public in many countries and cultures."

"Every living being is connected intimately, and from this intimacy follows capacity of identification and as its natural consequences, practice of non-violence."

FOR NORWEGIANS, Arne Naess's reputation is unimpeachable: he will remain a great public figure, a riddle and an inspiration. But whether Naess's reputation will abide beyond the shores of his native country is a more vexed question. Will his coinage of the term 'Deep Ecology' ensure his immortality as a philosopher? Will the myth that has been woven around him continue to entice people to his work?

Responses to Naess over the years have been nothing if not multifaceted. He has been variously labelled as a 'guru', an 'eco-fascist', a 'prophet' and a *panzercharakter* (meaning a person with a personality like a tank). His life has run the gamut from contemplation to robust recreation: he began as a mountain-climbing philosopher, who studied in Vienna, partly for the peaks, and fell in with a sombre 1930s philosophical circle called the Logical Positivists. Then he raced off to California and attracted attention by conducting psychological studies of rats. Norway enticed him back by offering him a Professorship of Philosophy at Oslo University, where he produced vast tomes on the philosophy of science, semiotics and scepticism. In the 1960s he began moving towards environmental philosophy. During all this deep thought he climbed, devoutly and expertly, some of the highest mountains in the world.

He is well known among environmentalists for having coined the term 'Deep Ecology' to distinguish eco-centric environmental arguments from 'shallow', anthropocentric ones. Naess holds that industrialised society has lost touch with a crucial portion of human experience: the ability to be 'alone' and yet 'not alone' in nature, to subsume one's own sense of identity into the common mass of creation. The world has changed immeasurably since Naess crafted his definition in the 1970s. Does the Deep Ecology message continue to ring resonantly?

It certainly did for me, and his arguments formed a substantial portion of the patchwork of reasons why I left London and moved to Norway. I met Naess several times while in Oslo.

The most memorable of these encounters was not the formal meeting in the lecture theatre, but on a rainy day, when I took a train up the mountains outside Oslo, and asked Naess a few questions about his thoughts on the future.

Naess used to spend much of the year in a mountain retreat, on a virtually inaccessible peak. The old, slightly bent man who opened the door was just a little hesitant and frail, wearing a huge woollen jumper, staring around with pale blue eyes. But there was a residual wiriness, as he sat, a strength remaining from a lifetime of vigorous activity in nature.

Naess has consistently preached a doctrine of political, deliberate slowness. Life runs too fast, Naess insists. No one has a chance to stop, look, and be quiet in the woods. And this is why environmentalism continues to fail to seize the political centreground in Europe and North America. "There's always a sense of hurry, as if we are always on the way. But I say we are here, completely here. . . . I am always telling people to slow down, to enlarge on moments that have value; not to think 'What do I have to do now? What's the time?', but to think, 'This is something perfect.'"

The industrialised world wants us to speed up, speed away from nature, from moments of contemplation: "People are mostly not educated to experience nature. Parents must take their children into the woods, or anywhere that is not dominated by human activity, so they can learn to like to be in nature, to appreciate small things."

Deep Ecology might be seen as too mystical for the mainstream. The talk of a future in which the vast majority have reached 'ecological enlightenment' has been dismissed as utopian dreaming. But the Naessian world-view is still warmly applauded by environmentalists who work towards practical solutions.

It remains the case that environmentalists still prick up their ears on both sides of the Atlantic when Naess is mentioned; Deep Ecology remains one of the most quoted, if at times least understood, points of environmental philosophy. As the environmental situation worsens, popularisers of environmental thought will become more important. Naess has supplied a larger-than-life quality, and combined it with an incessant charm which has mollified many of his detractors. But in some ways, even if the mantra of Deep Ecology survives and flourishes, there remains a need for the next Deep Ecology movement: a new incitement to action and change of sensibility. Deep Ecology was a product of a particular coalescence of time and place and people—and the values at the core of the Deep Ecology movement could only be fostered and strengthened by a new, popular mantra for a more cynical, distracted age, which has little time for forests and quietness, but which fears the advent of global warming as much as does the smiling old man in his small log cabin.

Joanna Griffiths

JONATHON PORRITT
Catalyst of Change

"The creative force of capitalism should be used to transform capitalism itself and make it into an instrument of a genuinely sustainable economy."

"We [the green movement] have persuaded people that the world is in trouble and that's a huge achievement. The paradox is that having won the argument, we are still losing the world. So you've got to stop and say 'why?'"

JONATHON PORRITT made his name with twenty-five years of uncompromising campaigning on environmental issues, which began when he was a teacher with the Inner London Education Authority in the mid-seventies. In the early years he was an activist with the Ecology Party, the forerunner of the modern Greens, for which he stood repeatedly for election to local councils, the Commons and the European Union. He ended up as chairman of the party.

But eventually he lost patience with it. "He and other moderates failed to convert the party into something electable because of the wild, woolly, bright greens in it who wouldn't compromise their purist 'no leaders here' idealism," said one insider from those days. Porritt became frustrated with the tendency of the party to level down all talent. "He wanted to make it effective in political terms." He made some enemies.

Porritt quit party activism in 1984 to become director of a little-known pressure group called Friends of the Earth. "He thought he'd do it for three years and then go back to teaching," says one friend. But over the six years which followed Porritt transformed it into one of the most powerful lobbying and research organisations in the country. Under his leadership, its number of supporters rose from 12,700 to 226,300, and his personal profile rose.

But then in 1991 he left, and set to work establishing a charity called Forum for the Future, which aims to persuade individual businesses to improve their environmental performance. Since then, some of the green movement feel his influence has diminished. "He is not as important as once he was," says one leading environmental writer. "Once he was the top green in the country, really on the cutting edge. Nowadays, despite all the TV appearances and journalism, you're not really sure what he does."

If so, it is because Porritt has undergone a remarkable and rather admirable transformation. Certainly the radicalness of his views has not shifted much. But if his radical edge is undulled, his strategy has shifted significantly. "After twenty years of being against things, he decided that he wanted to do something positive," said one close friend. "An important part of his personality has been sidelined by his campaigning. It was the part that wanted to celebrate the good things in modern life. There was something about that relentlessly negative campaigning that had affected him spiritually. He needed to change."

What had motivated his campaigning was a powerful sense that beneath today's ecological crisis lies a crisis of the human spirit. "As we have degraded the Earth, caught up in a frenzy of suicidal consumerism, so we corrupted our souls," Porritt once wrote. What was needed was some kind of spiritual renaissance to address the crisis.

It is that combination of values and economic realism which undergirds Porritt's Forum for the Future project. There has been, he feels, a real change in the policies and performance of dozens of global companies. "To deny the importance of that contribution is dishonest," he has said. It is also highly damaging to the radically different approach which is needed to save the environment through what he calls a "cross-sectoral partnership" between governments, councils, the voluntary sector and the business community.

But engaging with business is a messy undertaking. "It is an extremely difficult enterprise, staying true to the business of 'speaking truth to power', and yet finding constructive opportunities to move things forward," says one of Porritt's closest colleagues. Forum for the Future works with individual companies "on training, capacity building and on specific projects", which means that Porritt "very often finds himself quite torn about whether certain organisations are appropriate partners" or whether they are just using him for a bit of PR. "In the end, it's a risk you have to take," says the colleague. "But he's had to change the way he works. Providing good stories to the media is now secondary."

Porritt's old world was one of black-and-white certainties. Now, he realises—as he has written—that "in fact, it is almost all grey out there." This new approach of positive complexity is what he has taken into the Government's new Sustainable Development Commission. "We see ourselves very much as action-orientated—the very last thing we want to do is spend our time preparing reports recommending action by others. Instead, we want to do things ourselves—working alongside policy makers, business leaders, and others whose actions can make a difference to sustainable development, helping and encouraging them to move in the right direction."

The tension of working with business is paralleled by the ambiguity in his relationship with the Government. He felt, he has earlier said, "some inevitable nervousness about the Commission's dual remit of acting as both an adviser to the Government and as auditor of its performance."

For Porritt, politicians' inability to distinguish between what's really important and what's just immediate is not the only problem. Sustainable development is not yet a central concern for this government, and certainly not the central organising principle, as he would want.

Paul Vallely

VANDANA SHIVA
Seed Sovereignty

"Over the past two decades every issue I have been engaged in as an ecological activist and organic intellectual has revealed that what the industrial economy calls 'growth' is really a form of theft from nature and people."

ANDANA SHIVA IS A WOMAN creating a revolution at the grass roots. She is a fearless and passionate campaigner for the land, forests, women, countryside, small farmers, biodiversity, indigenous values and right livelihood; a peaceful warrior against the onslaught of economic globalisation, the dominance of multinational corporations, the industrialisation of agriculture and the commercialisation of basic human necessities such as food, water and shelter. She is a saver of seeds and a conserver of cultures.

Having studied both philosophy and physics, Vandana is able to marry traditional with modern attitudes and seek a synthesis between the rational mind and the feeling heart. In consequence she is as much an activist as a scientist, and able to back her intuitions with empirical evidence.

When we first met we started to talk about the famous forest resistance, known as the 'Hug the Trees movement', led by women including Vandana. "What was the occasion which precipitated that resistance?" I asked.

"In the seventies, the central government in New Delhi and the state government in Lucknow had given licence to the logging companies to cut down large parts of the Himalayan forest, which provided food, fodder, shelter and livelihood to local people," said Vandana. "When the devastating news of this commercial project reached the region, the women got together and planned to stop the loggers. Time was against them. There was no possibility to contact government officials nor to engage in any formal protest, so they simply decided to 'Hug the Trees'. They resolved to remain by the trees until the loggers left the area."

"How did they do it?" I asked. "The women—hundreds of them—tied themselves to the trees. They sang songs and chanted mantras to honour the forest. There was neither hatred, nor anger, nor abuse. The women simply said, 'Trees are our bodies. If you wish to cut down the trees, your chainsaws have to go through our bodies. We will live or die with our trees. We are born in the forest, we live with the forest and we will die for the forest.'"

"What was the reaction of the loggers?" I asked. "They were stunned and surprised. They did not know what to do. They waited for days in the hope that the women's patience would run out. But little did they know that these Himalayan women have a Himalayan resolve! Days and nights passed. Women organised a rota for being in the embrace of the trees. Men organised a support system to cook and feed the women as well as the children and themselves. The protest turned into a festival," said Vandana. "The occasion proved a training ground and a learning opportunity for many of us. Eventually the loggers and their chainsaws were defeated. Their trucks arrived empty and returned empty. The women won the battle of the forests. They saved their livelihood and their culture while saving their trees."

We travelled to Vandana's farm, some ten miles outside the city of Dehra Dun in the foothills of the Himalayas, surrounded by mango groves and natural forest. Here she has acquired thirty acres of land on which she has established a centre for research, experiment, study and living called the International College for Sustainable Living (Bija Vidya Peeth). It offers an education for Earth citizenship through the knowledge of 'seeds, seasons and soil'. Courses are held on how to ensure sustainable and ecological food production and how to set up seed banks and seed networks. For Vandana, seeds are the symbols of self-reliance and sustainability.

"How different is your research from that of the universities and government institutions?" I asked.

"Our research is not done in a vacuum," said Vandana, "as it is designed to be relevant to the lives of people. Universities carry out academic research in the abstract and impose their findings on people. This is how the disastrous 'Green Revolution' was brought about, and that is how genetically engineered seeds are now being imposed on farmers. Establishment scientists and the farmers live in two different worlds. Most scientists are cut off from the realities on the ground. Our research is based on the land and the people working on it. Here village people themselves participate in the research, gathering data and analysing it. We are concerned with measuring and evaluating the success of traditional methods of farming, such as crop combining. We monitor the food value yielded by a variety of different plants growing together, as compared with the food value of mono-crops."

Vandana and her colleagues are recording the knowledge of local people which the scientific establishment has ignored. "Local knowledge of farming and forestry maintains diversity," said Vandana, "and diversity is the mother of abundance—whereas academic science insists on mono-crops, the cause of scarcity. The system of diversity reveals that when one crop fails there are other crops to provide sustenance—whereas in the mono-crop system, the failure of one crop means the failure of the whole harvest; there is nothing to fall back on."

Vandana further observed, "Diversity has been the basis of traditional Indian agriculture. There are thousands of varieties of indica rice alone which grow in India, and then there are thousands of varieties of millet, pulses and cereals that have nourished our vast population for millennia. Traditional farming systems have always practised mixed cropping, rotations and green manuring. Even on small plots of land, trees like neem and plants like perennial basil (*tulsi*) have been used as a protection against pests and diseases."

Vandana Shiva's life and work are based upon the world-view of biodiversity. Through campaigning, research and teaching she is developing the practice and philosophy of the gift economy, and spreading her knowledge among others.

Satish Kumar

DAVID ABRAM
Sensuous Experience

"Each ecology has its own psyche, and the local people bind their imaginations to the psyche of the place by letting the land dream its tales through them."

"We humans have negotiated relationships with every aspect of the sensuous surroundings, exchanging possibilities with every flapping form, with each textured surface and shivering entity that we happened to focus upon. All could speak, articulating in gesture and whistle and sigh a shifting web of meanings that we felt on our skin or inhaled through our nostrils or focused with our listening ears, and to which we replied."

D AVID ABRAM'S SKILL as a sleight-of-hand magician (it was his profession for nine years) led him to embark on a series of journeys among traditional oral cultures in Indonesia and Nepal. There he met traditional magicians and medicine people. In the course of living with a number of these practitioners,

Abram found his own sensory experience of the material world beginning to shift and transform.

Abram challenges those of us born into literate, industrial civilisation to awaken our direct sensory experience of the world around us, and so to ground our flights of intellect and reason in the ongoing reciprocity between our breathing bodies and the animate natural world. The following is a short extract of an interview he gave outlining some of his thoughts on the impact of changing our forms of interaction from oral to literate.

How is it that language can either link us with the natural world or sever us from it?

We in Western, literate culture spend a great deal of time talking about the natural world. Indigenous peoples spend just as much time talking to the surrounding world. They experience the natural landscape as a living community of beings with whom they are engaged in an ongoing conversation. For them, it is the animate earth that speaks; human speech is just but one part of that vaster discourse.

Does this lead oral peoples to speak differently from us in the literate world?

Language in an oral culture tends to remain tuned to the particular rhythms and resonances of the local soundscape. It is influenced by the cries of birds and other animals, by the whoosh of the local winds through the trees and the particular patterns of light and shadow that move across that land. For oral peoples, language is an active speech—a shout, song, and sigh. To speak is to participate directly in the dynamic life of the land, which has its own ways of speaking, its own modes of expression.

But those of us born into literate, alphabetic civilisation tend to assume that language is an exclusively human property. When we speak, we do not feel that we are participating or conversing with the rest of an animate world, but rather that we are 'representing' the world, standing apart from it, looking at that world from outside. Language does not join us to the more-than-human terrain, but rather separates us from it. This is simply a very different way of experiencing language than was common to our oral ancestors.

We are then living in a very different sensory world.

Yes. For indigenous, oral peoples, all things accessible to our senses are experienced as animate, alive, even aware. Touching a tree, we spontaneously feel that the tree is touching us; gazing into the depths of a forest, we feel that we are also being watched by the forest.

But in learning to read and to write with an alphabet, we have to break the spontaneous participation of our senses in the natural surroundings, in order to recouple our eyes and our ears on the flat surface of the page.

With the advent and spread of the alphabet, the natural landscape gradually loses its voice, and soon comes to be experienced as a purely passive set of objects. The compelling fascination that the animate natural world once had for our oral ancestors is now experienced by us only in relation to our own signs.

The human intellect is really bereft if it doesn't remember its debt to sensing, breathing, and to the many tastes of the bodily world; it's so important to me to revalue our direct sensuous experience. The sensuous world is not the global world—not that dimension of distant events that we hear about through the newspaper or the radio or the television: the sensuous world is always local. The sensuous is the particular ground on which we walk and the particular air that we breathe, the specific smells that reach us from the surrounding plants and soils. To live close to our senses is to begin to ground ourselves deeply within the local world we bodily inhabit.

To the extent that we are now spending more and more time online, to the extent that our kids are actually growing up online and getting much of their education through the computer screen (and the television screen) rather than in direct, flesh-and-blood interaction with other embodied persons interacting in the depths of the sensuous world, then we are robbing our children, and our grandchildren, of the possibility of an ethical, sustainable world in which to live. We cannot learn how to interact with each other respectfully and with restraint without directly interacting with one another, bodily and sensorially, in the depths of a living world.

Interview by Jim Cummings

ROBERT HART
Forest Gardener

"The forest garden is far more than a system for supplying mankind's material needs. It is a way of life and also supplies people's spiritual needs by its beauty and the wealth of wildlife that it attracts."

"For those with eyes to see, this Ecological Renaissance is already in progress. In moving away from the machine and all it stands for, human beings must come to realise that the 'miracles' achieved by physical scientists can be dwarfed when more attention is focussed on the infinite potentialities of Life."

WHEN WE VISITED Robert Hart in the mid 1990s, his forest garden was lush in late summer when a small group of us set up camp between the sequoia and the Ethiopian juniper, and helped ourselves to currants from the surrounding fruit bushes. This garden, begun thirty-three years ago on Wenlock Edge in Shropshire, had become a model of temperate-climate agroforestry, attracting visitors from all over the world, inspiring many who would otherwise despair of any effective measures against consumerism and high finance. Robert himself became, by virtue of his creation of the garden and of his own courtesy and kindness, a mentor for those working for humane and sustainable designs for living—a concept now loosely encompassed by the term 'permaculture'.

Agriculture came late into Robert's life. He

was born in Kensington, to a private international lawyer and a strong-minded woman with a fine soprano voice. When his younger brother was born severely mentally and physically handicapped, Robert's mother was told by the hospital, "There's nothing you can do except take him home and give him all the love you can," and the family began a lifetime quest for healing. After Westminster School and a law degree at King's College, London, Robert was articled to his father's office, but rejected the artificiality of the City, and by the time his father died, was an up-and-coming sub-editor at Reuters.

While still at Reuters, Robert had come across an article by Gandhi: "All I can remember now is that it used the word 'love' in connection with politics. It was a revelation to me, and not long after, Ruth Frye sent me a book called *The Power of Non-violence*, written by an American disciple of Gandhi. That again was a revelation to me, the idea that non-violence could be a positive power." His understanding of world affairs had led him to decide to specialise as a writer in the problems of food production: now he began to apply Gandhian ideals to all his thinking.

Robert was still not remotely interested in actually planting crops himself. During the 1950s, a series of broadcasts by John Seymour on self-sufficiency became the catalyst to turn Robert's principles and theories about food-production into practice. For three years he organically farmed eight acres in Somerset, concentrating on blackcurrants and raspberries.

Robert's farming methods gradually moved from the incorporation of livestock and milk production to absolute veganism. Typically, this commitment to veganism combined ethical consideration towards animals, conviction about the nutritional benefits, and dedication to his brother, who, as farm-work failed to work the miracles that Robert and his mother had hoped for, needed the time that tending livestock demanded of Robert. Year by year his brother's invalidity bene-

fit was invested into creating the forest garden, which is in effect a memorial to him, to Robert's mother, and to other loved friends. It became a model for agroforestry and permaculture projects throughout the UK and worldwide.

In the forest garden, with about 300 different varieties of plant in less than an acre, Robert recreated the self-sustaining abundance and diversity of the natural forest which once formed the protective 'skin' of the Earth. Trees of all kinds—exotic and familiar, fruit bushes, plants and herbs—grow closely together, forming a web of mutually beneficial relationships with each other and the accompanying wildlife. The result is a natural larder, a pharmacy, and a place of spiritual refreshment—a living manifestation of the ideals to which Robert dedicated most of his life.

For thirty years, until his brother's death, Robert combined devotion to him with dedication to refining a system of organic food production. He always maintained his belief in the possibility of healing his brother, who for twenty-two years after the death of their mother depended entirely on him. Music, especially singing, always had a beneficial effect on him. "On the night before he died we were singing together." Robert's rewards were of the simplest: "When he gave me one of his loving smiles it reminded me that nothing else matters more than loving our fellow beings."

Robert minimalised his needs and lifestyle, and became fit and handsome on an austere diet of which more than 90 per cent was raw fruit, vegetables and herbs, with non-gluten cereals. He tended the forest garden each day, wrote, and was an attentive host to his visitors. "I've had some marvellous young people visit me, who fill me with enthusiasm and hope for the future." He became immensely heartened by the global mushrooming of forest garden and permaculture projects, and saw them as "nuclei of a new world order".

Hilary Armstrong

DONELLA MEADOWS
The Limits of Growth

"Speak the truth. Speak it loud and often, calmly but insistently, and speak it, as the Quakers say, to power. Material accumulation is not the purpose of human existence. Not all growth is good. The environment is a necessity, not a luxury. There is such a thing as 'enough'."

"Your paradigm is so intrinsic to your mental process that you are hardly aware of its existence, until you try to communicate with someone with a different paradigm."

"TWENTY YEARS IS ROUGHLY the doubling time of the world economy," notes Donella Meadows, an American biophysicist, syndicated newspaper columnist, and environmental studies professor at Dartmouth College, USA, as she assesses the future for progressive movements. "That means twice the number of cars and twice the tons of coal burned. So twenty years from now, if we don't do anything, there will be twice as much pollution and drawdown of resources as today. My agenda for the next twenty years is: let's not have the next doubling, because the Earth almost certainly can't bear it."

If that sounds like an intimidating goal—convincing industrialists and investors as well as indigent people in slums and villages around the world to settle for less (less production, less profit, less Pepsi)—keep in mind that Meadows is no stranger to controversy. In 1972 she co-authored

The Limits to Growth, a slim volume sponsored by the Club of Rome that sold 9 million copies in twenty-nine languages, with the message, based on sophisticated computer models, that the world economy could not expand endlessly without severe environmental strains and eventual social collapse.

"From my point of view as a scientist," she recalls, "there was nothing more stupidly obvious to say than the Earth is finite and growth can't go on forever. It was like saying the sun rises in the East. I was simply astounded at the number and power and loudness of people who wouldn't accept that."

In 1992 she, her ex-husband Dennis Meadows, a systems management professor at the University of New Hampshire, and Norwegian business executive Jorgen Randers updated their work, using new computer models, and came to the conclusion in *Beyond the Limits* that the day of environmental reckoning is closer than they originally imagined. "Things moved a lot faster toward limits than we thought, and some new ones have appeared, like ozone layers, that nobody knew about."

One thing that didn't change was a flurry of outraged criticism. "We got back the same arguments as before. 'Technology will solve all our problems.' 'The price system will solve all our problems.' 'We have to grow in order to end poverty.' We've had 250 years of industrial growth. Poverty is still with us. How much growth is it going to take?"

"I am very disheartened", she adds, "to hear the political debate just talk about growth, growth, growth, growth, and to hear nobody stand up and challenge them. Growth of what, for whom, for how long—and why is that so good? Nobody can do that. You are just not permitted in the United States in the public media to challenge the basic tenets of industrialism."

But, having done exactly that with *The Limits to Growth* and *Beyond the Limits*, Meadows says

she's learned about the immense power of mind-sets in dictating how people see the world, and how social and environmental issues are discussed. "I learned about mindsets because, of course, I started putting forth information that didn't fit into the 'industrial growth-forever' mindset."

"We all have mindsets," Meadows adds, admitting that for many years her scientific training prevented her from appreciating the value of spirituality. The whole diversity debate, she thinks, represents a dawning recognition that there are many mindsets out there among the American people.

"My greatest wish", she says, "is that I will see in this diverse world a hugely enhanced skill in dealing with diversity. I see people understanding that they have mindsets and that other people do too, and that they can get beyond their mindset to the level where they can talk and respect each other, even though they deeply differ in their world-views."

In her own experience, Meadows remembers moderating a debate about abortion where the photos of bloody foetuses foisted by anti-abortion activists deeply challenged her own world-view. "I still ended up pro-choice, but I ended up finding some common ground with those people—although it's hard to do, with pro-life people. I want there never to be an abortion in the world. I'm not willing to outlaw it, but I'm willing to do all kinds of things to make sure that a woman never has to face the choice of abortion."

To Meadows, that means wider access to birth control, good sex education in the schools, and campaigns against irresponsible sex. Because of this she supported the crusade against Calvin Klein jeans ads with half-dressed teenagers in seductive poses. "That's a big change from the mindset I once had."

Jay Walljasper

PAUL SHEPARD
Field Biologist

"The generic human in us knows how to dance the animal, knows the strength of clan membership and the profound claims and liberation of daily rites of thanksgiving. Hidden from history, this secret person is undamaged in each of us and may be called forth by the most ordinary acts of life."

"MAN IS IN THE WORLD and his ecology is the nature of that inness," wrote Paul Shepard. "He is in the world as in a room, and in transience, as in the belly of a tiger or in love. What does he do there in nature? What does nature do there in him?" (from *The Subversive Science: Essays Toward an Ecology of Man*) As prophetic and clarifying today as it was in 1969, the essay, presaging deep ecology, avows that among the living, self and other are bound in an evolutionary, ecological continuum.

From *Man in the Landscape: An Historic View of the Aesthetics of Nature* to *The Others: How Animals Made Us Human*, Shepard richly articulated the

nature of our "inness". Lyrical, astringent, erudite, and profoundly subversive of human exceptionalism, Paul Shepard's opus is a great fugue of natural science, the work of a rare genius.

Max Oelschlaeger, editor of *In the Company of Others: Essays in Celebration of Paul Shepard*, writes: "Shepard is one of a very few intellectuals who has the psychological wherewithal and the intellectual courage to take nature seriously." Depth psychology, child development, ancient history, anthropology, ethology, primatology, mythology and art were among the subjects he studied and incorporated in his work. Above all, Paul Shepard was an avid naturalist, a field biologist, and from childhood onwards a student of wildlife. All these bodies of knowledge were digested to form a strong, supple, human-species consciousness: we are "space-needing, wild-country, Pleistocene beings", a species that emerged from "small-group, leisured, foraging life-ways with natural surroundings". At this point in our tenure on the planet, we are "trapped in overdense numbers in devastated, simplified ecosystems".

Thus it may be far more critical that we understand ourselves as a species with an organic identity than that we embroider our separate, deformed psychologies or demented nationalisms any further. Civilisation is a relatively brief episode of our species' experience, and cannot by any ecological criteria be regarded as evolutionary. In no sense has it fitted us better for life on a planet long given to biodiversity.

Shepard, observes Oelschlaeger, "takes time seriously". Thus the core understanding that our species' niche and destiny are for hunting and gathering, not peasanthood or technocracy. Shepard's scholarship culminated in the existential theory "that the human species emerged enacting, dreaming, and thinking animals and cannot be fully itself without them". He refers not to domesticated animals or pets, the enslaved "genetic goofies" of farmstead or apartment, but to the wild animals that sing and teach in all their mystery and plurality of difference. Prey and predator, all beings are dignified, not as ascending links in a great chain of being that culminates in modern humanity, but as participants in a sacramental gift exchange that has been going on for millions of years.

It is axiomatic that what we do to nature—to places and animals—we do to ourselves. As we gradually learned, over several millennia, to domesticate and so infantilise the plants and the beasts and denude our surroundings, so have we stunted our maturation and maimed our psyches. "Programmed for the slow development toward a special kind of sagacity," wrote Shepard in *Nature and Madness*, "we live in a world where that humility and tender sense of human limitation is no longer rewarded. Yet we suffer for want of that vanished world, a deep grief we learn to misconstrue."

This is not nostalgia, but a time-respecting exhortation to acknowledge our origins. Since the Neolithic Age, hunter-gatherers have been warred upon, condemned as savage, condescended to as primitive, too brutish to step on the escalator of Progress. Much of Paul Shepard's writing overturns this linear dogma of history. With its richly substantiated case against the pastoral, *The Tender Carnivore and the Sacred Game* is thoroughly unsettling, detailing the havoc wrought by sedentarisation upon all the species involved, including upon the inner life of *homo sapiens*.

Our species' sanity (or current lack thereof) was a central concern of Shepard. *Nature and Madness* begins with his asking: "Why do men persist in destroying their habitat?" Shepard says, "It is hard to be content with the theory that people are bad and will always do the worst," and he locates the psychopathology in the philosophies and theologies that apotheosise the abstraction and subservience that make agriculture, and thence civilisation, tick. Feminists, animal rights activists, back-to-the-landers, wilderness preservationists, vegetarians and monotheists, indeed any followers of any world religion, each and all will find their ideologies qualified, if not subverted, by Shepard's account of human ecology. All of which begs his question: "What can one say of the prospect of the future in a world where increasing injury to the planet is a symptom of human psychopathology? Is not the situation far worse than one of rational choices in an economic system or the equilibration of competing vested interests? . . .

"The problem may be more difficult to understand than to solve. Beneath the veneer of civilisation . . . lies not the barbarian and animal, but the human in us who knows the rightness of birth in gentle surroundings, the necessity of a rich nonhuman environment, play at being animals, the discipline of natural history, juvenile tasks with simple tools, the expressive arts of receiving food as a gift rather than as a product, the cultivation of metaphorical significance of natural phenomena of all kinds, clan membership and small-group life, and the profound claims and liberation of ritual initiation and subsequent stages of adult mentorship. . . .

"This means that we have not lost, and cannot lose, the genuine impulse. It awaits only an authentic expression."

Stephanie Mills

TERRY TEMPEST WILLIAMS
Intimacy with the Land

"To be whole. To be complete. Wildness reminds us what it means to be human, what we are connected to rather than what we are separate from."

"Our sense of community and compassionate intelligence must be extended to all life forms, plants, animals, rocks, rivers, and human beings. This is the story of our past and it will be the story of our future."

IF YOU WANT TO KNOW why we so badly need Terry Tempest Williams and her voice in the world, read 'Labor'. Read anything she's written, but particularly that lyric essay, written by the Utah-born nature writer at the age of forty-four at the turn of the millennium.

How we write is who we are, and 'Labor' is the very music of Terry Tempest Williams, the meaning her life makes, transposed to paper. 'Labor' is the polemical poem of her life. What it says is

who she is; what it says is how we might learn from the land to live more wisely, more beautifully and sustainably than we do; what it says is be swept away, be eroded and renewed. Start again.

We can begin to live differently, she repeats plaintively through this poem of a creed of a manifesto, set in the belly of Kane Creek Canyon in the womb of her home country, the redrock desert of the Colorado Plateau. And this is what Terry has been writing, one way and another, now directly, now allegorically, from the beginning—in books like *Pieces of White Shell, Coyote's Canyon, An Unspoken Hunger, Red*, and especially *Refuge*. We can be unmade by the world's forms and remade to bring to birth a new kind of community of beings, in which all life, not merely human needs and desires (but also those), might be sustained forever. Saving the Earth, starting right here on our own home ground, giving the more-than-merely human beings a voice, we can save ourselves, too, and find, while we're at it, a model for the kind of democracy the world seems to have forgotten the meaning of just now.

We can give birth to creation, she hopes. We can wake from our fear and slumber; we can let ourselves be spent and eroded; and we can rise again to know the rest of creation as our family, as our community, our elders—as our Self. In our politics, then, at home and abroad, and in our daily lives, we may recall biology in every phrase we utter, the brevity and beauty of each human (and each non-human) life; and we might learn the kind of humility that geomorphology and the natural history of erosion can teach us. Intimacy with the land can teach us the sense of perspective and proportion that seems to have been lost in the shrill politics of these days.

The eldest of four children, the rest of them boys, Terry was born to Mormon parents in Salt Lake City on 8 September 1955. Her father worked and her brothers still work in a family business, now four generations old, laying pipe in the desert. Terry is a child of that desert as much as of those parents and that desert-grounded faith. She inherits the feeling for magic and shape-shifting that the Great Salt Lake shares with the desert, with its first peoples and its Mormon immigrants. Unlike her forefathers, though, Terry is a pantheist and spiritual ecologist, Franciscan in her sense of kinship with other beings, and pagan in her celebration of the human body. She digs in the desert like her family, but metaphorically, and she finds in it stories of consolation, hope and transformation. She even finds in it her syntax and diction. Though she has, for now, moved out of the desert to Wyoming, where, with her husband, she continues the work of "inspiring people to act mindfully on behalf of wild nature" in new ways at the Murie Center, Williams, one suspects, will always speak as the deserts speak.

Terry Tempest Williams is an environmental writer who understands that the roots of the ecological crisis we live within reach down to a deeper spiritual disorder. We are alienated from our bodies; our bodies and minds have grown estranged from the rest of creation; we have forgotten that all human wisdom has always arisen out of fellowship and intercourse with the land, with our sister moon and brother sky and mother earth, with our beloved, the world. Her work is as political as it is poetic; as psychologically literate as it is nature literate; as spiritual as it is personal; as erotic as it is intelligent; as beautiful as it is urgent. Because it is all these things, because she speaks out of everything and every place and everyone she has ever been and still is—woman, mystic, naturalist, folklorist, Mormon, activist, Southwesterner—and because she communicates with such heart and care, her words have touched millions in the US and beyond, and changed as many lives. Hers is the kind of prophetic writing and speaking that lets readers—and the students and lovers and children of those readers—imagine another possible world, and see how they might help bring it into being, starting now, through what Terry calls "Home Work" and "bedrock democracy".

Kim Stafford, the American poet and essayist, uses the phrase "the musical arrangement of passionate fact" for a certain kind of creative nonfiction. He might have had Terry in mind, for this describes her work perfectly, and why and how it speaks to so many.

I will leave the last words to Terry:

"We can navigate ourselves out of the current. We can pull ourselves out of the river. We can witness the power of erosion as a re-creation of the world we live in and stand upright in the truth of our own decisions. We can begin to live differently. We can give birth to deep change, creating a commitment of compassion toward all living things. Our human-centered point of view can evolve into an Earth-centered one. Is this too much to dream? Who imposes restraint on our imagination?"

Mark Tredinnick

JACQUES COUSTEAU
Saviour of the Seas

"What is a scientist, after all? It is a curious man looking through a keyhole, the keyhole of nature, trying to know what's going on."

CALYPSO, JOHN DENVER'S famous hymn to Jacques Cousteau's famous ship, is corny, overwrought, and has a weird, wordless, half-yodelled chorus which suggests that the singer has found his favourite dog dead by the roadside.

Though *Calypso* is not a great piece of music, it has echoed around Jacques Cousteau's myth because it encapsulates the popular idea of what Cousteau was doing: gallivanting whimsically around the world, sharing his adventures, a sort of avuncular buccaneer carrying cameras instead of cannon. "True as the tide and free as a wind swell," as Denver had it, "joyful and loving in letting it be."

Denver was about half right. Cousteau was certainly an intrepid guide to the oceans, and a powerful communicator, equal parts explorer and evangelist. However, he was driven to a large extent by a darker vision of the value of his work. Along with Cousteau's material inventions—the

Aqualung, underwater film photography, a jet-propelled one-man submarine, the first liveable underwater habitats—he could also claim, as much as any one person could, to have pioneered the inescapably influential modern creed of apocalyptic environmentalism. Jacques Cousteau was one of the first to popularise the idea that we were poisoning our planet. "If we are not willing to change," he said, in a quote which sounds rather better when imagined in a gruff Gallic snort, "we will disappear from the face of the globe, to be replaced by the insect."

Cousteau saw the sea not just as a research project, but as a potential habitat; not only a nice place to visit, but somewhere we might all end up living. In the epilogue of his book *The Silent World*, he wrote, "Obviously man has to enter the sea. There is no choice in the matter. The human population is increasing so rapidly, and land resources are being depleted at such a rate, that we must take sustenance from the great cornucopia." As Cousteau saw it, his enormously popular books, films and television programmes were showing us not just an unexplored aspect of our planet, but our destiny. He'd just got there first, an astronaut in flippers.

Jacques Cousteau was born in 1910, in St André-de-Cubzac, near Bordeaux. His professional life underwater happened, literally, by accident. Though he'd been sufficiently nautically inclined as a young man to join the French navy, he was training to become a pilot. This ambition was ended by a serious car accident after which, to strengthen his shattered arms, Cousteau took up swimming. The legend has it that the inspiration which guided his life came from the goggles he developed to give him vision under the water. Photography had also been an early passion of Cousteau's: he'd bought his first movie camera as a boy, and he figured that if he could get a camera to see as clearly below the waves, he could let the whole world in on the spectacle. Cousteau's first film, 10 *Fathoms Down*, was made in 1942. Incredibly, it was shot entirely with breath-hold diving, every sequence limited by the air the camera-operator could hold in straining lungs. The search for a solution to this problem led to one of the most important inventions of the twentieth century: the Aqualung.

The Aqualung, developed by Cousteau and his friend Emile Gagnan, was the first self-contained underwater breathing apparatus, now known by the acronym SCUBA. Before the Aqualung, undersea explorers and budding undersea film-makers had been confined to heavy diving suits, into which air was pumped manually from a ship's deck, or had taken their chances with primitive, dangerous, re-breathing contraptions, which used lime to convert exhaled carbon dioxide to pure oxygen (oxygen is poisonous at some pressures—Cousteau nearly died more than once experimenting with such devices). Cousteau's Aqualung set divers free; men now had wings to fly underwater.

The Aqualung was immediately worthwhile, employed by frogmen to clear German mines from France's harbours (this was far from Cousteau's first important service to his country: he was decorated for his work as a wartime spy).

In 1950, financed by a wealthy admirer, Loel Guinness, of the Anglo-Irish brewing dynasty, Cousteau bought a decommissioned Royal Navy minesweeper, which was working as a passenger ferry in Malta, and which he had refitted as a combined oceanographic laboratory and film studio. The 400-ton wooden craft was called *Calypso*.

Calypso was Cousteau's headquarters and trademark for the next forty-six years. His passion for his subject, and knack for quirky self-promotion—he insisted on a peculiar crew uniform of overalls and red woollen hats—made him a superstar. His films and television programmes, most notably the 1956 cinema epic *The Silent World*, and his series *The Undersea World Of Jacques Cousteau*, which ran for seven years, were narrated with infectious wonder, and won Oscars and Emmys. His books, including the twenty-volume *The Ocean World of Jacques Cousteau* and twenty-six-volume *Planet Ocean*, sold colossal quantities. Cousteau was to the oceans what David Attenborough would become to the land: the one man who had, simply, seen more of it than any other person who'd ever lived, and was blessed with the ability to tell the rest of us about it.

Calypso sank in Singapore harbour in January 1996, after a collision with a barge (it was subsequently refloated). Cousteau died the following year, aged 87.

In 2004 it was announced that Loel Guinness, grandson of the original financier of the *Calypso*, had sold the rotting vessel to the Cousteau Society for a symbolic price of one euro; the intention was to restore it as a floating museum. The following year, Wes Anderson's film *The Life Aquatic* paid an oblique homage to Cousteau, with a lead character called Steve Zissou, an explorer with a penchant for red woollen hats, who sailed on a ship called *Belafonte*. Cousteau's stature is proving resilient, and he deserves no less. If Cousteau's overarching theory is correct, and man one day relocates to the deep, his name will become as ineradicable from history as that of Yuri Gagarin, his equivalent pioneer of space. And even if he was wrong, and people only ever visit his silent world as tourists, then he bequeaths a legacy of countless millions of tickled imaginations, and that amounts to a more than worthwhile lifetime's work.

Andrew Mueller

DAVID BOHM
Scientist of Interconnectedness

"The ability to perceive or think differently is more important than the knowledge gained."

"Suppose we were able to share meanings freely without a compulsive urge to impose our view or conform to those of others and without distortion and self-deception. Would this not constitute a real revolution in culture?"

"Thought is creating divisions out of itself and then saying that they are there naturally."

DAVID BOHM'S GENIUS lies in generating new metaphors to help us understand the nature of reality. The history of science tells us that new proposals always demand new metaphors of the physical world to become widely acceptable. It is no coincidence that Newton's use of the 'world as machine' metaphor gained ground in an era on the edge of industrialisation. Bohm's metaphor of the universe as a 'hologram in motion' is most promising, especially in an era when the essential connectivity, subtle interdependence and dynamics of human and planetary systems are becoming evident.

His metaphor is the 'hologram', but not just a hologram: one which is dynamic, a hologram in motion.

DAVID BOHM

A hologram is a three-dimensional projection from a two-dimensional photographic plate. The plate makes no sense to us until a concentrated beam of light is shone on it. A true hologram has a number of interesting features apart from being an unfolded form. Cutting away a chunk of film does not destroy the image. Any part of the original film can still unfold the whole image, although detail degrades; thus every part of a hologram is embedded within every other part. It is truly interdependent. A hologram is dependent upon the background from which it emerges. Bohm uses these ideas when he talks about the multi-layered reality out of which the material universe, or the universe we can measure, continually unfolds and re-enfolds. The holographic image is fixed, but Bohm's holographic universe is fundamentally a dynamic whole out of which particles, energy and whatever else are coming into being and disappearing from view continually.

Another analogy he uses is of the ocean wave: it looks like a separate thing, but is entirely dependent on the actions of the whole ocean for its existence. Water molecules move in and out of the wave, but the form remains—it is the abstraction we talk about as 'the wave'. Bohm holds that all that we ever discuss is an abstraction from a moving, internally interdependent whole. Everything is connected internally, just as the plate of the hologram contains information about the whole in every part; so this connectiveness is fundamental—profoundly so, and not at all like the billiard-ball universe of the mechanistic model.

Now all this is consistent with the science we have, it seems, yet it is a model which is, he claims, more inclusive and better suited to understanding a dynamic universe. These insights are of little value unless they generate fresh insights into our everyday life and living—after all, this is what Newton achieved long after his mathematics was relegated to the specialist. One particular application of Bohm's general idea might be a revisioning of 'the environment'—the physical chemical, biological, social and other 'surroundings' of our life.

The environment, using Bohm's model, might look rather different. It is no longer 'out there' as something we interact with in a naïve mechanical sense, but the context within which we find ourselves. Now, if there is a vast implicate order continually explicating us, our thoughts and the environment, it follows that there is a movement in the opposite direction. The wave depends upon the ocean, but the wave also affects the ocean. All that we do 'to' the environment is affecting the enfolded or implicate order, and is thus affecting the further unfoldment of us, our thoughts and the environment in quite subtle ways.

We do not, it seems, have much idea about these subtleties, but we can be assured that an effect or effects are real enough. This should add weight to our growing precautionary attitude towards the environment. In a holographic universe everything matters, and everything matters in ways which in terms of first principles we cannot fully understand, predict or control. Therefore we must tread carefully, out of humble self-interest. It adds another level of debate about the wisdom of intervention in the environment with novel molecules and new life-forms. We simply don't know what effect this might have on the enfolded order, and it won't be a question of 'if' but 'when' we detect the fruits of such change once more in our unfolded world.

Bohm claimed that his model asserts wholeness, internal interconnectedness, movement and thus change as fundamental features of the universe rather than secondary features: it is a turning of the mechanistic world on its head. Sure, the parts still matter and the reductionistic study of parts has a value, but in placing these values they are now some way down any hierarchy of meanings. If Bohm was right, then the calls for systemic thinking, for putting connectedness and meaning first, for integration, co-operation and holistic thinking, pave a stronger base than hitherto because they use the holographic universe as a metaphor. In this exploration of a new picture of reality we have perhaps the best hope for encouraging others to reassess their assumptions, give strength to holistic thinking and bring about, as Bohm termed it, "a creative surge along new lines".

Ken Webster

BILL MOLLISON
Permaculture

"Rather than asking 'What can I get from this land, or person?' we can ask 'What does this person, or land, have to give if I co-operate with them?'"

"We have sufficient to do everything possible to heal this Earth. We don't have to suppose we need oil, or governments, or anything. We can do it."

"Beware the monoculturist, in religion, health, farm or factory. He is driven mad by boredom, and can create war and try to assert power, because he is in fact powerless."

IN 1972, BILL MOLLISON had been teaching in the University of Tasmania for about five years. Then, like Lao Tzu, he withdrew from society, cut a hole in the bush and disappeared into it. From one Friday to the next Friday, working with two friends, he built a large two-storey barn, mulched a half-acre of ground and planted a total food-system. For the next two years he started to

think up the system which he called Permaculture.

Mollison had a little house on a mountain near Hobart, which is the capital city of Tasmania. It was an open-house situation. One of the people who came there was a young man with a broken arm and nowhere to sleep. He was David Holmgren, then a young man of about 19, and he provided a sympathetic ear to Mollison's developing theories of permaculture. David and Bill built several instant ecosystems. They had little half-acre systems of 300 species, from ground-covers to productive canopies, and it was working fine, so in a couple of years they were fairly certain that they were on to a good thing, but it was rather tentatively that they proposed a system which became permaculture, and published it.

In 1975 Mollison had some study leave, so he went to Oxford for a while, but just before leaving Australia he gave a short one-and-a-half hour evening national radio programme on the concepts. As a result he received 9,000 letters.

By 1976, when he had returned from sabbatical in Oxford, demands for books were coming in. About twenty-six publishers had written to him—the thing seemed to have its own life. People started to ask him to design their properties, which he found terrifying, because really permaculture is simply a proposal for change, not a manual for design.

The first design Mollison ever did was at the end of 1975 at a small community in urban Melbourne, and it has developed ever since, and it's been one of the real joys of his life. For a long time he kept a little hut in the middle of it, and would stay there when he was passing through Melbourne and would further develop it. It has never finished its development.

Mollison says, "You will never see a completed permaculture—that won't happen. You'll never see a permaculture like any other permaculture—that won't happen. If you think of setting up a demonstration permaculture, let me tell you it'll just be another permaculture and there'll be nothing like it—it'll demonstrate nothing but itself." So when he had completed 800 designs, for no charge or just for his fares, he had reduced his teaching load to one hour a week at university. He lay in bed and sweated at night for about a month, and decided to leave the university. Here was a man of 52, due for retirement pension in two years' time, leaving the university where he had life tenure—to do what? To teach people, he thought, to design.

It was 1981 before he had developed a curriculum for a design course. Max Lindegger is one of those who came to that 1981 course, and people like Lindegger have been an influence beyond Mollison's wildest predictions. He has designed and works with hundreds of properties. Between 1981 and 1986 they trained about 1,000 people globally, fairly equally distributed between Australia and America, and with a slightly smaller number in Europe.

"To be effective, we need to have built a complex of all the necessary services of a society within our own system, whose purpose is permaculture, or stable systems. We need our theorists and researchers, by all means, but we also need our nursery people and horticulturalists, our soil scientists and hydrologists, civil engineers, architects and so on. We have about achieved this in parts of Australia, where there are as many as seventy to ninety people in a region—we have an almost total service organisation, that is, we have potentially our own banking and finance, educational and construction and rehabilitative systems, our own theorists and our own people to look after species or reserves of species.

"What are our future concerns? First, that we spread and locally develop the 'people polyculture'. Even the people you hate are good for something. Even greedy people are great, because you can put them in a money-handling situation and they can have the whole thrill of handling money, forgetting for a minute it's not theirs. Our concerns are to spread rapidly and therefore to develop teachers and teaching.

"We are not networkers, we are only work-netters. We do not connect to information systems, we only connect business to business, production to retail, teaching to students. No more networking. No more writing permaculture and hoping everyone would admire you and you wouldn't have to do anything? Only work-netting. The time for networking is over, the time for evidence is over. There is only time for action. No more spectators, only players. I'm a very simple person: all I want to do is to re-green the Earth, that's all. I don't want to do anything else, that's what I'm going to do all the time. If any of you feel inspired to do nothing else but that, it'll take three of us, I think we could do it."

Adapted from a speech by Bill Mollison at the 2nd International Permaculture Conference.

LAWRENCE D. HILLS
A Great Gardener

"Ours is a good world, with the right moisture, temperature range, and atmosphere for our kind of life to enjoy. It is ours to love and to cherish through the sunlit centuries."

"Those who think organically are united in their respect for the future. They think ahead to the fossil fuels and fertilisers running out, the toxic metals and industrial wastes in our rivers, seas and soils, and the persistent pesticides and other pollutants adding up to danger in the bodies of all the life with which we share one world."

"O BSERVE THE WORKS of God in humbleness" and "Search only for the truth that harms no man" are the maxims by which two special men lived their lives. They were Henry Doubleday, a nineteenth-century Quaker entrepreneur, and Lawrence D. Hills, the father of the organic gardening movement in Britain.

Hills came across the work of Henry Doubleday whilst writing his book *Russian Comfrey*. It appeared in print in 1953, and would change his life. Doubleday had been convinced that the high-protein plant, which had the potential to achieve crop yields of over 100 tons per acre, could feed a hungry world. Unfortunately, nobody took him seriously and he died in obscurity in 1902, his work forgotten.

Hills shared his vision for the wonder plant, and the amazing response to his book, which became a minor bestseller, determined him to set up an organisation to continue Doubleday's research into comfrey. In 1958 the Henry Doubleday Research Association was born, set up on the slender proceeds of the book royalties, with Hills as its sole (unpaid) employee; its remit expanded to include research into improving organic horticulture. This was an incredible gamble, for not only did the organisation have no financial backing, but it was also flying in the face of the prevailing agricultural orthodoxy, which dismissed organics as little more than 'muck and mystery'. This was quite a burden for someone whose health had never been good. Ever since childhood Hills had suffered from chronic digestive problems, which remained undiagnosed until his mid-fifties. He didn't go to school, being taught at home by his mother, who nurtured in him a love of books and encouraged his prodigious and encyclopaedic memory.

To try to improve his health his early career had involved outdoor work, in plant nurseries throughout the south-east of England. During the long spells of convalescence that followed the periodic breakdowns in his health, he had worked as a successful horticultural journalist.

So, with nothing more than the income from his gardening column in *The Observer* newspaper and the support of a handful of enthusiastic comfrey growers, Hills launched the HDRA (as it soon became known) into a hostile world.

Throughout the 1960s a series of campaigns kept HDRA in the public eye and steadily garnered support. These included opposing atmospheric testing of nuclear weapons, which resulted in alarming genetic mutations in plants, and the use of DDT and other persistent pesticides.

At his two-acre trial ground at Braintree in Essex, Hills carried out practical experiments into ways of improving soil fertility and controlling pests and diseases without using harmful chemicals. In this he was helped by HDRA members who were encouraged to try things out for themselves in their own gardens. He was also an active collaborator with other organic agriculture pioneers such as Sir Albert Howard and Lady Eve Balfour, working closely with the Soil Association to produce the first organic standards.

In 1971, his book *Grow your own fruit and vegetables* was published, becoming a bible for home gardeners, self-sufficiency enthusiasts and the new breed of commercial organic growers. Many were inspired by the book to take the plunge and 'go organic'.

Three years later, I met Lawrence for the first time. My wife and I had been lured by a characteristic advert for help that he had placed in the personal columns of *The Times*. "Young couple wanted to work on organic research station; full board, no pay." At the interview, we were bowled over by this idealistic, enthusiastic man, talking at machine-gun speed. We agreed to join him, thus beginning our thirty-year commitment to HDRA.

That same year a piece of idiotic legislation emanating from Brussels, outlawing the sale of historic varieties of vegetables, drew Hills' fire. He was quick to see that not only was this a huge infringement of the rights of gardeners to grow what they wanted in their own gardens, but that it would also endanger the world's gene pool. Undiscovered traits, such as genes for disease resistance, that might prove vital to future plant breeders, would be lost forever if varieties were allowed to go extinct.

His response was to call for the setting up of a vegetable gene bank where seeds could be preserved in a deep frozen state for decades. This finally came to fruition in 1980. Meanwhile, we discovered a loophole in the law and promptly exploited it by setting up HDRA's Vegetable Seed Library—'lending', rather than selling, forbidden varieties.

In 1985, with Lawrence's blessing, Jackie and I moved HDRA's headquarters from Braintree to Ryton, near Coventry, and Britain's first organic demonstration gardens were created. At the age of seventy-five Hills stood down as director to make way for Jackie and myself to take over the running of the Association. As the acknowledged 'grand old man' of the organic movement, he was then able to enjoy seeing his life's work culminate in a sea change in the public's attitude.

Alan Gear

JULIA BUTTERFLY HILL
Protector of Trees

"The corporate and political power has made us feel like our voice and power has been taken away from us. But the power of the individual, the universal power that lies deep within each and every one of us, can outweigh any other force out there if we just grab hold of it and run."

"I gave my word to this tree and to all the people that my feet would not touch the ground until I had done everything in my power to make the world aware of this problem and to stop the destruction."

IN THE CANOPY of a 200-foot ancient redwood, Julia Hill, nicknamed 'Butterfly', gazes out over the sinuous Eel River near Scotia in northern California. Second-growth forest and the burnt-out stumps of trees, residual remains of recent clearcutting, are ranged on the slopes and in the valley below. It's been a year.

And, like Italo Calvino's 'Baron in the Trees', Julia won't come down. Her feet won't touch the ground, she states emphatically, until the tree known as Luna is safe from the chainsaw.

For the giant Pacific Lumber Company, which employs 1,600 workers and whose warehouses and lumber stacks stretch out along the valley below, the tree that it owns—Julia's adopted home—is money: US$100,000 to be precise. Indeed, had Julia stuck to her original plans to travel the world, this thousand year-old giant, like the hundreds of other recently-felled ancient redwoods, would in all probability be remodelled as ceiling beams and patio decking—ostentatious features in a new house or houses. Julia hopes that her action of tree-sitting will not only save Luna, but draw attention to the many other ancient trees and forests currently under threat.

The long journey, from small larva in Arkansas to inspired and inspiring 'Butterfly' in a California giant redwood, has been painful, certainly beyond the scope of ordinary endurance.

In July 1997, stopping to view ancient redwoods at Grizzly Creek in northern California, Julia became converted: "I felt spirituality like I never felt it in any church. I dropped to my knees, crying and laughing. There is no way to describe a part of yourself you never knew was missing. I knew nothing would be the same again." Then, following the path of Ralph Waldo Emerson and John Muir, Julia sought to redouble her joyful experience in a treetop: not to experience the sublime, but to save the tree. Briefly back in Arkansas, she sold everything she owned and moved out West and to the top of the tree.

Pacific Lumber have made several attempts to entice her down. They have attempted to stop supplies by sending guards to the base of the tree and menaced her with a twin rotor helicopter. Additionally, she has received lewd abuse from loggers, a cacophony of air horns to keep her awake and, worst of all, witnessed the clearcutting of trees all around her.

The weather too has shown little mercy. Two and a half weeks of furious winter storms left her with mild frostbite after four large broken branches destroyed her shelter. Through prayer and meditation she learnt the tree's secret: to bend with the storms and to relax. That's when she gave up wearing shoes and using a harness.

Since the hostile takeover of Pacific Lumber by the Maxxam Corporation of Houston, Texas in 1985, the company has sought to maximise profits by abandoning earlier sustainable-yield practices in favour of clearcutting on the unstable hillslopes of several river and stream catchments, including the Eel River valley. As a result, ten homes have been washed away through mudslides, and the siltation of the river and its tributaries has been so serious that the local Coho Salmon population has declined dramatically. For the many who testified at the public hearing in Oakland, these accumulated violations of the Forest Practices Act were paramount.

Before the arrival of Europeans 130 years ago, a contiguous strip of two million acres of redwood forest covered the northern coast of California and southern Oregon. Today only 4 per cent, 80,000 acres of unlogged old-growth forest, remains, mostly in State Parks such as the Humboldt Redwoods State Park and Redwood National Park.

Pacific Lumber owns the largest portion of unprotected ancient redwood forest. Clearcutting of unprotected areas not only disrupts watersheds but also destroys important plant and wildlife corridors that link fragmented species habitats together and therefore allow for gene pool replenishment and species survival. There are at least thirty-five species considered endangered, whose very survival is threatened. These species include the Northern Spotted Owl, the Marbled Murrelet and the Coho Salmon.

Many people living in northern California no longer trust the administration, still less the growing power of corporations. As Humboldt resident Rosemary Wolter testified: "I think that corporations are not only destroying our forests, but are also destroying our democracy." In a state that, according to economist Robert Ayres, spends more on prisons than on schools, and where a protester can wind up in jail for unfurling a protest banner without permission, those who do speak out are the courageous few.

And this is why Julia's defiant stance atop an ancient redwood tree has induced so much public sympathy, even in the mainstream media. In 1998 *Good Housekeeping* magazine's readers voted Julia one of their Most Admired Women—a treasured accolade in a place where keeping house, even in calm weather, is a challenge. But when the wind blows in gusts you hear coming as they roar through the valley, clinging on for dear life is the most you can do.

Stuart Franklin

PETER KROPOTKIN
Gentle Anarchist

"The law is an adroit mixture of customs that are beneficial to society, and could be followed even if no law existed, and others that are of advantage to a ruling minority, but harmful to the masses of men, and can be enforced on them only by terror."

"Have not prisons—which kill all will and force of character in man, which enclose within their walls more vices than are met with on any other spot of the globe—always been universities of crime?"

"Freedom of the press, freedom of association, the inviolability of domicile, and all the rest of the rights of man are respected so long as no one tries to use them against the privileged class. On the day they are launched against the privileged they are overthrown."

LIKE HIS FELLOW RUSSIANS Alexander Herzen and Michael Bakunin, Kropotkin was an aristocrat who became a revolutionary. Born in 1842, he served as a boy in the Tsar's Corps of Pages and as a young man travelled through Central Asia and the Russian Far East, gaining a reputation as a geographer. Involved in populist agitation, he was jailed for two years, and made a sensational escape from the prison hospital in St Petersburg.

In Western Europe he found his niche in the anarchist movement, arguing that the main obstacle to human liberation was the state, and that alternative forms of social organisation must be developed. After three more years of imprisonment in France, he settled in Britain, where, in 1886, with Charlotte Wilson, he founded the anarchist journal *Freedom*, which continues to this day. He had renounced both his title and his fortune, and lived on the income from his writings.

Kropotkin's advocacy of anarchism, of a non-governmental society, was built around his observations of the Russian peasantry and of the tribal people he had studied in Central Asia. He believed that in any society, people build up an elaborate network of social organisation based upon equality and reciprocity, but that government, imposed from above by local brigands, princes, or agents of far-away rulers, always destroys this delicately evolved harmony.

Similarly close to daily experience was his book *Fields, Factories and Workshops*, which is a key discussion of the quality of our daily lives. It remains the most widely translated and most influential of Kropotkin's works. I have seen it on the shelves of several generations of craftspeople, aiming at supporting their families through their skills in the studio and workshop, while reducing their costs through their vegetable plots and chicken-runs as well as by their automatic domestic philosophy of make-do-and-mend.

In a British context he argued, from meticulous statistical data, that the notion that Britain would remain 'the workshop of the world' was already out of date, as was the belief that imports would, for ever, meet British needs. He claimed that the vast urban population of great cities could be fed, not by imports from large-scale prairie farming, but by intensive cultivation in their own hinterland.

These were regarded as eccentric conclusions; but Jac Smit, co-author of the 1996 United Nations report on urban agriculture, told me how in the most crowded cities of the modern world, even Singapore uses 1,500 hectares for food production, while in Chinese cities 90 percent of vegetables are locally grown. Even Hong Kong, the densest large city in the world, produces more than half of its food. The reason for Kropotkin's earlier statistical exploration was not to praise self-sufficiency as an aim in itself, nor even as a revolutionary strategy, but to prove that it was possible for any of us to combine brain work and manual work. Most of us fail in this aim.

This provided the theme and title for Kropotkin's final chapter, where he urged that in life, as well as in education, there should be a combination of the two. Any artist or craftsperson knows this from daily experience, but the ideology of the secondary school has for decades been to regard manual training merely as a way to keep the non-academic children out of mischief in the final years of school. He said that "children long for the application of what they learn in school in the abstract, and how stupid are the educators who are unable to see what a powerful aid they could find in this direction for helping their pupils to grasp the real sense of the things they learn. In our school all was directed towards training us for warfare; we should have worked with the same enthusiasm at laying out a railway, and building a log house, or at cultivating a garden or a field. But all this longing of children and youths for real work is wasted simply because our idea of the school is still the mediaeval scholasticism, the mediaeval monastery."

Kropotkin's view was shared by William Morris and the other propagandists of the radical Left with whom he shared platforms in London. A useful opportunity to promote their ideas came when the London County Council started its Central School of Arts and Crafts and appointed W. R. Lethaby, who shared Kropotkin's educational opinions, as its first principal. He filled it with working craftsmen teaching their trades on a part-time basis, and the LCC was perplexed at having to devise an innovative pay structure. In its day it was seen as having developed into the best such school in Europe.

Kropotkin returned to Russia after the revolution of 1917, and died there in 1921. His fragmentary writings from his last years, which include his letters to Lenin and his 'Message to the Workers of the West', are of great interest, and appear in several modern collections of his writings. He is continually rediscovered as a thinker who challenges the assumptions of our working lives.

Colin Ward

WENDELL BERRY
Farmer Poet

"The care of the Earth is our most ancient and most worthy, and after all our most pleasing, responsibility. To cherish what remains of it and to foster its renewal is our only hope."

WENDELL BERRY IS A WRITER of many parts and, in a manner of speaking, a farmer of one: a novelist, poet, and essayist, he has given his life to tending a small hillside in his native Kentucky county, writing there by hand, and farming by hand- and horse-labour.

In seven novels and even more short stories, Berry tells with humour and affection the story of a small farming community, Port William, as it struggles to preserve its traditional ways against forces both outside and in. In more than ten volumes of poetry, he likewise celebrates (among other things) "the world of nature despite its mortal / dangers" in "a language that can pay just thanks / and honor for those gifts." In over twenty collections of essays, and in an idiom clear and uncompromising, he diagnoses our besetting ills, chief among them a blind faith in science, addiction to labour-saving devices, and dependence upon an extractive economy that "takes, makes, uses, and discards" and that moves therefore "from exhaustion to pollution". Against this he indefatigably defends a replenishing, agrarian economy—one that "takes, makes, uses, and returns" and that therefore pays its debts to the earth.

After earning A.B. and M.A. degrees from the University of Kentucky (1956, 1957), Berry went to Stanford University as a writing fellow in the famous Wallace Stegner seminar. He spent a year in Europe on a Guggenheim fellowship (1961-2) and then, from 1962-64, taught English at New York University before deciding to return to Kentucky. "At a time when originality is more emphasised in the arts, maybe, than ever before," he wrote, "I undertook something truly original—I returned to my origins." Berry then taught at the University of Kentucky (1964-77, 1987-93), all the while improving the farm on which he and his wife Tanya still live and work. But it is a mistake, Berry says, to characterise this story as a return to the simple life. It is a story of return, to be sure, and it is one of the oldest and most instructive in the western tradition, but there is nothing simple about it. Berry returned, he says, to a far more complex life, a life that he sustains and that in turn sustains him—not by purchase and haste but by work and patience; not by easy acquiescence to a centralised economy, but by careful attention to local ways and wisdom.

This commitment to local ways illustrates a salient theme in Berry's work: that our lives must be built, and our problems reduced, to the scale of human competence. Cities must not be so large that local agriculture cannot sustain them. The current 'economy' (Berry notes the etymological impertinence) must consist of smaller, local economies that attend to local needs and capacities. Citizens must act according to what they can know not in the abstract but in concrete particulars. If they cannot act in a manner commensurate with their capacity to know and to do, if they give themselves over to abstractions—which, Berry says, are always conducive to abuse—they will necessarily abuse the sources they live from: water, soil and air.

For Berry, there is no better example of this than the American farm crisis, which is characterised by the imposition on small farmers of the 'advice' and whims of distant, disinterested agribusiness corporations that since World War II have enlarged their profits by destroying small family farms and farmland. Berry criticised this government-sanctioned practice in what may be his most important book, *The Unsettling of America* (1977), now a kind of fixed star from which American agrarians take their bearings.

Among the many correctives Berry has proffered, two recur frequently: the acquisition of skills, not money, and the practice of restraint, not extravagance. In a characteristic phrase he has said that "we must achieve the character and acquire the skills to live poorer than we do." But Berry believes neither is possible apart from "culture-borne"

instructions. Nor does he believe our ecological crisis is a crisis of knowledge only: "Rats and roaches live by competition under the law of supply and demand," he says; "it is the privilege of human beings to live under the laws of justice and mercy."

Berry's politics, closely tied to his economic critique and his distrust of organisations, are complicated by the fact that America's two major political parties increasingly resemble one another. He calls himself a Jeffersonian and a democrat. He is a Jeffersonian inasmuch as he supports decentralisation and the proliferation of as many small landholders as possible, and he is a democrat inasmuch as he was born into, and comes out of, the New Deal. He holds that a responsible government will protect small businesses and craftsmen against the ravages of the 'free' market which, far from being free, gives the wealthy and powerful easy permission to become wealthier and stronger. He believes that democracy cannot survive apart from a well-informed citizenry that heeds the available moral instruction. But he has been clear on many occasions that he speaks for neither the liberals nor the conservatives as they currently understand—if they understand—themselves. Both are beholden to an economy intent on destroying whatever it can in its effort to support a standard of living that destroys whatever is.

As for his religious sympathies, Berry admits that Christianity, "for better or worse", is the religious tradition he is heir to, but he also confesses a debt to other religions—Buddhism, for example—that provide useful correctives to our most grievous faults. He seems less and less likely to countenance claims of religious singularity, given the pattern of warfare that follows from such claims. Nevertheless, Berry has consistently declared fealty to the literary and religious tradition to which Dante, Spenser, Shakespeare, and Donne—among others—belong.

Looking back over his work, Berry says, "The work that I feel best about I have done as an amateur: for love. But in my essays especially I have been motivated also by fear of our violence to one another and to the world, and by hope that we might do better."

Jason Peters

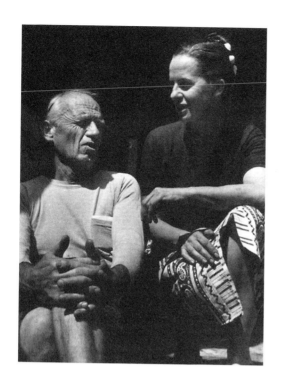

SCOTT AND HELEN NEARING
Earth Heroes

"The good life is never stable, never secure, never easy and never ended. It is a series of steps or stages, one leading into the other and all, in their outcome, adding, not subtracting; augmenting, not diminishing; building, not destroying; creating, not annihilating."

"Do the best that you can in the place where you are, and be kind."

WHO WILL BE THE GREAT folk heroes of the twentieth century? Who of our time will our great-grandchildren look back to? Surely, if a conserver culture prevails—and it's hard to see that humanity can continue otherwise—we will have to recognise the people who were pivotal in changing our direction. With this in mind, Scott and Helen Nearing, who are still much better known in the US than in Britain, deserve our full attention. Together they have been a powerful voice for energetic pacifism, animal rights, social involvement and backing out of consumerism. Between 1915 and 1993 they wrote about fifty books, lectured widely, consulted on a range of things and above all lived by example, publicly exposing every aspect of their half-century of experiment in lifestyle.

SCOTT AND HELEN NEARING

Born in 1883, Scott was a thorn in the backside of the Establishment for seventy-five years. Outspoken pacifist, total vegetarian, socialist, a farmer and prolific author, he died in 1983, consciously and deliberately, by a fast begun on his one-hundredth birthday. By 1910, as a university lecturer, he was already a controversial voice for a rational approach to life. He openly opposed US involvement in the First World War, and at the time of the Russian Revolution came out as a Soviet supporter.

His wife Helen Knothe came from a prosperous, intellectual East Coast family. At seventeen she met the young Krishnamurti, fell in love with him (he was outrageously handsome), and spent several years close to him and his emerging philosophies. After Krishnamurti moved away from her in the 1920s, she gradually became involved with Scott, who was twenty-one years her senior.

In 1932, with Scott having been thrown out of both the University of Pennsylvania and Toledo University, tried for sedition and persecuted as a Communist, they together gave up city life and bought a run-down maple syrup farm in Vermont, "preferring to be poor in the country than to starve in the city". Their book on that experience, *Living the Good Life*, inspired countless Americans to give up meat, stop exploiting the land, and move out to the country.

It's now easy to scoff at their rigorously high principles and scout-like zeal, but in the depths of the Depression it took great courage to embark on such an enterprise. They grew their food organically, almost all of it, in a dreadfully hard climate. Scorning machines, and refusing to employ draught animals, they pulled their own plough and hauled all their own fuel, sourced from trees off their own land. Determined to live by honest labour and social justice, the Nearings set a standard for uncompromising principles which was to mould four generations of Americans. They can be credited with impelling the post-war Back to the Land movement which was central to US culture in the sixties and seventies. It led to repopulation of huge tracts of rural land by people with post-industrial values, out of which has grown much of our maturity in conservation, rural sociology and deep ecology.

Against all predictions of ruin, their farm prospered. Gradually they built solid stone houses to replace wooden shacks, quarrying their own stone and building for themselves, without training or experience. In winter Scott did lecture tours, Helen wrote and hosted visitors. They deliberately sought out true quality in their lives, at every level.

At a time in history when we talk of the burden of an ageing population, Scott particularly stands out representing great age without senility. One wet winter night in 1978 I trudged through the chilly Californian rain to hear him speak, one brief stop on a national lecture tour, this time to a huge crowd at the University of California at Davis. The subject, said the poster, was 'Three Revolutions'. I wasn't expecting a great deal, and almost stayed at home by the stove.

The talk was a personal record of the effect of the French, Industrial and Socialist Revolutions on the history of the world, and within that, on the life of one man—himself. One statement comes back, almost two decades later: "It is 200 years since each of these revolutions began and I have lived through half of that time."

His style was compelling, his assertions provocative. At question time students, professors and the Press pounced on him, sharp young people trying to ridicule and discredit him, an old radical whose time had gone. Scott took them on one by one, neatly demolishing each opponent like a master swordsman, dodging, slicing and running them through, an unforgettable exhibition of verbal dexterity. His logic, authority and experience were awesome. Only afterwards did I realise that this agile talker was ninety-four years old. He was beginning to look elderly, sure, but his behaviour was that of a wise man just coming into his full power.

Helen's biography tells of each of their backgrounds, then covers the deliberate rhythms of their life together. Finally she writes on the calm and loving preparations they made together for Scott's passing. Here is an unparalleled model of control, acceptance and welcome for the only certainty in life, that it is a temporary condition.

Ianto Evans

RICHARD ST BARBE BAKER
Man of the Trees

"Today it is the duty of every thinking being to live, and to serve not only his own day and generation, but also generations unborn by helping to restore and maintain the green glory of the forests of the earth."

RICHARD ST BARBE BAKER'S vision was that trees were essential to the well-being of the earth. The analogy he used was that if a man loses a third of his skin he dies. Would it not be reasonable to suggest that if the earth loses more than a third of its tree cover, it will die?

He was born in England, and grew up in West End, which is now a suburb of Southampton, but in his books he writes as if Southampton hardly existed and West End was a quiet little backwater in the midst of woodland. His family included many parsons, but his father was a forester and nurseryman, so he grew up with a close affinity with the land and growing things. Once he was fired with an idea, he pursued it—whether taking up beekeeping aged 12, or with the idea of pio-

neering in Canada aged 17. This early experience in Canada, where he spent three and a half years as a homesteader, farmer, lumberjack and bronco buster, clearly shaped him for the future. On his return to England he went to Cambridge University, but it was not long before the outbreak of the Great War. He joined the cavalry, where his ability to manage both horses and men was extremely useful.

After the war he returned to Cambridge to read forestry, and seems to have rapidly become involved in using his practical experience and persuasive abilities to the benefit of the Agriculture department. The cost of studying at Cambridge worried him, and in a moment of inspiration had an idea for making caravans from surplus aircraft parts, so he set up a company and solved the problem of university fees. On completion of his forestry degree he applied to become a colonial forester, and was posted to Kenya. He had a natural ability to talk and listen to anyone and everyone. He also had an ability to pick up languages, so he could communicate in Swahili soon after reaching Kenya. He was probably unusual in his time for the way he would spend the evening round the camp fire not only talking with the Africans who accompanied him on his forest tours but with anyone else who joined them. When he saw the problem of deforestation and soil degradation in Kenya, it was his understanding of Kikuyu culture that provided a solution. Planting crops was men's work, whereas planting trees was God's work, so he conceived the idea of a "dance of the trees" to initiate tree planting. Thus, the "men of the trees" were born.

His visit to Palestine in the 1920s was another deeply felt experience. As the descendant of clergymen and preachers, he was familiar with the Bible's description of the trees of the holy land, but what he found was a lifeless landscape with ruined soil. The High Commissioner for Palestine had invited him to help establish a forestry movement. Again, his persuasive abilities enabled him to get Christians, Muslims and Jews to plant trees. In particular he involved schools. In Palestine he addressed huge numbers of people, including the leaders of the various faiths, universities and city governments.

In America his lectures were well received. Through the contacts he made, his message was broadcast there, and once convinced that he should write a book he set to the task with amazing vigour. Wherever he went he took photographs and films, which he used to illustrate his talks and show people the destruction of forests taking place. This message was not doom and gloom, but inspiring and positive: that people could do something about the problem—plant trees.

In the United States he was overwhelmed by the majestic redwoods, but realised that the last and best of the coast redwoods were in danger from logging, so he campaigned for their conservation, directly contacting President Roosevelt and getting his support. He saw this as an issue of world importance, not only for the USA.

When visiting different countries, several times

he found that forestry schools, universities and experimental stations were not receiving government support, and he immediately set out to explain to those in charge of the purse strings why this was short-term thinking, and why opportunities were being wasted. His worldwide travel gave him a perspective that few others had, so that he saw the global value of the study of trees: forestry education and an understanding of trees and their requirements was a cornerstone of his message.

Wherever he went he was appalled by the way trees were felled with no thought for the future, and how the soils would then be vulnerable to impoverishment and erosion so that even if replanting was contemplated in the future the soil might not then be suitable. He was also very practical, and looked at trees as sources of income for communities as well as protectors of the environment.

His travels in Africa led to one of his greatest campaigns: he realised that desertification was a massive threat to Africa, and that a green front should be established to halt the southward spread of the Sahara. To learn more he travelled across the Sahara to record the state of the desert and gather information for his campaign.

He realised very quickly not just the value of communication with those he met but that the media enabled him to reach a vast audience. His first experience of the power of radio seems to have come as a surprise, and he was apprehensive about the first request that he should write a book, but eventually writing became a essential part of his campaigning. At the time of his death, aged 92, he was writing his thirty-third book.

His vision is still valid today, and needs to be pursued with even more vigour. Worldwide, we destroy trees at an even greater rate than in his lifetime. Why do we do it? We still take trees for granted, and thinking is still short-term: trees are felled without replanting, and even though there are agreements to replant following logging, these are not effective. Desertification remains a massive problem, now exacerbated by the threat of climate change. St Barbe Baker would say that planting trees on a massive scale is the answer to the problem of global warming.

A. C. Warne

VIKTOR SCHAUBERGER
Water Guru

"This civilisation is the work of man, who high-handedly and ignorant of the true workings of Nature, has created a world without meaning or foundation, which now threatens to destroy him, for through his behaviour and his activities, he, who should be her master, has disturbed Nature's inherent unity."

"WE MUST RECOGNISE that it is Nature, not Man, that is omniscient on the Earth, but that if we continue to flout her laws, humanity is undoubtedly doomed." This was the startling declaration of Viktor Schauberger (1885-1958), whose life was dedicated to unlocking the secrets of Nature's energies and making non-destructive energy available to society.

Viktor Schauberger made an extraordinary contribution to knowledge of the natural world. He is celebrated for his discoveries in the water sciences, in agricultural techniques, and in the energy domain—what enhances and what harms life. Schauberger provides us with a comprehensive and holistic approach to understanding Nature.

His insights form the foundations of what might be called a 'Science of Nature'. He developed energy generation devices, using Nature's methods, to release people from enslavement to destructive sources of energy. He developed agricultural methods to enhance the quality of soil and crops.

Viktor's father urged him to follow his brothers to university, but seeing how their theoretical studies inhibited insight, he elected to follow his intuition to study Nature's processes in the then unspoilt wilderness of the Austrian Alps, following his forebears who had been custodians of the forest. His scepticism of the scientific world-view made him hard to work with. After he had been forced to develop a flying saucer programme for the Third Reich, and an American group tried to steal his ideas, he suspected everybody's ulterior motives. He insisted that understanding Nature must come before developing free-energy machines.

Inspired by Goethe, da Vinci, Paracelsus and Heraclitus, Schauberger was a visionary who saw life's processes as an indivisible whole, linked by continually spiralling movements. He found two forms of motion in Nature: outward, expanding flow that is used to break down, and inward-spiralling which Nature uses to build up and energise. Minute changes in temperature affect the outcome of an energetic process. The balance between the attraction and repulsion of polarised atoms is the engine of creation.

One of the scientists observing Viktor studying a stream's flow was astonished that a tiny change of temperature, only 0.1°C, could make a large difference to the quality of the water. These three characteristics—movement, polarity and temperature—need to be studied simultaneously for a natural process to be understood, for they determine whether a process is working towards enhanced order and stability (evolution of life) or towards disorder and chaos (death).

The revelation that opened his eyes to the miracle of movement came when, as a young man, he disturbed a trout that darted quickly upstream against a swift current. How could it do this? Even more challenging was to discover how a salmon could leap up a high waterfall against the power of water falling by gravity. This led him to discover the complement of gravity—levity—as a powerful compensating force in the centre of the falling column of water, which can pull the heavy fish up to the top of the falls. Viktor's engineer's mind wanted to understand how things work in Nature.

Schauberger saw water as an organism—the blood of the Earth—which carries information as well as nourishment to all life. He believed that the degeneration of our society stems from our mistreatment of water. He described three forms of life energies: those that determine quality, those of dynamism and those that encourage fruitfulness. He observed that Nature uses the egg-shape to give birth to and to contain energy. His knowledge of what is required to help healthy, sustainable growth of organisms was formidable; as was his

understanding of bioelectricity and biomagnetism in the soil and in trees. He describes the intimate interchange between cosmic and planetary energies—how cosmic movements are mirrored at the micro level.

Today's scientists are trained in the particular, not the general. They are expert at splitting, but they are limited by the physical, the surface appearance, and have difficulty in understanding that the energies that create matter work at a higher level of being than matter, which is only decaying energy. Schauberger frequently castigated conventional thinking, insisting that we have to think an octave higher.

In the last 200 years, the application of increasingly complex technologies has greatly accelerated, overwhelming the far more subtle energy systems of Nature, with dire consequences for us all. For while some will argue that these have brought benefits to many on the material level, the quality of life on the planet has seriously deteriorated, with severe damage to ecosystems and to essential biodiversity. No one explains as convincingly as Schauberger just how this came about. The energy our technology propagates is destructive of the evolutionary impulses in life forms, precipitating instead a downward spiral in the quality of organisms, and in human quality of life.

Schauberger argued that when the natural ecosystems are in balance and biodiversity rules, there is great creativity and evolution of higher and more complex life forms, but there is also order and stability. When humans walked lightly on the Earth, we co-operated with Nature. Although still part of Nature, we behave as though we are above it, dominating and abusing it. Viktor warned eighty years ago that if we continued to go against Nature, the Earth's eco-systems would become sick, the climate destructive and human society would break down, with extreme violence, greed and pandemic illnesses. His insights are vital for us today when the prevailing scientific paradigm sees the Earth as inert matter, and Nature observed as a mechanical system, its resources exploited for humanity's benefit, contributing to the appalling desecration of the environment, and to climate change.

Alick Bartholomew

ALBERT HOWARD
Soil Scientist

"Soil conservation, in the sense of counteracting the destructive effect of rain on cultivated soil, has been an essential, albeit sometimes incidental, feature of all successful agricultural systems. It was nonetheless essential for being incidental. As long as men, guided by intuition and with crude implements helping the work of their hands, treated the soil to their best advantage, soil conservation looked after itself."

I F A VISIONARY is a dreamer and, by implication, remote from practical affairs, then Sir Albert Howard was no visionary. Only someone with a firm grasp of administrative procedures and of agricultural methods would have been appointed, as Howard was in 1905, First Economic Botanist to the government of India when that country was still the jewel in the crown of the British Empire. Although a servant of Empire, Howard learned much from the cultivators of the sub-continent, and returned to Britain a quarter of a century later with views on farming which offered a distinct alternative to the industrialised methods then emerging. His approach was a vision of an agriculture which worked in harmony with nature's laws: a marriage of science and spirituality.

Howard's boyhood on a Shropshire farm shaped his scientific attitudes, giving him a robust contempt for 'the laboratory hermit'.

Nobody, he believed, had the right to be an agricultural scientist, who lacked practical farming experience. Such criticism was not the product of ignorance of scientific method, as Howard had taken first-class honours in Chemistry at the Royal College of Science (significant in view of his later hostility to chemical farming) and was first in all England in the Cambridge University agricultural diploma.

In 1899 Howard took up his first post, serving as a mycologist (expert on fungi) in the West Indies; then, from 1902 until his appointment to India, he worked at Wye Agricultural College in Kent. Influenced by the Cambridge botanist Marshall Ward, he was developing the idea that parasites are less likely to attack healthy plants. Another important influence was Gabrielle Matthaei, who encouraged him to study plants in their ecological context and whom he married in Bombay cathedral in 1905. They worked as a team to produce many scientific papers.

From 1905 to 1924 the Howards ran the experiment station at Pusa, concentrating on wheat and cotton, and from 1912 to 1919 oversaw the fruit experiment station at Quetta. Howard believed that Asian agriculture had much to teach about keeping soil fertile and crops healthy in difficult conditions, and he attached great importance to ensuring that his research helped cultivators.

Unhappy with the over-specialised approach of Western science, the Howards established the Institute of Plant Industry at Indore. They believed that food grown in humus-rich soil was likely to promote animal and human health, and developed a system of composting based on oriental methods, which transformed the surrounding land.

Gabrielle died in 1930, and the following year Howard returned to England, married her sister Louise and published *The Waste Products of Agriculture*, intended as his final contribution to science. Such was its impact, though, that he spent the 1930s advising cultivators in Asia, Africa and Europe on adapting the Indore Process to their conditions; his expertise helped save Costa Rica's coffee industry from collapse.

By the mid-1930s Howard was speaking at many venues, including the Farmers' Club and the Royal Society of Arts. He reviewed the Indore Process's achievements in *An Agricultural Testament* (1940). His converts included Lady Eve Balfour and the horticulturalist Lawrence Hills. As the pages of *Farmers Weekly* demonstrate, his views aroused considerable wartime controversy.

Although a chief inspirer of the Soil Association, Howard declined to be involved, unhappy at its scientific work being subject to control by laymen. He edited his own journal *Soil and Health* until his death in October 1947. This was the year that the Agriculture Act was passed, confirming British farming on its road of industrialisation.

Since Howard's methods had proved effective in various conditions, why were they not more generally adopted? Howard thought the answer lay in the vested interests of Big Business, though he suggested—somewhat charitably—that the motive behind mass-production of fertilisers and sprays was a desire to avert starvation in an insecure post-war world. The problem was, in his view, that the approach of manufacturers and research institutes was based on a fragmented outlook. Apart from the possible harmful effects of chemicals, Howard objected to their use on the grounds that they were simply unnecessary.

Howard's vision of agriculture was holistic, based on the 'rule of return' of wastes to the soil. These wastes create humus, which preserves and enriches the soil; the humus-rich soil produces healthy, disease-resistant plants and crops, and they in turn transmit those qualities to the animals and humans who consume them. Agriculture thus becomes a primary form of preventive medicine. It works with nature, using scientific techniques to enhance and accelerate natural processes, rather than waging war on them.

In its most advanced form, industrial agriculture aims to separate itself entirely from natural processes and ecology. But its existence depends on the ever more insecure and expensive resource of oil, and when the day of reckoning arrives, Howard's alternative vision, or something akin to it, could point the way to a more viable future.

Philip Conford

TED HUGHES
Poet of the Land

"It is occasionally possible, just for brief moments, to find the words that will unlock the doors of all those many mansions in the head and express something . . . of the deep complexity that makes us precisely the way we are."

TED HUGHES WAS BORN in 1930 in Mytholmroyd, deep in the Calder Valley of West Yorkshire. Though he later described the area as "the cradle of the industrial revolution in textiles", it was not difficult to escape into woods or onto the high moors. He claimed that for him in childhood the word 'horizon' was the most magical in the language. His much older brother initiated him into the natural world by taking him as retriever on his hunting excursions. The split between the world of men and industry and the world of wild nature was particularly stark here, and imprinted itself on Hughes' psyche. Poetry came to seem for him the voice of wild nature trying to make itself heard above the cacophony of mills, schools and churches. It seemed to him an extension of fishing, which (especially in a deep forbidden pond at

midnight) is the projection of an antenna from the familiar world and the known self into the frightening primeval darkness. All animals seemed to him messengers from that darkness, which was also his own unconscious, bellowing the evidence that we seek to hide. Some animals, such as wolf and fox, became his familiars, guiding him, like a shaman, into the world Blake called "the Energies".

Nevertheless, he found himself 'in the cooker' of grammar school and university, the intellectual, academic life, and soon after married to another poet, Sylvia Plath, whose work was dedicated, at first, to fame and success. The responsibility of providing for wife and children tied Hughes securely to that world. Otherwise, he wrote, he would have been fishing in a boat off Western Australia.

From his schooldays Hughes was greatly attracted to myth and folklore. His English master's leaving present from Mexborough Grammar School was a copy of Robert Graves' *The White Goddess*, which replaced Henry Williamson's *Tarka the Otter* as his sacred book (to be replaced in its turn by *The Bacchae* of Euripides). At Cambridge he changed from reading English to Archaeology and Anthropology. His view of nature, which derived from the struggle for survival on the bleak moors, and was mediated by myth and folklore, was very far from the Wordsworthian pieties.

Hughes described his early poems as bulletins from the constant battle between vitality and death. From the first poem in his first book *The Hawk in the Rain* (1957), he was aware how tenuously and briefly life maintains its foothold against death. Unlike Tennyson, who was prepared to "let the tiger die" rather than accept nature red in tooth and claw, Hughes was determined to find a way to accept nature and live within her laws. But before he could accomplish this, the suicide of Sylvia Plath in 1963 plunged him into despair, and the world appeared to him to be made of blood.

Hughes felt that after the death of Sylvia, the rest of his life would be posthumous. But he found a great healing resource in fishing, which became almost a religion. To enter water and become continuous through his rod and line with the holy life of that magical element was a form of atonement, of receiving the blessings of an unfallen, Dionysian world. All fish which were not eaten were returned unharmed to their element. And writing poems was a parallel activity, projecting the imagination into darkness and otherness, which is simultaneously the Great Outer Darkness (GOD) and the small inner darkness of his own unconscious. "What we capture in the outer world is what has escaped from our inner world."

In *The Life and Songs of the Crow* Hughes tried to work his way through error and suffering towards rebirth. But a second tragedy in his life forced him to abort that epic project, and thrust him into a period of fatalistic world-denial. For years he struggled, through mythic means, to transform pain into illumination.

Though he did not change his views on the possibility of pain becoming bliss, Hughes fortunately found a less painful way of reintegrating himself with the given world. In 1970 he had married a farmer's daughter, Carol Orchard, and in 1972 he bought Moortown Farm in Devon, and ran it with Carol and her father until Jack Orchard's death in 1976. Farming literally brought Hughes down to earth after his rather too Blake-like excursions into prophetic books. It proved, for all the frustrations and losses, extremely therapeutic. From a world of blood he found himself baptised into a world of mud, of life at its most grounded in the land, animal life and the seasons. It bred in him the conviction that 'only birth matters'. Without that experience, I believe it unlikely that Hughes would have come through to write his finest poems, *Moortown Diaries, Remains of Elmet* and *River*. These are poems of raw, unmediated experience, of being reborn into a radiant world, a world of light.

Hughes believed that the free intelligence which has directed Western civilisation is uninformed by our genetic survival gear of senses and instincts, and cut off from spirit. It has fostered dualistic thought and the dominance of the hubristic, violent male, and has led us inevitably into our present crisis, despite the clearest warnings from imaginative writers, especially poets, ever since the ancient Greeks. They are still ignored, or damned with faint praise and consigned to a sideshow of 'poetry for pleasure'. How can a poet, Hughes wrote, "become a medicine man and fly to the source and come back and heal or pronounce oracles? Everything among us is against it."

Yet he inspired many readers, including children, budding writers and teachers, fertilised the work of other poets, artists and composers, and surely contributed more than any other poet of his time to our rapidly growing awareness of the interdependence of all life. No longer are poetic visionaries voices in the wilderness. Their holistic and biocentric vision, formerly seen as romantic or eccentric, is coming to be seen as the essential vision of a nascent world age.

Keith Sagar

PETER MATTHIESSEN
Spokesman of the Wild

"Soon the child's clear eye is clouded over by ideas and opinions, preconceptions and abstractions. Simple free being becomes encrusted with the burdensome armour of the ego. Not until years later does an instinct come that a vital sense of mystery has been withdrawn. The sun glints through the pines, and the heart is pierced in a moment of beauty and strange pain, like a memory of paradise. After that day we become seekers."

"One reason I like boats so much is that you have to pare everything down to the bare necessities, and there you are, the captain of a little boat, without a shelter, without a past, without future hopes."

IN SAGAPONACK, Long Island, eighty miles north of Manhattan, a cold wind blows hard out of the north-west, and Peter Matthiessen, at work on a book about cranes, is struggling to stay warm. Where he lives, just south of Sag Harbor, in country whose deep loam has, for thousands of years, been farmed for corn and potatoes and where the wealthy now retreat, it is late in the day, and the air outside has fallen below freezing. The weather is unseasonal. It stands as proof to Matthiessen that humankind has damaged the order of things profoundly.

Matthiessen is a naturalist, writer and sage of the wild. By the time he was thirty-two he had already written the definitive story of North America's wildlife and two acclaimed novels. He has dedicated himself since to a life of search and renewal that has clearly kept him limber. He has held to a difficult path—seeking depth far from home and simplicity in wild places, even as wildness retreats and modern life grows more abstract. "The world is losing its grit and taste," he says.

Over five decades he has practised an exacting discipline in his prose and his life, orienting himself toward truth and giving rise in his writing to a rare, stern kind of beauty, a pure kind of joy. "I had my first story published when I was fifteen," he says, "and I have just been writing ever since." Writing called him, as nature called him, from his earliest childhood, and he has simply stuck at it. I am hunting for a mission statement, but he shies away from grand claims. I notice, as he talks, how he avoids analysis too. He is impatient with abstractions, at ease with places and things and people. So, he speaks warmly and elegantly about Siberian tigers, blue cranes, kingfishers and copperheads. He tells short tales about his books, his wife, his friend Robert Hughes, and his publisher.

Then he says, "Albert Camus, when he won the Nobel, said that writers are obligated to speak for those who cannot speak for themselves." He falls silent, letting the words rest.

It strikes me they catch exactly what Matthiessen has been doing these fifty years—entering the lives of rivers and wild animals, of landscapes and mysteries, of people whose voices and values are dying; and writing, in prose from which any hint of cant or sentiment is banished, the true things they have to tell us. He writes in prose stripped clean of artifice—most strikingly in the novel *Far Tortuga* (1975). Matthiessen, a Zen master and a naturalist used to keeping quiet in the presence of wild things, has become practised at stilling his mind and uncluttering his sentences to hold, without distraction, the speech of those who have no words.

Matthiessen sees himself mostly as a writer of fiction. "I only write non-fiction to pay my way," he says. That is how it began with *Wildlife in America* (1959). Yet it is for his non-fiction that he is best known: *The Cloud Forest* (1961), *The Tree Where Man Was Born* (1972), *The Snow Leopard* (1978) and fourteen others, all of them crafted with immaculate care. In his writing, the spirit of a place, its gesture, finds body in a prose both restrained and truthful, formal and wild.

Tigers in the Snow, with astonishing photographs by Maurice Hornocker, celebrates the work of the Siberian Tiger Project in the Russian Far East, and describes the terrible decline of the tiger across the world in this century. Many of its races—the Bali, Caspian and Javan—are already gone, and the others, including the Indian and the Amur (Siberian), number at most a few thousand each, as the woodlands that support them are logged or cleared for farming. Matthiessen's tough and tender book filled me with grief, but left me with a timid hope that the project in the Amur-Ussuri watershed and the prose of Peter Matthiessen may keep the tiger from extinction. If not, life's vividness will dim some more.

In the handwritten note he faxed me overnight, Matthiessen suggested I catch him before he goes on the road again. It turns out he is off skiing in Colorado with his neighbour, the writer James Salter. He, too, is in his seventies.

There have been harder journeys—by foot across Tibet and Nepal in search of the snow leopard, by boat through South American wilderness, by small plane and old Landrover through East Africa, and many times by sea in search of whales, white sharks and other gods.

A life spent cutting against the grain of modern convention, leaving safety far behind, can, apparently, bestow a quality of wellbeing and wonder on a person, and it is this, perhaps, that has aged Matthiessen so kindly. He has always sought out places where the manners and connections he was born to in New York won't help him. He hasn't lost his manners, but he's transcended them, as YOU must when you turn to the wild world and stay true to it for life. "There is so much to see and speak for," he says, "I could happily live 300 years."

Mark Tredinnick

CAROLINE LUCAS
Planet Politics

"Quite simply, if politicians see their job as helping business and industry sell more and more goods, then the planet will force us to change our ways—rather as the hole in the ozone layer forced us to phase out CFCs, and climate change will force us to reduce CO_2 emissions."

"It is possible to be radical and effective. To be progressive and competent. And to bring honesty and integrity back into politics."

CAROLINE LUCAS IS AN unusual environmental campaigner, and an equally unusual politician. In the UK, many environmentalists choose to have influence in one of the country's major pressure groups. In organisations such as Friends of the Earth or Greenpeace, they can remain true to their beliefs and work hard to ensure the environmental message is proclaimed loud and clear. But deep down they know the dominant ideology in the mother of parliaments is one of forever promoting economic growth, and this all too often outguns policies to protect the environment.

Their alternative can be to join one of the large political parties, where if you're bright and able, you may attain the status of backbencher or MEP. But being a Green campaigner in these parties means abandoning the reality that our finite planet needs a stable economy to bring the country back onto a sustainable footing.

Caroline recognised early on that she has to be where the decisions are made if we are to change our society to one of environmental balance and social justice. She realised too that it is the policies of the large traditional political parties which are causing many of our problems. So as a Green Party politician she competes in elections, persuades the voters, and sits it out in parliament alongside members of other parties who either don't believe that the economy is a wholly owned subsidiary of the environment, or who are learning painfully slowly that their ideologies can't solve the problems our society faces. She knows she has to loudly shout that society has to make wholesale changes to the way it operates, if it is to survive.

Caroline is one of the UK's first two Green Party Members of the European Parliament, and her term of office has coincided with environmental degradation moving from being in the realm of prediction, to there being disasters and steady deterioration on a daily basis. Concurrently, the European Parliament itself changed from being a consultation body with no real powers to a legislature setting the framework for many of the laws which EU countries later introduce.

Caroline prides herself on never having given up being an activist for the environment and social justice. She recognises that campaigners are essential to counterbalance the powerful influence of business and industry. So she is often to be seen on official EU delegations to bodies such as the World Trade Organisation, and later the same day linking arms with demonstrators outside who remind the negotiators that our economy is despoiling the planet and patently not succeeding in lifting people out of poverty.

Caroline cut her teeth as an international trade expert for Oxfam. She also worked as national press officer for the Green Party, in the days when Green politics in the UK was seen as a fringe activity irrelevant to the real gritty subjects of economics, food, health, trade and defence. Twenty years later the analysis of the problems put forward by the Greens is widely accepted by government, business and industry. The challenge now, she says, is to get the powers-that-be to take on the solutions put forward by the Greens.

She is determined to be one of those powers-that-be because, as she says: "Politicians from the other political parties which seek a forever expanding economy will see their policies for protecting the environment doomed to failure. Quite simply, if politicians see their job as helping business and industry sell more and more goods, then the planet will force us to change our ways—rather as the hole in the ozone layer forced us to phase out CFCs, and climate change will force us to reduce CO_2 emissions."

Competing for election as a Green in the UK is still seen as an unusual activity, and it is often asked why Green parties in mainland Europe seem to get much more support—Greens have been in government in France, Germany and Finland, Sweden and the Netherlands, and there are Green politicians at every level in over twenty European countries.

Quite simply, says Caroline, Greens in mainland Europe do not enjoy more support than in the UK. The difference is that in Britain most elections—and particularly for national government—use a voting system set up centuries ago, which gives results entirely out of kilter with voters' wishes. The effect is that prospective Green politicians have to persuade the public of the wisdom of their policies, and also that they are worth voting for in a skewed electoral system.

The Labour government has been experimenting with different voting methods, and where they have introduced systems similar to mainland Europe, such as for the European Parliament, the Scottish Parliament, and the Greater London Assembly, Greens gain similar vote shares to their colleagues across the English Channel.

Caroline has grasped the nettle: she sits in the European Parliament and asks uncomfortable questions of politicians who years ago mocked the Green message. They are now having to deal with the climate changing, poverty increasing, and a myriad of other problems. Caroline is determined to continue asking those uncomfortable questions, and proposing radical and workable solutions.

Peter Lang

PETRA KELLY
Green Politician

"We, the generation that faces the next century, can add the solemn injunction: 'If we don't do the impossible, we shall be faced with the unthinkable.' "

"If there is a future, it will be green."

"A truly free society must not include a 'peace' which oppresses us. We must learn on our own terms what peace and freedom mean together. There can be no peace if there is social injustice and suppression of human rights, because external and internal peace are inseparable. Peace is not just the absence of mass destruction, but a positive internal and external condition in which people are free so that they can grow to their full potential."

ORN INTO POST-NAZI Bavaria in 1947, Petra Kelly's determination to succeed and her passion for hard work may well have stemmed from her early convent schooling. She spent her adolescence in America, acquiring linguistic and cultural skills vital for a career in international politics.

Like all successful women, Kelly had to be so much better than the men in her field to reach the top. A vibrant personality, beautiful and charismatic, she brought issues to life with an impact unrivalled by any earnest young man trotting out politically correct pre-edited texts. "It will be a great day when our schools get all the money they need and the air-force has to hold a bake sale to buy a bomber." Images like this brought the ideas home to ordinary people, making connections between sexual discrimination, civil and military nuclear policy, poverty and environmental degradation.

Kelly's political career was founded on experience at the heart of European administration, where she was one of only ninety-nine women senior administrators at the European Commission in Brussels. There, decisions affecting millions of people were taken "with as much emotional engagement as a twice-smoked kipper". As Kelly declared: "Europe is one big male supremacy bastion—the Church, the political parties, the trade unions, the national bureaucracies, the European institutions."

Her vision was of a world where people had responsibility for their own destiny; in her favourite phrase "power to—not power over". This classical anarchist stance sits uneasily with her ability to seek out those with "power over" in order to further the causes which she espoused. Fund-raising campaigns for the many individual and collective causes she championed depended on her wealth of connections. Following Thoreau, Rosa Luxemburg, Gandhi and Martin Luther King, Kelly's central theme was the importance of people taking responsibility for their own destiny. This could not be achieved within the massive bureaucratic structures which all existing political parties accepted. Hence the formation of the 'anti-party party' to fight for a nuclear-free Europe of the Regions.

A sub-plot to the story is the role of leadership in Green politics. Kelly's tragedy was that she succeeded as a leader in a country and within a movement where leadership was a highly suspect quality. Realising this, she advocated rotation of posts, failing to foresee that this was no solution, since successful community politicians do not necessarily make good media figures. On the 1990 defeat of Die Grünen at the polls, Kelly considered: "The Green Party has a very small chance to learn from its past mistakes and to begin accepting the fact that political programmes are communicated to others by persons, by human beings made of flesh and blood, each of us with our strengths and weaknesses."

Kelly's vision of a Green politics which transcends national boundaries and incorporates anti-nuclear, anti-military, anti-poverty issues, human rights and gender issues, flows throughout this narration of her life's work. As a woman in a man's world, Kelly's life was one of contradictions. She never had much time for those "dogmatic macho men (like Marx) theorising and philosophising about the working classes and capital and at the same time discriminating against their wives and children and leading the lives of 'academic pashas'." And yet, what is the alternative? She herself was forced to live a lifestyle traditionally more acceptable to men, working long hours with male colleagues, relying on them for emotional support, leaving day-to-day domestic and caring chores to others, dependent on a female in the family—in this case her famous "Green granny"—for administrative and moral support. For most women it is far easier to opt out of public affairs, a decision too readily accepted at face value by men. As the contributions to these pages demonstrate, women still find it more difficult to make the space to express their views in the public arena. The record of Petra Kelly's life may act as inspiration.

Frances Hutchinson

JOHN AND NANCY TODD
Eco-designers

"Ecology and biology should be the basis of all design and a framework for a new economic order. We need to recognise that Earth is a living entity, a sentient being. In this Gaian world-view our obligations are not just to ourselves but to all the Earth itself."

"It has become essential that we create a truly symbiotic relationship with nature. This relationship will be predicated on new, highly evolved technologies made up of plants and organisms—Living Machines."

"The twenty-first century will be the century of ecology and the environment. We don't have any other choice."

JOHN TODD IS NOT a famous celebrity, because he is a strange and alien creature in academic science; an intuitive generalist whose poetic stories about life are practical and can serve as the source for the entrepreneurial fortunes of the future. He is a Tesla in a world that only rewards Edisons.

The great entrepreneurial fortunes of the nineteenth and twentieth centuries were made on the 'conscious' transport systems of railways, motorcars and aeroplanes, and on the elemental energy systems in coal and oil that empowered these systems. But I believe that the great entrepreneurial fortunes of the twenty-first century are going to be made on the 'unconscious' transport systems of pollution and the invisible elemental domains of bacteria that empower them. Only John Todd has had the instinctive genius to recognise this and to design 'living machines' and 'bioshelters' in which the dark and fluid movement of all that we choose to ignore as pollution and excrement can be transformed into the processual architectures of new human settlements. By bringing bacteria and plants into the design of new kinds of architecture, John Todd is basically creating a new kind of immune system for a bacterially cultured human society. Now if one stops to think about the economic implications of bringing architecture, public health and industrial development together, then one should be able to see the enormous economic implications for the future of Todd's 'living machines' and 'bioshelters'.

Nancy Jack was the first to recognise the gifts of John Todd, the first to understand that this intuitive synthesis of biology and design called for a new way of living. In leaving the bourgeois life of the faculty wife in the suburbs to help found New Alchemy Institute a generation ago during the Vietnam war, she also served to found the new human science of social ecology. Throughout the decade of the seventies, the Todds' New Alchemy Institute was the leading pioneer in appropriate technology and sustainable culture. As her contribution to the life of the institute, Nancy Jack edited the book-length monographs of *The New Alchemy Journal* that articulated the new vision of 'the solar village'. Their ideas attracted the attention and admiration of E. F. Schumacher, Gregory Bateson, Governor Jerry Brown in California, and Maurice Strong in Canada. In the eighties, Nancy and John founded Ocean Arks with its Center for the Restoration of Waters. For this new effort, Nancy Jack founded and edited *Annals of Earth*, a journal that endeavoured to articulate the new relationships between feminism and biological design, to extend the meaning of ecological thinking to the transformation of the psychological pollution of men's dominance of women, children and nature. As a *sage femme*, Nancy Jack Todd worked as midwife to the birth of a new global culture, and this work took her to Costa Rica, Italy, Scotland, Sweden, Japan and the Seychelles.

The partnership of the Todds became a marriage of talents, for as John is the storyteller, he is a member of an oral culture and is not comfortable at a desk, working to produce a book; but Nancy Jack is the writer, the interior sort of person who creates social relationship out of solitude through writing. She was the one who kept the books coming: *Tomorrow is Our Permanent Address* and *Bioshelters, Ocean Arks, City Farming: Ecology as the Basis of Design*. The latter has been revised, updated and re-released under the title *From EcoCities to Living Machines: Precepts for Ecological Design*.

In the Reagan and Bush era of military development and environmental deconstruction, the Todds' home had to be mortgaged and re-mortgaged to keep their Center for the Restoration of Waters afloat. In risking their own home to support the development of new ideas, technologies and strategies needed for our survival, they proved that they were serious when they talked about the planet as our home.

More recently the idea of Living Technologies has begun to take hold. The technologies have been licensed and are being used in ten states and in Canada in a wide variety of applications. Living Machines are being used successfully to restore polluted lakes, wetlands and rivers; to purify human, industrial and dairy wastes, to demonstrate the function of ecosystems in museums and, in classrooms around the country, to teach students from kindergarten to university an experiential understanding of ecology. In that, the Todds have come to terms with adapting human technologies to the living world. We could return the compliment by recognising that inasmuch as they have designed the forms of human settlement for our future, it is fair to say that whatever will become of them will happen to us.

William Irwin Thompson

MARY MIDGLEY
Ethical Philosopher

"We cannot dismiss our emotions and the rest of our non-intellectual nature, along with the body and the earth it is fitted for, as alien, contingent stuff. We have somehow to operate as a whole, to preserve the continuity of our being."

L IKE ALL GOOD VISIONARIES, Mary Midgley has a habit of seeing the significance of things before the rest of us. At a time when ethical theory was still firmly entrenched behind human lines, she wrote *Animals and Why They Matter: A Journey Around the Species Barrier*, joining Peter Singer in taking seriously the idea that ethical obligations extend beyond our own species. Moreover, Midgley has addressed more theoretical tasks, such as unravelling the implications for conventional Western approaches to ethics and trying to track down the intellectual confusions that lead to a denial of inter-species ethics.

Unusually for a professional philosopher, she constantly returns to the wider context, addressing questions such as the place of humans and their activities (including, crucially, science) in the general scheme of things, and in particular the relationship between humans and the environment.

Seeing things in their context has enabled her to show that apparently conflicting positions are in fact complementary aspects of a wider whole; and that these positions can and should be reconciled. She has argued in this way against the polarisation of animal welfare and environmental concerns which, tragically, have frequently been understood as presenting a need to take sides.

Another example is found in *Beast and Man*. Here, Midgley uses a wider focus to reveal the ways in which philosophers have typically taken an excessively abstract approach to the human mind, hence obscuring important features of the way it functions. She shows us instead the human mind in its evolutionary context and, in the process, forges a reconciliation between reason and emotion, and emphasises the importance of imagination in our reasoning processes. And she argues powerfully in recent books

(*Science and Poetry* and *The Myths We Live By*) against the alleged opposition between science and myth, and science and spirituality.

In all these cases it is a mistake to be bullied into the position of having to treat these as either/or choices. This, she argues, is "intellectual tribalism", where one perspective or dimension of an issue is taken to be the whole story and is then ranged in battle against other perspectives. This mistake can only be noticed when the wider context is brought into focus. Once this is done bridge-building and reconciliations are possible, and this in turn has tremendously constructive implications, both practical and theoretical.

Midgley graduated from Oxford in Philosophy and Ancient History in 1942. She was a civil servant and a teacher during the war, married in 1950 and moved to Newcastle, where she focused on reviewing books and starting a family. In 1963 she took up a lecturing position in the philosophy department at Newcastle University. After 'retiring' in 1980, Midgley stayed in Newcastle and continues to work with great success as one of a very rare breed—a freelance philosopher.

When James Lovelock's book *Gaia: A New Look at Life on Earth* was first published in 1979, it was widely considered to lie somewhere between fantasy, lunacy and, worst of all, spirituality. Midgley read it and immediately saw that it made sense. In *Science and Poetry* and in the Demos pamphlet *Gaia: The Next Big Idea* she argues that this way of looking at life on Earth can provide a much needed prompt and source for challenging some of the assumptions behind the practice of contemporary science. More generally, it can inspire us to rethink some of our broadest patterns of thought.

This brings us to the most literal sense in which Midgley is a visionary. She is a person who works with visions. Her writing consistently offers us a vivid understanding of the ways in which our intellectual frameworks and patterns of thinking affect the way we live and act. We live our entire lives against the background of a guiding vision or worldview. This has immense implications for how we behave, think and live. But it is often an unnoticed part of the background to our lives; and so, too, are the problems within it. Bringing to the surface any given vision and patiently opening it out to critical scrutiny is thus a crucial precursor to change—and is the point at which philosophy becomes truly political, in the broadest and most constructive sense.

In the context of environmental and social justice issues, the need for new mental models is as crucial as new technology. Western societies still struggle with corrosive forms of social atomism and individualism that militate against sustained and concerted effort to deal with collective human problems, for example, hunger, at a global level.

Helping us rethink these visions is perhaps Midgley's most crucial contribution. Here, she draws on Gaia theory as a key source, giving us the conceptual wherewithal to adapt our background vision in ways that will not only be more truthful but will afford profound understanding of our environmental problems—and inspire us to act. The Earth is not a lifeless jumble but an immense complexity of interrelated systems. And we are not independent from this living whole but deeply immersed in it. We are part of ecological systems and not apart from them. Once this simple truth is truly understood—emotionally as well as intellectually, with imagination as well as with reason—then our reasons for taking care of the environment as an overriding priority become utterly and compellingly clear.

Midgley's work of re-evaluating our background visions reveals philosophy's potential as a radical activity, affording us the much needed ability to rethink our economic, social and political institutions when they become problematic as well as the very patterns of thought that have led to these institutions and particular ways of life in the first place. 'Thinking about thinking' is thus a profoundly radical activity when approached in this way.

Tragically, however, liberating philosophy's full potential often requires extracting it from its commonest setting—academic institutions—where it can, like all subjects, become excessively specialised and far removed from practical problems in the real world. Midgley's philosophy is not about abstraction and playing intellectually beautiful but largely irrelevant games. It is about wisdom, and it is about change. And it is absolutely necessary.

Kate Rawles

ALDO LEOPOLD
Noble Naturalist

"A thing is right when it tends to preserve the integrity, stability and beauty of the biotic community. It is wrong when it tends otherwise."

"We abuse land because we regard it as a commodity belonging to us. When we see land as a community to which we belong, we may begin to use it with love and respect."

"In June as many as a dozen species may burst their buds on a single day. No man can heed all of these anniversaries; no man can ignore all of them."

"We shall never achieve harmony with land, any more than we shall achieve absolute justice or liberty for people. In these higher aspirations, the important thing is not to achieve but to strive."

ALDO LEOPOLD

ALDO LEOPOLD (1887-1948) is rightly and widely credited as being one of the founding fathers of the modern environmental movement. Born in Burlington, Iowa in the United States, he discovered his passion for the natural world during his boyhood wanderings in the wild country around the Mississippi river. After graduating from the Yale forestry school in 1909 he worked with the US Forest service in Arizona and New Mexico, where he was rapidly promoted, at 24 years of age, to the position of Supervisor of the Carson National Forest. He was centrally involved in developing proposals for the creation of the Gila Wilderness area in 1924, the first of many wilderness areas that now exist throughout the United States. In 1933 he published the first textbook in the science of wildlife management, a discipline that he founded virtually single-handedly.

Leopold was one of the first nature writers in the West to propose that our ethical sensibilities should extend beyond the human realm to encompass the whole of nature. His book *A Sand County Almanac*, published in 1949, is a classic in the field of ecological writing. In it, with great insight and simplicity, he describes the experiences in the natural world that led him to develop his 'Land Ethic', the nub of which is that humans are just "plain members of the biotic community". The land ethic hinges on the insight that humans are not the pinnacle of creation, and that it is a mistake to think of ourselves as the masters, stewards or controllers of nature; ideas rejected by a society that sees the more-than-human world as no more than a set of resources to be exploited for human benefit and economic gain. In this sense his views were advanced forerunners of the deep ecology perspective later developed by Arne Naess, the great Norwegian philosopher, whose key insight is that all life has intrinsic value, irrespective of its usefulness to humans. Like Naess, Leopold stressed the importance of affection and aesthetics in our relations with the more-than-human world. Perhaps Leopold's two most characteristic dictums in this regard are: "A thing is right when it tends to preserve the integrity, stability and beauty of the biotic community. It is wrong when it tends otherwise," and "We can only be ethical in relation to something we can feel, understand, love or otherwise have faith in."

Leopold's scientific thinking was also well ahead of its time. He thought that biodiversity conferred stability and integrity to ecological communities, making them more resistant to change and better able to recover from disturbance, a proposal denied by mainstream ecologists for many years but which has recently been vindicated by scientists working with grassland communities in the field, with laboratory microcosm experiments and in the mathematical modelling of complex ecological communities. Leopold had a sophisticated view of the thermodynamic and cybernetic nature of the land, which, for him, "is not merely soil, it is a fountain of energy flowing through a circuit of soils, plants and animals". He pioneered the restoration of degraded ecological communities, putting his ideas into practice on a damaged piece of land alongside the Wisconsin River so badly farmed that much of the sandy soil had been blown away by the wind.

His deep connection with the world of nature led him to develop a notion that the planet as a whole could be considered as a single living entity with tightly coupled interactions amongst its biota, air, rocks and waters, an idea prescient of James Lovelock's Gaia theory.

Leopold's message has major implications for our efforts to live harmoniously with the Earth, for nothing of lasting value will be achieved unless we begin to treat the wild world not as a slave to be subdued and exploited, but as a 'person' in the widest sense of the word. Leopold believed that "no important change in ethics was ever accomplished without an internal change in our intellectual emphasis, loyalties, affections and convictions." He emphasised the fact that hands-on experience of ecological restoration could help to bring about this radical inner reorientation—a task carried on to this day by the work of the Aldo Leopold Foundation on the land that he so passionately helped to restore, and on which he so tragically died whilst helping a neighbour to extinguish a grass fire.

Stephan Harding

LADY EVE BALFOUR
Organic Pioneer

"My subject is food, which concerns everyone; it is health, which concerns everyone; it is the soil, which concerns everyone—though they may not realise it."

"Soil fertility can still be maintained by obeying nature's law of return, and by this means vitality in soil, plant animal and man results."

ORN IN 1898, EVE BALFOUR'S close male relations included a viceroy, two prime ministers (one a renowned world statesman), and several distinguished academics. Her female relations, formidable in intellect and action, included Eleanor Balfour, founder of Newnham College, Cambridge; her sister Alice, a gifted artist, author and lepidopterist; and leading suffragette Constance Lytton. With this background it might have been expected that such a vibrant and striking girl would have married early, and but for the First World War, this might have happened.

From the age of eight, however, Eve, with her older sister Mary—who was delicate and almost always in the protective shadow of her younger sibling—had expressed the desire to farm. An explanation for this then unusual ambition may have been that their uncle A. J. Balfour's mansion lay above the rich pasturelands of East Lothian, 'the garden of Scotland'. On leaving the estate, the vista of busy, fertile farmland, with horse-drawn ploughs at work or rows of men scything the crops laid out in front of young impressionable children, must have seemed magical. "One day we will have our own farm," they declared, with youthful single-mindedness.

It says much for her determination that at the age of eighteen Eve became one of the first female graduates in agriculture at Reading University, where Mary also took a course in poultry breeding. Eve was then appointed wartime manager of a requisitioned Welsh farm, overseeing delinquent girls older than herself assigned to agricultural work. Soon after the war she and Mary, with the help of a loan from their parents, bought a farm in Suffolk with a moated Elizabethan farmhouse, but no sanitation or running water. Against the odds, their dairy farm survived the post-war slump years when agriculture was severely affected, but to do so Eve formed a jazz band, performing professionally, and wrote thrillers.

In the 1930s, now styled Lady Eve, following her father's succession to the earldom that had been awarded to his brother, A. J. Balfour, she led the almost forgotten but finally successful battle against payment of tithes on farm land and incomes. Obscured today by the outbreak of the Second World War, this was at the time an epic struggle against the all-powerful forces of the Church. On successive days Eve appeared in court on charges of public order offences (on which she was acquitted), and then gave evidence before a Parliamentary Commission, when her straight talking swayed the result.

With world events moving inexorably towards war, and her farming showing every sign of success, she turned to the larger picture. She became inspired by Lord Lymington's book *Famine in England*, and the research of Sir Albert Howard and Sir Robert McCarrison on the effects on health of farming, diet and the results of composting waste materials. In conjunction with her neighbour, Alice Debenham, and with Mary's support, she decided to put these methods to the ultimate test by donating the two farms to an Experimental Trust to compare side-by-side the results of organic farming and mixed farming with chemicals. Despite the outbreak of war and death of her co-founder Alice Debenham, she successfully formed the Haughley Trust, accepting a farm labourer's wages as Manager of the Experiment.

In 1943 she published her book *The Living Soil*, extolling the virtues of compost and the all-important connection between a healthy soil and healthy crops, animals and people—then a revo-

lutionary concept. It was an instant success, selling over seven editions. With the support and encouragement of many of those who had read and approved of it, including the leaders of the Peckham Experiment, she organised a meeting in 1945, when the Soil Association was formed under her chairmanship.

A natural leader and organiser—although as she herself admitted, not a good chairman—she soon accepted the role of organising secretary. The Soil Association itself eventually gravitated to Haughley, taking over the Trust. Like many such bodies composed of disparate enthusiasts, it tended to lack cohesion. Eve's enthusiasm and drive, however, kept it going through its many vicissitudes. The major problem was that its message to the farming community seemed directly opposed to that of the giant combines such as ICI, which were producing chemical fertilisers that promised increased yields and hence higher incomes. She and the Soil Association were quickly labelled as cranks and publicly derided, yet she resolutely toured the agricultural shows and built up a punishing yearly schedule of lectures at venues from village halls to university agricultural courses as the voice of the organic movement, stoutly representing the Soil Association.

The Haughley Experiment was finally wound up due to a lack of finance, but not before some important results had been achieved. Undaunted by the many financial crises of the Soil Association, Eve toured the USA, Australia and New Zealand, Kenya, the near East and Europe, mostly on a shoestring, supporting herself by lectures and forging alliances and contacting like-minded people on the way. She persevered as organising genius of the Soil Association into her late seventies when it moved from Haughley, and even in her retirement she had a worldwide correspondence and following. For over forty years she was a voice in the wilderness, but she had the satisfaction of knowing that the message she had proclaimed so indefatigably—that soil and health are one and indivisible—had finally been acknowledged on a world scale. She was a visionary indeed, but with her feet firmly in the soil.

Michael Brander

EDWARD GOLDSMITH
Original Ecologist

"The crisis we are facing today is not caused by a lack of material goods, nor yet by a lack of technology; it is caused by the social, biological and ecological disruption we have inflicted on the world in our relentless pursuit of material 'progress'. It can only be solved by re-establishing the social, biological and ecological systems we have disrupted. Only then can we hope to achieve a sustainable, just and self-reliant society."

TEDDY GOLDSMITH was born in Paris in 1928. His mother was French, and his father British, of German Jewish descent. Since the Middle Ages, his father's family had been prominent members of the Jewish community in Frankfurt. With that background, it is hardly surprising that Teddy should have some of the characteristics of the 'Wandering Jew', not accepting as read the accepted wisdom of his contemporaries, but instead keeping his mind open to fresh ideas, to other ways of 'seeing'.

It is precisely that broad vision that led in 1968 to his founding *The Ecologist* magazine. In so doing he undoubtedly ruffled the feathers of those ivory tower biologists who insisted that ecology was their domain and theirs alone. Teddy was certainly one of the first to see ecology writ large. He realised that ecology was the overarching discipline, with biology taking its place, with the rest of the biosphere, under its mantle. As such, an ecology of necessity had to encompass human actions upon the environment.

Given that understanding, it is hardly surprising that Teddy should have embraced Lovelock's Gaia Hypothesis. The logic of Gaia was close to his own concept of life on Earth. Teddy believes that the parts support the the whole, in a set of nested living entities, each interacting with the other, and in turn impinging upon the environment, the conditions of which are then altered to suit life itself.

He has also always fervently rejected the notion—inherent in neo-Darwinist theories of evolution—that randomness, a hit-and-miss event on a gene, is the prime driver of evolution. The very idea that the extraordinary adaptations of life and the relative stability and longevity of living systems should be simply the result of random mutations appeared to him as unutterably ludicrous.

Instead, he realised that life, from the cell to the organ, to the whole organism and on to the community, would always seek to stabilise the environment surrounding it. Like Lovelock and more or less at the same time, Teddy extended the notion of the *milieu intérieur*, the internalised physiology proposed in the nineteenth century by Claude Bernard, to the external environment, the *milieu extérieur*. That is Gaia, and it becomes clear that evolution does not occur through haphazard mutations, independent of environmental changes, but is a planetary-scale process in which feedbacks in both directions occur between the whole and its component parts.

Teddy read Philosophy, Politics and Economics at Magdalen College, Oxford. What he gained from his time in Oxford was an incredulity that people would actually believe that human activities on the Earth could be classified as 'progress', without taking into account the devastating impact of modern life on life support systems. Classic economics, based as it is on the notion of a bounty of limitless resources waiting for the ingenuity of man to exploit them, was seen by Teddy as wholly unsustainable.

The Ecologist was one of the first magazines of its kind to reveal the dangerous shortcomings of the nuclear industry, and again I remember Teddy taking the stand in front of the perimeter fence of what was then Windscale, just before the 1977 public inquiry, and putting some life into what had been until then a rather damp protest.

In 1972, Teddy co-authored *A Blueprint for Survival* which declared that our planet, as a life-supporting system, could not survive untrammelled growth, and that we had better orchestrate a move towards a sustainable economy. Just how to do that was spelt out and it included the return to a healthy agriculture, to greater self-sufficiency at the local and regional level, and ways to curb transportation. The accelerating move towards global free trade and the ever greater integration of national economies are diametrically opposed to the prescriptions for survival as laid out in the *Blueprint*. The publication of the *Blueprint* had considerable impact. It was published in fourteen countries and translated into many different languages. It spawned a number of Green Parties, the first in New Zealand. It also aroused scorn and derision among people such as John Maddox, then editor of *Nature*, who saw no limits to human ingenuity in overcoming bottlenecks, in spurring on growth and simultaneously in protecting the environment.

In fact, the real limits to growth are beginning to manifest themselves, not necessarily as was thought thirty years ago through shortages of raw materials, but through the impact of fossil-fuel-based economies on global climate. And it is not just greenhouse gas emissions but the destruction of ecosystems, such as the great tropical forests of the Amazon Basin, that are bringing about abrupt, devastating change to weather patterns and climate.

Teddy, as inspirer, activist and ecologist *par excellence* was honoured in 1991 with the Right Livelihood Award and one year later with the Chevalier de la Légion d'Honneur. He has written innumerable articles, ranging from the meaning of society within the context of the environment, to the impact of development and free trade, never afraid to speak his mind and challenge the orthodoxy of the idea of a world steadily progressing to the pinnacle of human fulfilment and wellbeing. His books, all conceptually challenging, include *Can Britain Survive?* (1971), *The Stable Society* (1977), and perhaps best encapsulating Teddy's way of thinking, *The Way: An Ecological World View* (1992). He has also contributed to and edited *The Earth Report* (1998), *The Case against the Global Economy* (1996), and *The Social and Environmental Impacts of Large Dams* (1984).

Peter Bunyard

JOSÉ LUTZENBERGER
Green Agronomist

"The most profound spirituality consists in feeling part of this marvellous and mysterious process that characterises Gaia, our living planet: the fantastic symphony of organic evolution which originated ourselves together with millions of other species. And it means feeling responsible for its continuous unfolding."

"Modern intensive agriculture, along with the economic policies that reinforce it, are responsible for the mass uprooting of small farmers and migrations from the land to the cities."

JOSÉ LUTZENBERGER will go down in history as an extraordinary visionary, genius and orator. Born in Brazil in 1926 of German parents, he was trained as an agronomist, and lived through the transition from culturally diverse regenerative agriculture to the predominance of industrial chemical agriculture.

Lutz, as he was affectionately known, was a passionate man, with a deep sense of moral indignation at injustices inflicted on human beings, other species, or indeed the planet herself. He brought all these dimensions of vision, pragmatism, determination and compassion to every situation with which he engaged. He said of himself, "I became an environmentalist out of despair. I'm the kind of person who, when confronted with something that can be changed for the better, will get a very bad conscience if I do not act."

He lamented the fact that so many people are illiterate in natural history. "They do not realise what a unique and beautiful evolutionary story we are experiencing, which began four and a half billion years ago, when our solar system was born. It took hundreds of millions of years and many explosions to put the elements into the atmosphere that make life." He had a way of explaining this miraculous story, using his scientific rigour, that would bring himself and his audience to tears at the wonder of creation. "Real scientific enquiry makes one humble and in awe of this beautiful universe," he said.

Lutz believed that our major challenge now is to break the techno-bureaucratic infrastructure set up by corporations. Technology ensnares us in ever more complex structures.

We have a techno-dictatorial world governing system, controlled by corporations in all areas of human life. They promote technology that is good for technology, not for genuinely solving human needs. But they pretend that they are trying to solve the problems which technocracy created. Their answer: more technocracy. The technocrats claim that poverty is the problem and genetic engineering is the solution to feed the hungry. But it is industrial agriculture which created poverty in the first place.

We do not need mass production, but production by the masses. It is so much more efficient because production is close to the individual; thus it is more flexible, more adaptive, more complex and thus more intelligent. It implies Earth democracy in that there is a more equitable spread of decision-making, self-reliance, people thinking for themselves and taking responsibility for themselves, being closer to the Earth and living dynamics.

Lutz believed that the most important is the necessary rethinking of our cosmology. The anthropocentric world-view has allowed our technocrats and bureaucrats to look at planet Earth as if it were no more than a free storehouse of unlimited resources to be used, consumed and wasted to indulge our most absurd or stupid whims. We have no respect for creation. Nothing in nature is sacred.

With very few exceptions indigenous people developed mythologies, taboos, rituals and attitudes that made their existence compatible with the survival of the ecosystems they depended on, usually enriching them. In modern terminology, we would say that their lifestyles were sustainable.

We need a new frame of reference, to put it in more technical terms. If I said "mythology", many scientifically minded people might protest. James Lovelock suffered stinging attacks from people because he used mythological metaphors. But his concept of Gaia, the Earth as a homeostatic system that regulates itself, is both a strictly scientific interpretation and a mythological way of looking at the world, which is what most people need.

Lutz was also a successful businessman, and he set up his own waste management company. His attitude with regard to pollution was to try to co-operate with large companies and change them from within. For many years he fought Riocell, a large cellulose and paper factory in southern Brazil, because of the way it polluted the environment, but he always remained on speaking terms with the factory's director. Eventually he was hired as a consultant, with dramatic results. He set up a system whereby 99.6 per cent of the company's waste is turned into fertiliser and other products for organic farming.

Lutz died on 14th May 2002. These words from Melissa Holloway, a student of Lutz, sum up the feelings of all who knew him:

"The sadness for us and the world is to lose such a shining soul. I remember the passion, the fire in his voice, the tears as he spoke of Gaia and what we have done to her. I like to think of Lutz as a giant, wise oak tree, who dropped many, many acorns in the fertile minds of those who listened to him. He is now gone, but a whole forest of people touched by his vision and wisdom remain. We now have a responsibility to carry his message forward to the next generation."

Liz Hosken

JANE GOODALL
Champion of Nature

"I think one of the most exciting things is this feeling of mystery, feeling of awe, the feeling of looking at a little live thing and being amazed by it and how it's emerged through these hundreds of years of evolution."

"The least I can do is speak out for those who cannot speak for themselves."

DR JANE GOODALL is best known for her work with chimpanzees at the Gombe National Park in Tanzania. The study that she began in 1960 continues today and has taught us a great deal, not only about our closest living relatives, but also about our own position in the natural world. But while Jane has become the world's best known primatologist, she is more concerned today with saving primates than studying them: her focus is on the terrible harm that we have inflicted on the environment worldwide.

Jane's love of animals began when she was a toddler, watching worms and sparrows outside her London home. Indeed, Jane attributes much of her success to her mother, Vanne. Not only did she encourage Jane's childhood dream of going to Africa to live with animals, but when the British authorities of what was then Tanganyika refused permission for a young girl to go to Gombe alone, Vanne volunteered to accompany her for the first few months. Once there, Vanne started a little clinic for the fishermen and thus established the good relations with all the villagers which so facilitated her daughter's work.

Jane refers to some chimpanzees as "friends", but says that such friendship is not comparable to that between humans. Yet it can be intense and moving. David Greybeard was the first chimpanzee who lost his fear of Jane. One day, as she sat near him, she noticed a palm nut lying on the ground. She held it towards him on the palm of her hand, but he turned away. When she held her hand closer he looked into her eyes, took the nut, dropped it to the ground, then gently squeezed her hand in reassurance. The primeval communication was simple: Thank you, I am not in the mood for the nut, but I appreciate the offer. Among all her experiences with chimpanzees, this stands in her memory as the most significant.

It brings up the question of our whole relationship to other animals. Is there, as some would say, a sharp line between animals and humans? Jane says emphatically no. Chimpanzees have personalities; minds capable of rational thought and emotions. Like us they are capable of violence on the one hand, love and altruism on the other.

Yet even the famous Gombe chimpanzees are endangered. Outside their tiny national park all the trees are gone. Human populations there have increased, as they have worldwide, and there has been a massive influx of refugees. There are more people in the area than the land can support. Survival here, and across Africa, is a struggle. Habitats are destroyed and animals are hunted. Worst is the bushmeat trade—the commercial hunting of wild animals for food—made possible by foreign logging companies that bulldoze and chainsaw their way into the forests making roads that enable hunters to follow. They shoot everything from gorillas and chimpanzees to birds and bats, load them onto trucks and sell them to the urban elite, who pay more for the meat than for chicken or goat. At current trends, up to 90 percent of the apes' remaining habitat will be lost and they themselves will be almost extinct by 2030—or, says Jane, even sooner.

A visionary does not merely record the passing of events. Jane's vision for change involved working with the local people, improving their lives in practical ways that they might help conserve the natural world. TACARE (Take Care), a programme of the Jane Goodall Institute, works to improve the lives of people in twenty-four villages in the Gombe area. It is holistic, including reforestation, soil erosion control and the revitalisation of farmland. It provides microcredit loans to women, primary school scholarships for girls, HIV-AIDS education, primary health care, hygienic latrines and family planning. TACARE, now run entirely by Tanzanians, has arrested the rapid degradation of natural resources. "We need to put TACARE everywhere," says Jane.

Jane recognises that we are living in dark and frightening times. With global warming, the looming water crisis, loss of biodiversity, genetic modification of foods and all the results of human cruelty and violence, it is not surprising that so many young people blame us for compromising their future. When Jane looks at her three young grandchildren and thinks how we have harmed our planet since she was their age, she is saddened, angered and determined more than ever to do all she can to fight such evil. We can only succeed, she believes, if we have hope, without which we become depressed and fall into apathy.

To counteract this, Jane initiated Roots & Shoots, an environmental and humanitarian programme for young people. Its main message is that every one of us makes a difference every day. It began in Tanzania in 1991 and has grown to more than 8,000 groups in ninety-six countries. Roots & Shoots has programmes for pre-schoolers through university. Each group chooses three hands-on projects to make the world a better place, for the human community, for animals—wild and domestic—and for the environment.

It is knowing that young people—enthusiastic, energetic, determined, courageous—are actually changing the world each day that gives Jane the energy to carry on with her gruelling schedule. She alights, occasionally, at home in Bournemouth on England's south coast, where she does her writing. She gets to her beloved Gombe just twice a year for only a few days at a time. Yet those short visits, when she can spend time in the forest, in solitude, serve to recharge her spiritual batteries.

Bob Lebensold

MASANOBU FUKUOKA
Natural Farmer

"The ultimate goal of farming is not the growing of crops, but the cultivation and perfection of human beings."

"If we throw mother nature out of the window, she comes back in the door with a pitchfork."

IMAGINE YOU ARE a bird flying over farmlands somewhere on Earth. What do you see? Long straight rows of a single vegetable—say cabbages, carrots, or corn—or perhaps vast square fields of wheat. Patterns are geometric, regulated, artificial, clean-cut, and maintained with big petroleum-powered machinery. Water is piped from distant reservoirs. Chemical pesticides eliminate insect life. For Masanobu Fukuoka, the legendary Japanese sage-farmer now in his 90s, who developed the 'natural' or 'do-nothing' approach to farming after countless seasons of patient observation and subtle experimentation, this is a dying landscape, a vista of auto-destruction.

From a bird's-eye view, the agriculture based on Fukuoka's farming principles would, on the other hand, resemble nature gone wild—a rich and dense 'untidy' tapestry or scraggly patchwork of orchards, a great variety of fruits and vegetables, weeds, grains, insects, clover, spiders, microbes, fungi, worms . . . in other words, an uncontrolled, self-regulating, teeming community of life. Like a landscape-altering earthquake, Fukuoka's simple 'unorthodox' methodology shook up and overturned the very assumptions upon which our entire modern, agricultural monolith had been built and maintained. This humble, white-bearded gentleman has prepared the soil for a sustainable, robust and socially beneficial agriculture that will take root, and hopefully help restore wholeness to our planet, in this century.

Fukuoka originally trained as a plant pathologist and worked as a research scientist. Plagued by self-doubt, he quit his job, suffered a life-threatening bout of pneumonia, and then at the age of twenty-five spent a sleepless night under a tree—where suddenly the true nature of things was revealed to Fukuoka in a flash of *satori*. He comprehended the wholeness of all existence, an experience that was to profoundly alter his view of farming forever. He brought this fundamental outlook back to his father's land on the island of Shikoku in 1938, became a farmer and experimented with 'natural farming' for the next forty years. Before the Westernisation of agriculture in Japan, first in the Meiji era (around 1868) and then again after World War II, land in Shikoku had pretty much been cultivated by natural methods—the close observation of cycles and seasons—for almost 1,400 years. This tradition must have also been a strong influence on Fukuoka's thinking. The translation and publication of his book *The One-Straw Revolution* by Rodale Press in 1978 added momentum to an already growing worldwide movement towards alternative agriculture.

Fukuoka's profound insight is that 'nature, left alone, is in perfect balance'. Nature cultivates excellent soil on her own. Why meddle? His second great insight, which contains the seeds of great spiritual and social revolution as well, is that humans should farm with nature as she is. Work alongside nature with humility, sensitivity, and gratitude. Any kind of tampering to 'improve' or control her processes is invasive, and will only introduce disorder into a biological community that is already a dynamic, self-regulating, self-creating system. Interference is only futile and self-defeating. We do not grow food; nature grows food! Fukuoka's harvests consistently are equivalent to or surpass those from the cultivated plots of nearby agri-biz farmers, yet he has never ploughed his land, composted, pruned, fertilised, or used machinery, herbicides or pesticides. His Four Principles of Natural Farming are:

- NO CULTIVATION: No ploughing or turning of the soil. As Fukuoka observed, the Earth has been cultivating its soil for millions of years through the penetration of root filaments, decay, the activity of micro-organisms, fungi, and earthworms. It's an expert!

- NO FERTILISER OR COMPOST: Soil already maintains fertility through the cycles of plant and animal life. Be a careful observer of these cycles!

- NO WEEDING: 'Weeds' are members of the ecosystem too, and should not be eliminated. Instead, assist the ecosystem by finding the most 'co-operative weeds'. Fukuoka eventually settled on straw mulch, a ground cover of white clover, and temporary flooding to attain sufficient productivity without resorting to herbicides or weeding.

- NO CHEMICALS, NO PESTICIDES: In Fukuoka's own words: "Harmful insects and plant diseases are always present, but do not occur in nature to an extent which requires the use of poisonous chemicals. The sensible approach to disease and insect control is to grow sturdy crops in a healthy environment."

In later years Fukuoka developed a technique of packing up to a hundred seeds into small balls of red clay. He then broadcasts these 'seedballs' onto unploughed land. The clay protects the seeds from being eaten by animals, but when exposed to rain, it melts and releases nutrients, allowing the seeds to germinate. This technique has been seen as a possible method to build soils and reverse desertification in places like Africa. Fukuoka in fact visited Somalia, making gifts of seedballs to hundreds of poor children. Fukuoka was recognised as a pioneer of sustainable agriculture when he received the prestigious Ramon Magsaysay Award for Public service in 1988, and 'Fukuoka Societies' continue to sprout in countries around the world.

Significantly, it is not the quantity of food produced by Fukuoka's methodology that is most important, but the quality of life that results from its practice. The food is healthy and organic, a greater community of life is served, and labour is light, leaving much time for art-making (ink painting is one of Fukuoka's favourite pastimes), walking, laughing, visiting friends, telling stories, playing music, or watching the starry night sky. Fukuoka's methods leave us rich in time, although he insists that "there is no such thing as time". A richer soul, a richer society—all based on rich, natural soil left to do what it does best.

John Einarsen

KARL-HENRIK ROBÈRT
The Natural Step

"Business is the economic engine of our Western culture, and if it could be transformed to truly serve nature as well as ourselves, it could become essential to our rescue."

"I think most people in business understand that we are running into a funnel of declining resources globally. We will soon be ten billion people on Earth—at the same time, as we are running out of forests, crop land and fisheries. We need more and more resource input for the same crop or timber yield. At the same time pollution is increasingly systematically and we have induced climate change. All that together creates a resource funnel."

K ARL-HENRIK ROBÈRT is not easily described. Whilst the awards and accolades steadily mount as tributes to his remarkable achievements, he remains in so many ways a very simple individual; simplicity without reduction is a favourite phrase of his, and in some ways it describes him perfectly.

Karl-Henrik, Kalle to his friends, is as honest and straightforward a person as you will meet anywhere. That is my meaning in describing him as 'simple'. It certainly does not refer to his intellect. There is such unquestioning commitment from Kalle to the cause he has chosen, or which has chosen him, that at times he can be infuriating in sticking to his analysis. There is no dissimulation with Karl-Henrik. I cannot think of anyone less likely to thrive in politics, for he simply does not have the self-interest that seems to be needed for that kind of role. On the other hand I cannot think of anyone I would be more pleased to have in the trench with me when things get tough.

The enduring strength of this straightforwardness is remarkable. Can you imagine one scientist asking others to agree upon what it is makes the world tick? Yet that is what he did. And he kept on asking that question, until the non-negotiable truths of our unsustainability became exactly that—irrefutable and utterly compelling in their simplicity. As Paul Hawken has said, "The whole world has dreamt of a solid definition of sustainability that would allow systematic step-by-step planning. When the definition arrived, delivered by The Natural Step, it was remarkable to see how simple it was. Why hadn't anybody thought about it before?"

The story of how this remarkable individual went about his one-man crusade to get answers to his questions has been told many times. It began in Sweden, and it is interesting to wonder if it could have happened anywhere else at that time. Fifteen years ago the world was struggling to understand the unending chain of environmental impacts triggered by our human economies. Much had been done by science to understand the basic cycles and services of nature. Some economists had realised for many years that unrestrained economic growth was a dangerous mirage. But nobody had put these together in a way in which made sense for those who were making decisions everyday. No real attempts had been made to produce an explanation, in the midst of such complexity, that people could actually use. Therein lies the real genius, in my view, of Karl-Henrik's pioneering work. The Natural Step's System Conditions have been elaborated and incorporated in a wider Framework these days, but even in their original raw form they were laid out brilliantly. They took the science, and built a perfectly clear bridge to human actions and behaviours. The communication of that science was very cleverly done. The trick seems to have been in forging a marriage between natural science and systems thinking, which makes it all so clear and so accessible. It is the systems approach, at which Karl-Henrik really excels, that has been the foundation of the way he inspires so many others. The pedagogy of TNS is a shining example of how to communicate science in a way that lets others get to grips with the consequences.

As well as that extremely strong and deeply thought-through systems approach, there are other ingredients to the TNS package, also purpose-built from the very start, which have ensured its lasting significance. Understanding and responding to the way people learn was another fundamental part of the way Karl-Henrik went about his creation. And it works, as many of us can testify. You can 'get' sustainable development, using the Natural Step Framework, in all kinds of ways and to many varying degrees. I have personally seen the light bulb go on for people who probably never had to spell photosynthesis before, as well as for leaders and intellectuals in all walks of life. It is as if Karl-Henrik created a crystal with many facets. Whichever one you choose to look at, the story is clear. You can take it deeper and it still makes sense, or you can stick with the basic unreduced principles. It is probably because of this clever construction that The Natural Step as an organisation has been so successful in getting the sustainability message to so many businesses and communities around the world. It engages people, no matter where they are coming from.

Of course that has also been a part of the individual brilliance of Dr Karl-Henrik Robèrt. He is charismatic, to use an overused word in an apt description for once. He has so much faith and absolute commitment to what he is doing, furthering the cause of sustainable development, that audiences respond to him as a person as well as to his message. Both are accessible. Both the person and the message are totally vital, and must be heard.

Karl-Henrik will go on receiving awards for what he does and for what he has created. He, and the organisation dedicated to promoting The Natural Step, will go on exploring the art and the science of sustainable solutions. Long may they run.

David Cook

RUPERT SHELDRAKE
Morphic Resonance

"My aim has been to try to find a wider picture or paradigm for science that is not constricted to an inanimate, mechanistic view of things. In a way, the bigger picture is the idea of the whole universe as a living organism."

"I'm talking about science on the leading edge, where it's not clear which way things are going because we don't know, and I'm dealing with areas which we don't know about."

"Most of nature is inherently chaotic. It's not rigidly determined in the old sense. It's not rigidly predictable."

"The idea is that there is a kind of memory in nature. Each kind of thing has a collective memory. So, take a squirrel living in New York now. That squirrel is being influenced by all past squirrels."

RUPERT SHELDRAKE

RUPERT SHELDRAKE'S IDEAS challenge not only the accepted theories of science, but the way in which science is done and the power structures that govern it.

The basis of his work is a new way of looking at causality—at the way in which the universe hangs together. Conventional science is based on unchanging natural laws, coupled with chance—the randomness of the timing of a radioactive decay, or of the positions at which genetic mutations arise on a strand of DNA. To these, Sheldrake adds a new fundamental principle called formative causation. According to this, forms that occurred often in the past tend to repeat themselves in the future.

A 'form' can be a shape, such as the shape of a crystal, or of the early stages of a developing embryo (including its internal structure), or a form can be a pattern of change in time such as a particular sort of learnt behaviour. Formative causation does not act explicitly on individual particles as do the forces of conventional physics, but it steers the growth of large-scale patterns down a particular route in situations where chance has opened up many alternative possibilities. It is not limited by time and space: once many instances of a form have occurred in the past their influence is available everywhere, at all later times.

Formative causation works through a process which Sheldrake calls morphic resonance. When, perhaps through chance, a form appears that matches the very first stages of some particular process of development that has occurred in the past, then formative causation latches onto this correspondence, like a musical string resonating to the sound of a corresponding note, so as to increase the tendency for the later stages of the process also to appear. An example is the growth of an embryo. When a fertilised egg starts to grow, an initial sphere of cells forms which then develops a characteristic shape by folding in on itself. The correspondence between this shape and millions of identical occurrences in the past then sets up a tendency in the space around the embryo for the past patterns of development to repeat themselves. Sheldrake calls this guiding tendency in a region of space a morphic field.

Morphic resonance applies to minute systems like atoms as much as to organisms, and so in his later books Sheldrake argues that what have been thought of as the 'natural laws' of physics are in fact instances of formative causation. So the universe is governed not by abstract eternal laws, but by a web of habits maintained by morphic resonance.

This theory came to be seen by orthodoxy as a dangerously subversive heresy, in part because of the striking and easy ways that Sheldrake devised to test it. He organised experiments as part of TV programmes in which the viewers could post in their immediate results which provided the data for research. Now school children can send for a pack of instructions and verify the effects in their classrooms. Science suddenly escapes from privileged laboratories and becomes the property of everyone.

All his work is directed by a true scientific empiricism. He never dismisses any theory or anecdote out of hand, but looks to see how it can be tested. Neither is he willing to accept received dogma unless it too has been tested. As a result he presents a world-view that is both scientific and yet radically different from the mechanistic character of the conventional picture. It is non-mathematical, based on perceived qualities. It is non-local, morphic resonance being indifferent to time and space and acting on extended forms. When, in his book *The Sense of Being Stared At*, he connects the morphic fields of our own minds, fields which extend outside our bodies, with the process of vision, he confirms our intuition that our minds themselves extend beyond our bodies. He thus gives us a world where we are intimate neighbours with everything that our minds can reach out to and touch, a world where ecological concern is as natural as concern for our own bodies. This vision is itself a spirituality, and perhaps a reflection of the mystical strand of Christianity that has always underpinned his life.

Despite its current hostility to formative causation, it is to be hoped that as conventional science moves towards an increasingly connected picture as a result of its own development, and begins to assist society at large in framing a new world-view, so Sheldrake's position will be seen as one of the main foundation stones of an eventual synthesis between science and the spiritual vision.

Chris Clarke

THOMAS BERRY
Earth Theologian

"We cannot obliterate the continuities of history, nor can we move into the future without guidance from existing cultural forms. Yet, somehow we must reach even further back, to where our human genetic coding connects with the other species codings of the larger Earth community. Only then can we overcome the limitations of the anthropocentrism that binds us."

THOMAS BERRY WAS BORN in North Carolina in 1914. His early years as a Catholic priest were those of a contemplative monk. In 1948 he completed his doctorate in comparative history of religions, and went on to become a cultural historian of religions of the world. His library gives one an inkling of his depth of understanding of the world's spiritualities: he has written on Buddhism, Confucianism, Christianity, Hinduism and the spiritualities of indigenous peoples. He is also a writer of books and essays, and a poet.

However, the most important sense of who Thomas Berry is can only be grasped by the personal impact that he has had on so many lives. The only way that I can convey this dimension of his 'presence' is to give the reader a sense of how he changed the course of my life. What follows next is my first personal encounter with Thomas Berry in 1978 during a series of seminars at the Holy Cross Centre at Port Burwell, Ontario, Canada.

By the end of his first talk I knew that Thomas Berry was going to have a profound influence on my life. His opening statement anticipated the expansiveness of his vision. As Thomas put it, the governing dream of the twentieth century appears as a kind of ultimate manifestation of that deep inner rage of Western society against its earthly condition as a vital member of the life community. At such a moment a new revelatory experience is needed, an experience wherein human consciousness awakens to the grandeur and sacred quality of the Earth process. Thomas later would refer to this as a "moment of grace". This awakening is our human participation in the dream of the Earth, the dream that is carried in its integrity— not in any of Earth's cultural expressions, but in the depths of our genetic coding. Therein the Earth functions at a depth beyond our capacity for active thought. We can only be sensitised to what is being revealed to us. Humans have probably not had such participation in the dream of the Earth since earlier shamanic times; but therein lies our hope for the future for ourselves and for the entire Earth community. This is the vision and challenge he put before all of us who attended his summer seminars at Holy Cross.

At the very first Berry summer seminar series I was asked to make a final reflective response to Thomas's presentations. Because of the richness, diversity and depth of his presentations, I knew I would need a guiding focus to hold what I would have to say. The guide turned out to be what he called the three operating principles of the universe at all levels, namely differentiation, subjectivity and communion. Throughout his lectures, Tom had cautioned against the creation of monocultures. Instead of seeing difference in a dangerous light, we were invited to entertain the idea that all of the creative processes come to us as difference and variety. As Thomas would say, "The universe abhors monoculture."

But the universe brings us much more than worlds of difference. There is a deep order of subjectivity or what Thomas would say, quoting Teilhard de Chardin, there is a "within of things". He also referred to it as the dimension of interiority. There is an 'inscape' as well as a 'landscape' to attend to, and it is this deep order of 'interiority' that attunes us to the deep mystery of things. This depth dimension opens us up to the domain of the sacred where awesome mystery pervades.

Having said all that, Thomas then went on to say that all of the differentiated powers of creation, in the deep depths of their mystery, ache and arc towards connection. He called it the compassionate curve of gravitational attraction. I could sense that we were being invited out of the anthropocentric confines of the human community into the wider matrix of the Earth community and the universe itself. We should consider ourselves as 'earthlings' bonding in the wider community of the 'web of life'. This sense of the wider community moved us from a restricted sense of human history to a wider expansive framework of an evolutionary universe history. Our own personal consciousness is webbed into the 'great story' of the universe.

With my first encounter with Thomas Berry's work, I was very aware that I was being challenged to move toward a new order of consciousness. More importantly, there was also the challenge to move to a new order of valuing. The challenge that Thomas ventured toward his listeners went to a level of core values. It was a fundamental challenge to our professional life, given the state of the planet. His opening sentences were as follows:

"The glory of the human has become the devastation of the Earth. The devastation of the Earth is becoming our destiny. Given this state of affairs, it is fitting that all human institutions, programmes and activities must now be judged by sustainable human/Earth connections."

This applied to all of the professions. Law, theology, education must move forward to face the challenges of our historical ecological crisis. The culture was at a decisive turning point, and we were challenged to view our professional commitments within the light of ecological sustainability.

My friend Stephen Dunn, who first introduced me to Thomas, observes: "It is his ability to enter deeply into so many other worlds of thought, discourse and activity which has encouraged many 'worlds' of affirmation, challenge, articulation and mission. . . . In ways without number, Thomas Berry's guidance and friendship has been productive for the Earth." Yes, guidance and friendship. The only title that Thomas will allow is that he be a friend and mentor. An Amazing Life, a Great Work as a Person, a Great Soul!

Edmund O'Sullivan

LYNN MARGULIS
Scholar of Symbiosis

*"Admonish your students, friends and family:
Study nature in nature."*

*"Amid all the recent interest in complexity, many point out
that the future of science belongs more to biology,
the study of complex systems, than to physics."*

LYNN MARGULIS HAS HELD the title of Distinguished University Professor in the Department of Geosciences at the University of Massachusetts, Amherst, since 1989. She is the author of over 150 published articles and author or co-author of over forty books, with more honours and appointments than would fit this page.

Her topics include original contributions to cell biology and microbial evolution. Perhaps Margulis's most dramatic contribution, her theory of symbiogenesis put forth in *Acquiring Genomes*

(2002) co-authored with her son, Dorion Sagan, is still challenged. It states that evolution, or more accurately speciation, does not occur by random mutation alone but by symbiotic detente reached by organisms of different taxa to create new species. She postulates that it is an intimacy of strangers which becomes part of the engine of life and moves onward to accelerate the process of change. She claims that ancient symbiosis generated the cells of all the species we can see with the unaided eye. In fact the fossil record does not show gradual changes between closely related species but rather a jump from one to a different species. There is no evidence that gradual accumulation of random mutations by itself, she says, leads to new species.

Hers is a revolutionary theory even today! Scientists, like the rest of us, hold their cherished beliefs tightly. Lynn Margulis moves too quickly for that. There is simply no time to hold on to beliefs. New information and theories demand that they be fluid.

Fluent in Spanish and French, Margulis was raised on the south side of Chicago, where she received a solid liberal arts education. After years as elementary school and college student at the University of Chicago, she graduated at age nineteen. She moved on to the University of Wisconsin in Madison where she studied genetics and zoology, much of it under the tutelage of Professor Hans Ris. Margulis's research on chloroplast DNA at the University of California, Berkeley, led to her PhD in genetics.

Scientific researchers in the real world, she discovered, can be contentious. Scientists can be arrogant, ambitious, political and idiosyncratic, particularly the very talented ones at institutions of higher learning. After thirty-four years of uninterrupted NASA funding for her research, Margulis now receives no public money. She failed 'peer review' and is grateful to the University of Massachusetts and two private donors for providing the wherewithal to continue her radical science.

A groundbreaker in so many ways, since the mid-1970s Margulis has aided James Lovelock in documenting his Gaia theory, a way of looking at the Earth as alive. Gaia theory posits that the Earth's surface interactions among living beings, sediment, air and water have created a vast self-regulating system.

A generation ago all life was classified as either plant or animal. That was how it was assumed to be, and taught in schools everywhere. In part as a result of her challenge to that assumption, the living things of the Earth are now classified in five kingdoms, or three, but not in only two. Fungi are not plants without chlorophyll; amoebae are not single-celled animals. A universe of single and multicellular organisms with and without nuclei exists in addition to animals, plants and fungi. Those lacking nuclei are the bacteria, without which there would be no life anywhere on Earth.

Margulis's classic book, *Five Kingdoms: An Illustrated Guide to the Phyla of Life on Earth*, third edition (1998), co-authored with K. V. Schwartz, provides a consistent formal classification of all our planetmates. Her *Symbiosis in Cell Evolution: Microbial Communities in the Archean and Proterozoic Eons*, second edition, (1993) is the precursor and logical basis for this work. Having established the bacterial origins of both chloroplasts and mitochondria, her current work is to prove the last postulate of her cell symbiosis theory: oviduct cilia, rod and cone cilia of the retina, sperm tails and the "waving feet" of protists—structures identical to each other when viewed at very high magnification—began as the same free-swimming bacterium.

These wily, mud-dwelling and tissue-penetrating bacterial ancestors, by hypothesis, belong to a group called spirochetes, many kinds of which thrive today. She and her colleagues and their students collect and study spirochetes from mud flats in Spain at the delta of the Ebro River and from microbial mat communities near Woods Hole, Massachusetts. They take photographs of spirochetes and other bacteria that grow and incessantly swim in the back end of the digestive system (the hindgut) of wood-eating termites.

Except for a few scientists and close friends familiar with certain arcane facts in the professional biological literature, nobody agrees with her spirochete hypothesis of the origin of cilia.

Margulis now helps with the exhibit on the diversity of life that opens in the magnificent, expanded Barcelona Museum of Science (Spain) in late 2006. She is very enthusiastic about this newly furbished museum, which she calls utterly amazing. The classification in the new biodiversity exhibit of bacteria, protoctists (algae including the seaweeds, slime molds, water molds), fungi, animals and plants reflects the scheme presented in the Margulis and Schwartz book.

Margulis was elected to the National Academy of Sciences in 1983, and received the 1999 National Medal of Science from President Clinton. In 1998 The Library of Congress announced that it will permanently archive her papers.

Bob Lebensold

THE PRINCE OF WALES
It's All about Balance

"As I have grown older I have gradually come to realise that my entire life so far has been motivated by a desire to heal ... so that the temple of our humanity can once again be lit by a sacred flame."

T HE PRINCE OF WALES has long defended a spiritual vision against the prevailing secularism and scientific materialism of the contemporary West, which he is convinced has led to a grave lack of balance in our culture. There is too much emphasis on reason and scientific analysis at the expense of intuition and wisdom. At worst, reason severs itself from a deeper part of the human mind so we come to feel alienated and fragmented, uprooted from our natural as well as our spiritual roots:

"I believe that we need to restore the balance between the heartfelt reason of instinctive wisdom and the rational insights of scientific analysis. Neither, I believe, is much use on its own. So it is only by employing both the intuitive and the rational halves of our own nature—our hearts and our minds—that we will live up to the sacred trust that has been placed in us by our Creator— or our 'Sustainer', as ancient wisdom referred to the Creator."

We have focussed on the outer rather than the inner, on the head rather than the heart. Modernism, the Prince argues, has carried out a demolition job on Western culture by literally pulling up our traditional roots. This has affected "the very ground of our being which had been nurtured for so long in the soil of what I can only describe as perennial wisdom. And I think the destruction was utterly comprehensive and deadly in its effect and it has particularly affected the four areas in which I have battled away about for the last twenty-five years or so—that is agriculture, architecture, medicine and education."

Although the Prince himself argues for the importance of intuition and wisdom, he is clearly advocating a 'both-and' approach that values intuition and reason together, rather than privileging one mode of knowing over the other. This approach is reflected right across the range of his concerns—for instance in sustainable agriculture and integrated health. The Prince calls for a combination of the best of the old or traditional with the best of the new and innovative. He deplores the cult of the new when it means a wholesale repudiation of traditional wisdom, and often refers to the danger of throwing the baby of tradition out with the bathwater of superstition.

It is important to note the Prince's insistence on timeless principles. The timeless is not in the past, it is a perennial source; the so-called ancient wisdom is in fact timeless and perennial—meaning that it is relevant to all times. What we need are new forms appropriate to our time. In the Platonic view which the Prince upholds, the spiritual essence or principle is unchanging—Love, Wisdom, the Good, the Beautiful, the True—but the forms that it takes will change with the generations.

It is the contention of the Prince of Wales that the mechanistic and materialistic outlook is limited and outdated, and is being gradually supplanted by systems based on spiritual, holistic and ecological principles. He is in the forefront of this transition, articulating and embodying an integrated world-view in his philosophy and work that corresponds to a growing movement known as the Cultural Creatives who are harbingers of a new world system. While the Prince's critics overwhelmingly tend to advance mechanistic and materialistic arguments, his supporters embrace similar spiritual, holistic and ecological principles. This struggle or 'paradigm war' should not be simplistically reduced to a dichotomy of modern science versus traditional religion. The transition to a new world-view is occurring in science and medicine as well as in other areas such as psychology and the nature of spirituality itself.

The Prince puts his ideas into practice right across the board in what amounts to the largest one-man charitable enterprise in the UK. The integrity and consistency between the Prince's words and actions—his practical idealism—is truly impressive and inspiring. He has made his house, Highgrove, into a famous organic garden and has also converted the Duchy of Cornwall home farm to organic production; he founded Duchy Originals to market the produce, and the company now turns over more than £30 million, giving away more than £1 million of its profits to charity; he has worked tirelessly through the Prince's Trust to give young people better opportunities to fulfil their potential; he has supported the regeneration of local communities through his Business in the Community schemes and is now applying the same principles to rural life; through the Prince's Foundation he has been responsible by means of the Phoenix Trust and Regeneration through Heritage for the preservation or restoration of many historic buildings; he set up his own Institute of Architecture (now a part of the Prince's Foundation), has inspired the building of Poundbury in Dorset, and is Patron of the Temenos Academy, dedicated to the teaching and dissemination of 'perennial wisdom'; at the Prince's Foundation he has also set up a drawing studio and a degree course in Visual Islamic and Traditional Arts; he has established the Prince's Foundation for Integrated Health to encourage research in complementary medicine and forge a coherent future for healthcare as a whole.

There is nothing inherent in the constitutional role of the Prince of Wales that makes any of this work inevitable. As one young person remarked, "he didn't have to do it". But there is an inner drive in the Prince that has inspired him to initiate a multifaceted programme based on his desire to restore the balance between inner and outer, the intuitive and the rational, the traditional and the modern. The Prince himself embodies the kind of balance of qualities about which he speaks and which characterise his work: the practical idealist, the radical traditionalist, the contemplative man of action. He is a man rooted in timeless principles and living traditions, whose actions address the problems of the present and point towards a sustainable human future where we may succeed in living more closely in harmony with nature and with each other.

David Lorimer

WANGARI MAATHAI
Mother of the Trees

"The earth was naked. For me the mission was to try to cover it up with green."

"When you start working with the environment seriously, the whole arena comes: human rights, women's rights, environmental rights, children's rights, you know, everybody's rights. Once you start making these linkages, you can no longer do just tree-planting."

"African women in general need to know that it's OK for them to be the way they are—to see the way they are as a strength, and to be liberated from fear and from silence."

WANGARI MAATHAI, the first African woman and first environmentalist to be honoured with the Nobel Peace Prize, has always hewn out a singular path. The third child of a sharecropper father and farmer mother, Maathai began attending school at age seven. She excelled, and found herself drawn to the sciences. After graduating near the top of her class from a convent high school, she was awarded a US government scholarship to enable young Kenyans to be post-independence leaders.

Maathai studied in Kansas and Pennsylvania, earning bachelor's and master's degrees. In 1963 she watched Kenya gain independence on television, and returned home in 1966. Then in her early twenties, she joined the University of Nairobi as a researcher and then lecturer in veterinary anatomy. What followed was a series of firsts. In 1971, she became the first woman in east and central Africa to earn a PhD (in biological sciences). A few years later she was appointed the university's first woman department chair. She got married and had three children.

In was in the mid-1970s that Maathai became aware of Kenya's ecological decline: watersheds drying up, streams disappearing, and the desert moving south from the Sahara. On visits to Nyeri she found streams she had known as a child gone—dried up—and vast forests cleared for farms or plantations of exotic trees. Fast-growing and lucrative, most of these species drained the ecosystem of water and degraded soil.

Maathai began making connections that others hadn't. Through the National Council of Women of Kenya (NCWK), of which she was an officer, Maathai met rural women. "Listening to the women talk about water, about energy, about nutrition—it all boiled down to the environment—I came to understand the linkage between environmental degradation and the felt needs of the communities."

She hit on the idea of using trees to replenish the soil, provide fuel wood, protect watersheds and promote better nutrition (through growing fruit trees). "If you understand and you are disturbed, then you are moved to action," she says. "That's exactly what happened to me."

Maathai set up a tree nursery in Karura Forest on the outskirts of Nairobi, later shifting it to her backyard. But the idea did not catch fire. A number of people expressed interest in tree planting, but not one of them followed it up.

Disappointed, but not deterred, the NCWK urged her to pursue the idea and in 1977 the Green Belt Movement (GBM) was born. Over the years, GBM has incorporated other activities into tree-planting efforts, in order to address community needs. Among these are the cultivation of more nutritious indigenous foods, low-tech but effective ways to 'harvest' scarce water, training in entrepreneurship, and awareness-raising on reproductive health and HIV/AIDS prevention.

In the early 1990s, GBM launched a civic and environmental education programme. Maathai and GBM led high-profile campaigns to save Kenya's forests and green spaces—including, in 1991, Nairobi's Uhuru Park—from an enormous tower block that the ruling party wanted to build. The dictatorship was still strong, and the dictators were not amused. For their boldness, Maathai and her Green Belt colleagues were subjected to stints in jail and harassment, including death threats. Many nights, Maathai stayed in safe houses. She was ridiculed publicly by Parliament and President Daniel arap Moi, called a mad woman and a "divorcee". At protests, government security forces and hired thugs regularly inflicted beatings—once to within a panga (club) blow of Maathai's life.

And yet she was not put off. In 1992, partly as a result of Maathai's activism, Kenya legalised opposition political parties. In subsequent years, the regime, while still corrupt and cantankerous, showed signs of cracking. After a series of violent confrontations with Maathai and GBM over Karura Forest in 1999, the regime abandoned its illegal development plans. The forest stands today, vast and green, on the edge of Nairobi's throbbing streets.

As Maathai's Green Belt Movement grew, it joined other pro-democracy forces to challenge the autocratic rule of Kenya's former president Moi, the tree took on new meanings. It became a symbol of the movement for democratic governance. Trees also became a call for—and an active step towards—peace. In the lead-up to Kenya's 2002 elections, Maathai planted trees to urge a fair vote and a peaceful transition to democracy.

After a generation of repression, Kenya got just that. Maathai, now 65, also won—and won well. She was elected to represent Nyeri in Parliament with an eye-rubbing 98 per cent of the vote. Soon after, the new President, Mwai Kibaki, named her deputy minister for environment and natural resources.

Mia MacDonald

SOCIAL
VISIONARIES

A journalist: "Mr Gandhi, what do you think of Western civilisation?

Gandhi: "I think it would be a good idea."

MAHATMA GANDHI
Servant of the People

"Whenever you are confronted with an opponent, conquer him with love."

"There is enough in the world for everybody's need, but not for anybody's greed."

"Be the change you want to see in the world."

"Whenever you are in doubt whether your action is right or wrong, think of the poorest of the poor and work out if your action will help to uplift that person. If it will, you're on the right path."

"There is nothing that wastes the body like worry, and one who has any faith in God should be ashamed to worry about anything whatsoever."

WE ARE ALL RIGHTLY WORRIED about such issues as climate change, global warming, unsustainable economic development, overexploitation of natural resources and ecological imbalance. This raises two interrelated questions. First, what is the source of these dangerous developments? And second, what should we do to avert them? There are many answers, some more satisfactory than others. Mahatma Gandhi was one of the first to address these questions and to offer perceptive answers.

For Gandhi, two interdependent assumptions inspire these dangerous developments. First, the anthropocentric view of the universe. In this view humans are the centre of the universe, the crown of creation, and have absolute right over nature. Nature is an inorganic mass of material, which human beings are free to use as they please to satisfy their needs. Second, the consumerist world-view. Human beings are seen as desiring beings: desires make them feel alive, and are the driving forces of their lives. Desires or wants have no inherent limits. When satisfied, one desire leads to another, and the endless chain goes on till death. Obsession with the satisfaction of desires leads to consumerism, which in turn encourages a purely instrumental view of nature.

For Gandhi these two assumptions legitimise and drive modernity. Whether the latter takes capitalist or communist forms, its basic ethos is the same. Communism is not therefore an answer to capitalism; rather it functions within the same world of thought. The crucial thing is to question the very basis of modern civilisation and rebuild it on an alternative foundation. This does not mean rejecting modernity altogether, but rather selectively appropriating its worthwhile achievements and grounding them in a different view of the world.

For Gandhi, the anthropocentric view of the world should be replaced by a cosmocentric view, in which human beings are seen as located in a wider whole and related to its other members as equal tenants. Nature is not reduced to environment, because that puts humans in the centre whose 'environment' it is. Nor is it a 'resource' to be used as one likes. Rather, it is seen as a self-regulating system which human beings should respect and fit into. Human beings cannot survive without making demands on nature, but their demands should be limited to what is needed to lead decent lives. And they entail the corresponding obligation to take tender care of nature, and to replace whatever human beings have to take for their survival in all ways they can. For Gandhi, nature is a delicate ecological system. Whenever its internal rhythm is disturbed, it has disastrous consequences not only for the world but also for human beings in such forms as global warming, unexpected diseases, natural disasters, and pollution.

The idea of human beings as consumerists or desiring beings should be replaced, Gandhi argues, by a profounder view of human beings. This view sees humans as moral beings whose characteristic excellence lies in moral self-development, self-restraint, mutual concern, and a truly nonviolent way of life. Gandhi rightly argued that desires must be critically examined, regulated, disciplined and not allowed to become a self-propelling force. Material desires—that is, those for material objects—must be limited to those that humans need to lead decent lives, and which do not deprive others of what is due to them. As he said, "the world provides enough for everyone's need, but not for anyone's greed." Consumerism leads to exploitation, inequalities and injustices. By contrast, concern with self-development or moral growth paves the way for a just and non-exploitative society.

Although Gandhi's thought might appear demanding and even harsh, its basic thrust has much to be said for it. People's attitude to nature is bound up with their attitude to themselves, and vice versa. Both need to change. How to persuade people to do so is one of the greatest challenges of our time. Unless we find an answer to it and act on it, the future of humanity and the world remains in danger.

Bhikhu Parekh

MARTIN LUTHER KING
"I Have a Dream"

"Injustice anywhere is a threat to justice everywhere."

*"We must learn to live together as brothers
or perish together as fools."*

*"I believe that unarmed truth and unconditional love will have
the final word in reality. That is why right, temporarily defeated,
is stronger than evil triumphant."*

T HERE ARE TWO SIDES to Martin Luther King, Jr. as a visionary leader. One is the more familiar figure who led the civil rights movement and who was an apostle of nonviolence, charismatic orator, and campaigner for racial equality. The other is the less familiar, more radical figure, who criticised the war in Vietnam and who voiced doubts over the ability of capitalism to deliver social and economic justice.

Born in 1929 in Atlanta, Georgia, the twenty-six-year-old King shot into the national spotlight as leader of the Montgomery, Alabama bus boycott in 1955-6. The arrest of local black woman Rosa Parks for defying segregation laws sparked a thirteen-month community boycott of city buses, which eventually ended with the US Supreme Court issuing a desegregation order. Although the national press picked up on King's stress on nonviolence, it was the ideals of

Christian love and forgiveness, part of King's upbringing in the black Baptist church tradition, that were very much to the forefront.

National representatives of pacifist and civil rights organisations subsequently attempted to school King more formally in nonviolent techniques. However, King's understanding of nonviolence would take time to develop. Historian David I. Garrow has perceptively argued that this came in two distinct stages. From Montgomery in 1955 up to demonstrations in Birmingham, Alabama, in 1963, King followed a path of 'nonviolent persuasion', trying to convince whites of the moral rightness of the civil rights struggle.

However, in Birmingham King developed a more confrontational strategy of 'nonviolent coercion', which placed pressure on segregation through nonviolent direct action tactics such as sit-ins and marches. These campaigns forced local white communities to choose between introducing racial reforms or continued disruption. More importantly, the violence with which local whites often met demonstrations drew national media attention that brought brutal and overt southern racial injustices into the living rooms of a nationwide audience.

Between 1963 and 1965 King conducted a number of community-based campaigns to highlight the injustice of segregation and the denial of black voting rights. First President John F. Kennedy, then President Lyndon B. Johnson took up the civil rights cause. The resulting national legislation helped to achieve the central goals of King and the civil rights movement. The 1964 Civil Rights Act ended segregation in public facilities and accommodation. The 1965 Voting Rights Act provided federal assistance to black voters in a number of southern states. King's "I Have a Dream" speech at the 1963 March on Washington kept him to the fore as the conscience of the nation. His role in events was recognised with the award of the Nobel Peace Prize in 1964.

Just five days after the signing of the 1965 Voting Rights Act, the predominantly black Los Angeles district of Watts exploded in violence. King decided that the movement must now tackle the racial and economic problems of inner city blacks in the West and the North, as well as those of the segregated South. However, efforts to replicate his earlier southern campaigns in Chicago in 1965-6 revealed the deep-seated, often covert structural racism that pervaded the nation as a whole. King was forced to retreat from Chicago empty-handed.

Shortly after, King told white journalist David Halberstam, "For years I laboured with the idea of reforming the existing institutions of society, a little change here, a little change there. Now I feel quite differently. I think you've got to have a reconstruction of the entire society, a revolution of values."

This applied to overseas as well as to domestic matters. King had previously failed to take a firm stance on the war in Vietnam. He had been wary of alienating President Johnson, a key movement ally, and diverting attention away from the demands of the movement. However, on 4 April 1967, King broke his silence. In a speech at New York City's Riverside Church, he denounced the US as "the greatest purveyor of violence in the world today," and demanded a unilateral ceasefire and the withdrawal of troops from Vietnam. He also called upon Americans to conquer what he called the "giant triplets of racism, materialism and militarism".

King then began to draw up plans for a Poor People's Campaign to draw national attention to the plight of the poor in the US. He called for a coalition of blacks, whites and ethnic minorities to practise mass civil disobedience in Washington DC for better living conditions. Before he had a chance to lead that campaign, however, he was assassinated on 4 April 1968, while supporting striking sanitation workers in Memphis, Tennessee. King's death cut short his pursuit of a more radical agenda for domestic social and economic reform and challenges to existing US foreign policy. Although still popularly enshrined in his earlier "I Have a Dream" period, it is arguably in his later years, as an anti-war supporter and advocate of social and economic change, that King truly came into his own as a visionary leader.

John A. Kirk

E. F. SCHUMACHER
Small is Beautiful

"I have no doubt that it is possible to give a new direction to technological development, a direction that shall lead it back to the real needs of man, and that also means: to the actual size of man. Man is small, and, therefore, small is beautiful."

"Any intelligent fool can make things bigger, more complex, and more violent. It takes a touch of genius—and a lot of courage—to move in the opposite direction."

FRITZ SCHUMACHER FIRST CAME to Britain aged eighteen as a Rhodes Scholar at New College, Oxford. He then taught economics at Columbia University, New York, before returning to Germany and joining a small team engaged in international trade. To escape Nazism he cut short this successful business career and settled in England in early 1937.

With the outbreak of the Second World War he did a spell in a British internment camp and was released to become a farm worker in Oxfordshire.

A new career was launched when he wrote a paper setting out proposals for post-war international monetary reform. This was acclaimed by the economist Lord Keynes and political leaders of the day.

In 1949 Schumacher was appointed Economic Adviser (and later Head of Statistics) to the British National Coal Board, where he remained for some twenty years. In 1973 he published *Small is Beautiful: Economics as if People Mattered*, which caused a storm, even leading to death threats on his subsequent speaking tour of the US. "He changed the thinking of a generation," was how Barbara Ward summed up Schumacher's legacy when he died in 1977.

Schumacher's work in developing countries began in 1955, with a UN assignment to advise the government of Burma about its development programme. It was then that, as a student of Buddhism, he asked himself what an economics based on Buddhist values would look like. He concluded that at least in two fundamental ways it would be the exact opposite of conventional Western economics, the economic thinking that has resulted in 'globalisation'.

First, he argued, a Buddhist approach to economics would distinguish between misery, sufficiency and surfeit. Economic growth would be good only to the point of sufficiency. Limitless growth and limitless consumption would be seen to be disastrous. Secondly, a Buddhist economics would be based squarely on renewable resources: an economics of permanence. In contrast, Western economies are based on the ruthless exploitation of non-renewable resources; they do violent, possibly terminal damage to renewable resources such as agriculture, forestry and fishing; the technologies and systems employed are harmful to the great majority of people.

In his search for a new approach to development, inspiration came not from conventional economics but from Gandhi. Whereas the starting point of Western economics is always the production of goods, Gandhi's economic thinking always started with people—their needs, resources and skills. Schumacher made that his starting point, too. The challenge was how to make the poor more productive; and he was convinced that the answer must lie not in large-scale factories and mass production but in production by the masses.

Schumacher's opportunity to address this task came in 1962, when India's prime minister, Jawaharlal Nehru, having read his paper on Buddhist economics, asked him to advise on India's rural development. It was then that Schumacher came up with the idea of 'intermediate technology'. Typical rich-country technology, he argues, was very large-scale and very expensive, capital- and energy-intensive, and environ-

mentally damaging. There was no way it could provide the millions of new workplaces desperately needed in India and other developing countries. That need could be met only by technologies specially designed to fit into small rural economies. They would be relatively small, simple, capital-saving (instead of labour-saving) and environmentally benign: tools and equipment that could be owned and operated by poor people.

At the time of Schumacher's death, the world was at the high point of corporate organisation, of mass consumption, of mass employers, of geopolitical blocs. Big seemed destined to succeed. But in reality, this world was already starting to come apart. Since then, the large employers shed jobs, the state shed functions, mass production started to give way to mass customisation. The inhumanities and abuses of power have not gone away, but the new models of organisation are different, appearing to focus on networks rather than on hierarchies.

At a shallow level, from cars to computers, the new consumer society, oriented to the personalisation of goods and services, has embraced the allure of the small. And yet not all that is small-scale is human-scale, or carries the virtues of community, spiritual connection and ecological balance. The struggle for the kind of society Schumacher envisioned has moved on to new forms of articulation and organisation, while holding true to the same enduring truths and insights.

Schumacher's work lives on, not least through the UK and US Schumacher Societies and Schumacher College. The New Economics Foundation was started to take forward Schumacher's call for a new economics that gives human and environmental values a central place. The Intermediate Technology Development Group and the Soil Association also owe a debt to the work of Schumacher. Institutions like these, and many more across the environmental, labour and consumer movements rely not on the fat profits of economic success but on the vision and inspiration of leaders such as Schumacher. They are far more than a counter-narrative to the wrongs of today. They are our best hope of a better tomorrow.

Ed Mayo and George McRobie

ANITA RODDICK
Cosmetics with Conscience

*"If you think you're too small to have an impact,
try going to bed with a mosquito."*

*"Since the governments are in the pockets of businesses,
who's going to control this most powerful institution? Business
is more powerful than politics, and it's more powerful than
religion. So it's going to have to be the vigilante consumer."*

*"To succeed you have to believe in something
with such a passion that it becomes a reality."*

"The end result of kindness is that it draws people to you."

THE CHILD OF ITALIAN immigrant parents in an English seaside town, Anita Roddick was a natural outsider, and found herself drawn to other outsiders and rebels. As personal strength quickly became a characterising trait, the seedlings of a moral outrage were also awakened when she found a book about the Holocaust at the age of ten—a moral outrage that still motivates her today.

It is such inner strength that dictated Roddick's future career choices. Training as a teacher and taking up an educational opportunity on a kibbutz in Israel eventually turned into extended travel around the world. After returning to England, she turned her back on teaching and began a small cosmetics business that would not only change and influence the way that retail businesses were self-financed, but also would be the first of its kind to dedicate its business 'to the pursuit of social and environmental change'. Thus The Body Shop was born. Through its stores and products Roddick constructed a platform from which to help communicate human rights and environmental issues.

Roddick's early travels helped shape the destiny of the environmental activism of The Body Shop. Her travels had given her vital experiences in farming and fishing communities with pre-industrial people, and she had been exposed to body rituals of women from all over the world. These experiences, combined with strongly-held personal interests and convictions, helped inspire her work in community trade initiatives. Such initiatives have built up successful trading relationships with indigenous cultures and small-scale farmers all over the world, as well as helping to protect and preserve native lands and cultures from the onslaught of modern and unsustainable technology.

It is not just in the interests of The Body Shop and community trading that Roddick has campaigned for social and environmental justice. In the 1990s she led high-profile campaigns with other NGOs against the giant oil multinational Shell, which was ravaging the lands of the Nigerian Ogoni people in pursuit of oil exploration and production. Four years of continuing pressure on Shell resulted in a turnaround in company policy, with a subsequent greater emphasis on human rights and sustainable development. This is one such example of Roddick's commitment to her social and environmental vision—and another example of her self-confessed moral outrage.

Her vision is unrelenting. She has claimed that the older one gets, the more radical one becomes, quoting Dorothy Sayers in believing that "a woman in advancing old age is unstoppable by any earthly force". This would certainly seem true in Roddick's case. In true activist mode, she flew to Seattle in 1994 to speak out against the role of the World Trade Organisation, and witnessed the 'Battle of Seattle'.

In subsequent years Roddick has moved her work up a gear, publishing an autobiography, *Business as Unusual,* and editing the book *Take it Personally,* a collection of provoking thought pieces that challenge the myths of globalisation and the power of the WTO. Constantly confronting and exploring issues she cares about, she has also founded an activist communications centre, Anita Roddick Publications, where she says they like to manufacture "weapons of mass instruction". This play-on-words should not be taken lightly—Roddick is fervently passionate about the campaigns, which include exposés of multinational corporation sweatshops, and human rights campaigns on behalf of American political prisoners.

Roddick has pointed out that someone once said, "we are only limited by our imaginations". At present, there are no signs of her slowing down. Indeed, she has publicly spoken about her intention to continue fighting for human rights and against economic initiatives and structures that ignore them, for as long as possible.

Somewhat modestly, Roddick has not attributed the successes of The Body Shop, its community trade work and Anita Roddick Publications to just her own achievements. She states that her work is part of a massive global operation with thousands of people working towards common goals. She contextualises the foundation of The Body Shop through its timing; pointing out that The Body Shop arrived just as Europe was going 'green'. And yet one should really take heed of the opinion that this self-confessed 'radical' with a vision to transform the world really had no other destiny. Developed from survival-based necessity coupled with strong personal values, Roddick's campaigning and commercial strength has set her apart. Her work has united the social and environmental movement in a uniquely communicative way, and has done so at a time when it is needed more than ever.

Kate Hartgroves

AUNG SAN SUU KYI
Destination Democracy

"It is undeniably easier to ignore the hardships of those who are too weak to demand their rights than respond sensitively to their needs. To care is to accept responsibility, to dare to act in accordance with the dictum that the ruler is the strength of the helpless."

I N BURMA, IT IS EASY to mistake the snake for a rope. Burmese people seem unduly happy. Brought up in the Buddhist world of tolerance, acceptance, kindness and humanitarian values, they appear cheerful, friendly and welcoming. Yet behind the smiles there are countless stories of horror. Via a trusted interpreter, a house-cleaner told me in whispers that her son watched a small nonviolent demonstration in the capital when soldiers arrested him along with the marchers. At the brief trial, the judge asked whether he pleaded guilty or not guilty to being part of the demonstration. He

said: "Not guilty." The judge said if he had pleaded guilty he would have been sentenced to ten years imprisonment. Since he pleaded 'not guilty', he sentenced him to fifteen years. Sent to the far north of Burma, the prison authorities wrote to his poor, penniless mother demanding $800 for medicine or her son would die. Aung San Suu Kyi is the voice for such victims of repression.

Despite enormous pressure on her, Aung San Suu Kyi refuses to leave Burma, to conduct her nonviolent campaign overseas, since she knows that it would dishearten the citizens of Burma, and she would never be allowed back into the country. Suu Kyi is the mother of the nation, and a true mother never abandons her children.

For the first time in my life, I had a momentary feeling of being starstruck when I met her—she exudes a remarkable presence, very articulate, cheerful and breathtakingly beautiful. Aung San came out after a few minutes, invited me in, and we sat in a room with just a small colonial-style sofa, and not a single other item. It transpired that she sold much of her furniture during the time under house arrest to buy food, as she refused to eat the food that the military offered her.

I said to her it must be extraordinarily difficult making the transition from being the mother of two sons to becoming virtually overnight the mother of a nation. She said that in the late 1980s she had returned to Burma to visit her sick mother, and unexpectedly found herself invited to give a talk since she was the daughter of General Aung San, the hero of Burma's independence movement (he was assassinated on 17 July 1947). It seemed ironic that the generals who run the country today find themselves dealing with the daughter of the nation's hero and greatest general.

Once Aung San Suu Kyi had given her first talk, the Burmese people had found a leader to face up to the illegal and repressive military government, known at that time as SLORC (State Law and Order Restoration Council). The name sounds sinister, and it is. In May 1990, Aung San's party, the National League for Democracy, won 80 per cent of the vote but the military regime refused to relinquish their power, and kept Aung San Suu Kyi under house arrest.

She told me her faith in the Dharma, that is the teachings and practices of the Buddha, kept her steady. I asked Aung San how emotionally and spiritually she managed to survive this long period of being under house arrest. For two and a half years she was prevented from having any contact with her two children or her husband. She told me that it was Dharma practice that enabled her to continue to keep mind and body together through those years. As a Burmese Buddhist, she said she was familiar with the tradition of Vipassana, a teaching which encourages the practice of mindfulness, meditation, staying grounded here and now, living with imperma-nence, showing loving kindness and not clinging to anything whatsoever, past, present or future.

Aung San Suu Kyi insists that the nightmare of Burma must be resolved through dialogue with the Burmese government—which is nearly at the top of Amnesty International's list of countries that abuse human rights. With remarkable depth of detachment, she refers to the government that has arrested, tortured and killed many of her friends and political colleagues, as well as numerous innocent civilians, as "the other group".

The government-owned media continues to ridicule and undermine Aung San Suu Kyi. The regime refers to her in a patronising way as "Little Sister". They claim she abandoned Burma in her twenties to marry an Englishman and took no interest in Burmese affairs until she got a taste for power. They claim that democracy is a Western concept unheard of in the Burmese tradition or in Buddhism. Not only does the regime show a warped view of Burmese religious and national history, but it uses its arguments to justify keeping the military in power with its countless privileges, luxurious lifestyle and regular overseas trips for the generals and their wives.

I asked her if she had much opportunity to leave her home in the short periods when the ban on her travelling within Burma was lifted. People were afraid to invite her to their homes, she said. She said she had made a visit to a respected *sayadaw* (a senior Buddhist monk), who advised her to become a vegetarian as an extra discipline for her spiritual practice—no easy task in Burma.

I mentioned to her the growing Western interest in Buddha's teachings and Vipassana (Insight) Meditation. Aung San Suu Kyi said she was happy for Westerners to come to Burma to practise the Dharma, but she said that tourism only supported the "other group". She added that she tried to observe noble silence for inner renewal and reflection as much as possible on a Sunday, "I am inspired by Nelson Mandela," she told me. "He spent 25 years in a cell on Robben Island. I remember him when I feel the pressure of being under house arrest year by year, and knowing that the plight of millions of Burmese people is far worse than mine."

Christopher Titmuss

BOB DYLAN
Musical Expeditionary

"You don't need a weather man to know which way the wind blows. Don't follow leaders, watch the parkin' meters."

"I consider myself a poet first and a musician second. I live like a poet and I'll die like a poet."

"Come mothers and fathers throughout the land, and don't criticise what you can't understand. Your sons and daughters are beyond your command. Your old road is rapidly ageing. Please get out of the new one if you can't lend your hand, for the times they are a-changin'."

BOB DYLAN OPENS Scorsese's film *No Direction Home* (2005) by saying "I was born very far from where I was supposed to be. So I'm on my way home." Born in fact into a Jewish family in Minnesota, he heard, aged ten, the song 'Drifting Too Far From the Shore', and it gave him the feeling that he was somebody else—not even born to the right parents, maybe.

He calls himself a musical expeditionary, with an agile mind able to memorise a huge number of folk songs and ballads on just one or two hearings. He heard in them something timeless: stories of struggle, strife, and realisation that are forever the same with only identities changing. He immersed himself "in their Napoleonic scope", learning and singing others' songs—not thinking he too might become a songwriter.

For a while Woody Guthrie was his king. "He had a radical slant. You could listen to his songs and learn how to live." But after time in Greenwich Village, New York, he found he had gone through Woody Guthrie without wanting to have done so. So he wrote 'Song to Woody' (1962). "I needed to sing it, so I had to write it."

Something began to happen very fast. He learnt showmanship early. "Come you ladies and you gentlemen, a-listen to my song" (1962). On stage he played many parts, a shape-shifter, without need of stable identity, beginning to voice songs (as Ricks writes) "variously extraordinary and insinuatingly true". They tumbled out of him, cannily crafted. "I wrote them anywhere . . . 'Blowing in the Wind' just felt right. I wrote songs to perform in a language I hadn't heard before." The sudden maturity of his lyrics took on any subject with a torrent of miniature carnivalesque vignettes linked in a field of thought by cascades "of skipping reels of rhyme" and rhythms that drove the points home—if you can catch them. He was touched by a capacity to organise chaos imperceptible to others. When Ginsberg heard 'A Hard Rain's a-gonna Fall' (1963), he wept "because it seemed that the torch had been passed to another generation from earlier beat illumination and self-empowerment." Dylan resisted others' interpretations. 'Hard Rain in the Cold War', when atomic warfare was feared and expected, was said to be about atomic fallout. "No", insisted Dylan, "it's hard rain."

At a civil rights rally in the South, he made everyone take note. 'Only a Pawn in Their Game' is about how an impoverished white murderer of a black is not to blame—he's doing his political masters' behest. Now fully in his stride, he sang at the Civil Rights March on Washington, alongside Martin Luther King. "I was up close when King made that speech; it still affects me profoundly." Dylan sang 'When the Ship Comes In' (1963), a gloriously youthful song about every kind of Goliath's days being numbered.

He protests that his protest songs are not political. "Being on the side of people who're struggling for something, doesn't mean you're political." This felt like betrayal to some in the folk movement, where issues were held dear. But he comes from another angle, tapping into the collective unconscious and articulating feelings in the spirit of the times. He articulated what many wanted to say but couldn't, giving inspiration to those whose burden it is to carry protest towards political solution.

Not to be trapped in anyone's script, he pressed on ("he who's not busy being born is busy dying"), causing uproar at the Newport Folk Festival. His acoustic concerts became second-half electric. The UK tour 1966 took its toll on him. "Judas", someone yelled. "I don't believe you," he replied darkly, "you're a liar", before pounding into 'Like a Rolling Stone'. Back in the States, after a motor-cycle accident, he retreated with the Band into making what became The Basement Tapes, music of mythic conspiracy.

Uncontainable in the protest movement— "Democracy don't rule the world / ... This world is ruled by violence / But that's best left unsaid"—he remains a potent force. His depth of reflection and the immediacy of image in his discs *Time out of Mind* (1997) and *Love and Theft* (2001) are evocative to the core.

He has a sinewy, feline, sometimes combative, appreciation of the feminine. His many love songs, of love found, lost, betrayed, and moved on from, attest to that. He knows that the feminine is a presence for good, something other than the unthinking masculine perceives. *License to kill* (1983) begins: "Man thinks 'cause he rules the Earth he can do with it as he please." The choruses are variations on: "Now, there's a woman on my block, / She just sits there as the night grows still. / She say who gonna take away his license to kill?"

Paul Zeal

FRANCES MOORE LAPPÉ
Food for All

"The act of putting into your mouth what the earth has grown is perhaps your most direct interaction with the earth."

"Even the fear of death is nothing compared to the fear of not having lived authentically and fully."

I T WAS THE LATE 1960s. Bell bottoms were big. The war in Vietnam was heating up, newspaper headlines were predicting imminent global famine, and Stanford professor Paul Ehrlich's *Population Bomb* was exploding in the popular press. At the time, my mother, Frances Moore Lappé, was twenty-six years old, and she'd just left graduate school, hungry for answers. Little did she know that her decision would set her on a lifelong path of onion-peeler (more on that later).

At the University of California at Berkeley she had been studying social work, believing this path would offer a way that she could help alleviate suffering in the world. But graduate school classes didn't help her answer her most burning question: What were the root causes of the hunger and suffering she saw all around her, and what path could she take that addressed those underlying causes?

She left the security of a degree, and entered the hushed halls of the university library. Using a research approach that she has since perfected over more than three decades and fifteen books, she followed her nose. What she uncovered in the stacks of the Giannini Library challenged everything she, and the rest of the world, were hearing. There was more than enough food to feed the world. So, her question deepened from "Why hunger?" to "Why hunger, in a world of plenty?"

Answering this question led to her first book, *Diet for a Small Planet*. The 1971 classic—which began humbly, as a flier she intended to hand out to friends in Berkeley—went on to sell more than three and a half million copies. It became a bible for a generation. Its dog-eared, yellowed pages, cropping up in kitchens from Kalamazoo to Kansas City, helped spark a revolution in thinking about the root causes of hunger and the impact of our food choices.

In *Diet*, she showed how we squander abundance through the wastefulness of industrial farming, particularly grain-fed cattle. Factory farming, she explained, turns cattle into "protein-factories in reverse". Ruminants that had once turned inedible grasses into high-grade protein, now in the US feedlot system required roughly sixteen pounds of grain and soy to provide us just one pound of meat, not to mention the water wasted and fossil fuels used up. To choose a plant-centred diet, she explained, is one way to align ourselves with what is best for our bodies and the planet.

This seminal book propelled her on a lifelong path of serial onion-peeler, stripping away layers of thinking to get at root causes and powerful solutions. In work ranging from *What To Do After You Turn Off the TV* (a collection of games and activities to play with your family when you pull the plug) to *Aid as Obstacle* (a searing critique of the damage of international food aid on developing countries) to *Democracy's Edge*, she has worked to awaken people to their own power, to demystify authority—even herself! I've heard audiences gasp when they hear her—an international bestselling author—say that she got a 'D' on her first college English paper. "I like to say I wanted to shock people with my ordinariness," she said, when I asked her about this theme in her work. "I like to believe that my self-taught life shows that any one of us can figure out what we need to know to make a difference."

Her two national non-profit organisations—the Institute for Food and Development Policy (or Food First, as it's popularly known) and the Vermont-based initiative, the Center for Living Democracy, also played an integral role in her efforts to educate people to become change-makers. In raising her two children (which, as one of them, I like to think she also counts among her life's greatest accomplishments), she also strived to show us the power of our own voices. Her third social-benefit organisation, the Cambridge, Massachusetts-based Small Planet Institute continues this work. This time it's a family affair. Institute associates include myself and my brother, Anthony Lappé, executive editor of the Guerrilla News Network, an online news service that 'lives democracy' by engaging its users as truth seekers.

She has carried through all of this work her insightful eye into the heart of democracy. When she realised thirty years ago that hunger is not caused by the scarcity of food, but a scarcity of democracy, she peeled back yet another layer to ask, then, "What is democracy?" Her latest book *Democracy's Edge*, and its conceptualisation of democracy as a culture of engagement—what she calls Living Democracy—is the culmination of her ruminations on this question. "Democracy is not simply elected government plus a market economy," she says. "Democracy is an evolving culture of trust grounded in the values of inclusion and mutuality. We shape its norms and expectations as workers, students, employers, parents, community members and clients, as well as citizens. Living Democracy is something we do. It is a practice; it is never finished."

"There is no road to democracy," she often says in speeches, applying Gandhi's wisdom to the challenge of our era. "Democracy is the road." But in order to travel this road, we must see the road and believe in it. Her life's work has been showing us that road. Her five-year national media initiative, the American News Service, publishing articles in 300 newspapers, the book we co-authored, *Hope's Edge*, and much of the rest of her work has helped bring to life the engagement of millions of people in Living Democracy.

My mother likes to say that if you're asking a question that can be answered in your lifetime, you are not asking big enough questions. Her courage to ask the 'big enough' questions of our era, to continuously peel off another layer of the onion and engage with what she finds, emboldens all of us to do the same.

Anna Lappé

R. D. LAING
Destroyer of Deception

"Insanity—a perfectly rational adjustment to an insane world."

"Madness need not be all breakdown. It may also be breakthrough. It is potential liberation and renewal as well as enslavement and existential death."

"The range of what we think and do is limited by what we fail to notice. And because we fail to notice that we fail to notice, there is little we can do to change; until we notice how failing to notice shapes our thoughts and deeds."

IN THE 1960s and 70s, when his star shone brightest, it seemed there was no limit to Ronnie Laing's potential. He stood for intense humanism against all forces of repression, applying his formidable intellect to a series of causes and conditions. The first of these was schizophrenia. As an army psychiatrist, he experienced the numbing effects of uniformity on those who became mentally ill, discovering in himself a strange and profound capacity to listen, that he did not wholly want. Then he trained as a psychoanalyst, and took a senior research position at the Tavistock Institute. His reckless side began to cause consternation amongst his colleagues, who advised him against the radical path he seemed set on.

In 1963 he founded the Philadelphia Association, London, in order to open idealistic communities for people in the grip of psychosis where there would be no distinction between staff and patient. This radical concept made headway in the opening of Kingsley Hall in the East End of London which became both haven and disaster, a very specific pocket in the unfolding chaos of the 1960s. He explored increasingly adventurous psychotherapeutic methods. He took LSD, and used his medical licence for its therapeutic use with patients and others, providing safe, quiet settings for the several hours of the trip. People reported revelatory experiences. Laing found in the *Tibetan Book of the Dead* a model for how to sit with people through their extremes.

He became increasingly interested in intra-uterine life as the precipitating matrix for the life that would be lived, and adapted a rebirthing method in which it seemed actual birth experiences were relived. Intellectually he went beyond the professional pale, exploring conception and implantation shock. He took up the cause of natural birth, making a very telling film about the negative impact of standardised medical interventions.

He tried to write from a timeless stance, and was totally without fear in his critique of family, social and national hypocrisies. A Glaswegian whose dark voice never lost its accent, God-fearing but often lacking faith, he was drawn to the eternal human verities of the Buddha, Socrates and Spinoza. He was a resolute intellectual, discontent with intellectual limitations on the wisdom of the heart and opposed to any form of mainstream compliance. "You can lead a thousand lives in one," he declared uproariously—indeed he developed several. Musician, poet, aesthete, philosopher, family man, and in his writings many voices: pulpit-thumping rhetoric, sinewy oriental mystic amongst them.

His career-long stance on schizophrenia was uncompromising. *The Divided Self* (1960) and *The Self and Others* (1961) are classics, as is the co-authored *Sanity, Madness and the Family* (1964), a close study of communicational double-binds in families that generate schizophrenia. He was remarkable for classics written while still young, fully informed by mainland European philosophical traditions almost unknown in the UK. His view was that although the schizophrenic is mad, in the family context that madness is intelligible. This caused outrage. Laing opposed the genetic view of schizophrenia: no schizophrenic gene had been found, and even if it were to be, there are still communicational systems to consider.

Having found his essential metaphor in the madness of sanity and the sanity of madness, he broadened his assault. He pursued the line that it is mad to be normal in a world where normal men and women killed perhaps 100 millions of their own kind during the fifty years covering the two world wars, and are destroying their environment. He strips away the self-deception and self-congratulation involved in education and manipulation of nature, and calls these activities violence masquerading as love. He used the inside-out myth of Plato's cave. Normal is really an ego-chained condition looking at self-deceiving reflections, taking them to be 'me' and 'you'; while the one who turns and looks toward the source of the light and is blinded and disoriented, nevertheless sees the truth. Laing turned toward the source of the light and, though burnt by it, articulated a path of sane simplicity that, even if he could not wholly follow it himself and never pretended otherwise, makes for aspiration in a despairing world.

Throughout his tumultuous career he was interested in the non-objective facts of experience, proclaiming subjectivity against all odds. His last major work, *The Voice of Experience* (1982), includes a chilling analysis of the scientific method's cold look at the world. "The world has already been destroyed in theory. Is it worth bothering to destroy it in practice? We and the world we live in faded out of scientific theory years ago." His answer was radical phenomenology: to be into every kind of felt, lived, embodied experience. He resisted the mechanisation and reification of humanity. His fundamental philosophy was that love—not violence that masquerades as love, but love that lets the other be—is the fundamental presence in both life and death.

Paul Zeal

MUHAMMAD YUNUS
Banker to the Poor

"This is not charity. This is business: business with a social objective, which is to help people get out of poverty."

"One day our grandchildren will go to museums to see what poverty was like."

"The oneness of human beings is the basic ethical thread that holds us together."

"I made a list of people who needed just a little bit of money. And when the list was complete, there were 42 names. The total amount of money they needed was $27. I was shocked."

MUHAMMAD YUNUS GREW UP in Bangladesh, and studied at the universities of the West before returning to Bangladesh as a professor of economics and government adviser. He began to question whether economists had got their theories right. Fifty years of international aid programmes, supposedly aimed at poverty reduction, had little impact on the poorest. He went out to investigate.

One example of what Yunus found was a woman who worked for a few pennies daily making baskets. Yunus asked her why she earned so little, when the baskets were of such beauty and good quality. She told him that she supplied them to the merchant who gave her the materials. He asked her how much she would need to buy these materials herself. It was next to nothing, so Yunus gave her a small loan. Freed from the merchant, she was soon able to buy her own supplies and to double her income by selling baskets herself. Within a few days she repaid the debt. Yunus did this again with others and found that credit worked for the poor.

He went to commercial banks to ask them to help in this project. They refused, saying it might work with one or two people but it wouldn't work with everyone. After all, they understood banking best. So he experimented with ten people, then a hundred, then in different localities, to prove it worked; yet the banks continued to refuse to take his success seriously.

Eventually he accepted that he would have to take on this project himself. After thirty years the Grameen Bank has over five million borrowers, and in 2005 lent as much as $600m. Its borrowers come from the ranks of the poorest, the landless. To join Grameen you have to be without assets. The initial loans average only £60 and yet this has enabled 75 per cent of borrowers to lift themselves out of poverty.

Yunus found it was the women who were the most successful and who would pass on benefits to their families. So, around 95 per cent of Grameen loans are given to women. Through a network support structure and insurance against misfortune, the system ensures that 98 per cent of loans are repaid with fair interest—a success unmatched by the commercial banks with supposedly secured lending.

Given time, borrowers became savers. They are then able to borrow larger sums to improve their homes, buy land or expand their enterprises. Further, the borrowers themselves have universally adopted a community-based programme for social change. They refuse to allow the benefits to be swallowed up by the dowry system which they reject out of hand. They improve their sanitation and health.

Given the success of the Grameen Bank, microcredit has been introduced elsewhere in the world. It is used to finance appropriate technology for threshing, milling, and stove-building, and to buy looms and sewing machines. Already there are 170 micro-enterprise projects worldwide, including the deprived inner cities of the US in the midst of a culture of crime and drugs. In the search to promote success through good practice, Yunus set up the Grameen Trust to train those wishing to set up microcredit projects and enable them to adapt schemes to local needs.

For some years now Muhammad Yunus has worked closely with Results, an international grassroots lobby organisation working to generate the political will to end poverty. With Results' help, Yunus gained $2m for the Grameen Trust from both the US government and the World Bank, the first outright gift of its kind. Yunus was key in the setting up of the Consultative Group to Assist the Poorest (CGAP) which further raised $100m in seed money for similar work, and to which the UK government has now signed its support.

Results has developed a non-confrontational approach to lobbying that builds relationships between ordinary people and their politicians. Personal approaches of Results activists to individual UK MPs and MEPs have helped to build a contingent of over twenty on the Council of Parliamentarians at the Microcredit Summit. They have initiated serious discussion of microcredit within the European Parliament.

If we want a world of peace and unity, then we need to remove the sources of conflict. There is no greater source of conflict than poverty. I believe there is no better way of addressing poverty than extending credit to the poor. Microcredit costs nothing once initial backing is given. Funds are constantly recycled, offering more and more opportunities. The small locally controlled enterprises created are at the root of truly sustainable development. It can help release poor economies from the vagaries of transnational companies within the global trading system. People can choose how to develop businesses they control and that best serve local community needs.

Andrew Pring

ARUNDHATI ROY
Conscience Keeper

"I do what I do, and write what I write, without calculating what is worth what and so on. Fortunately, I am not a banker or an accountant. I feel that there is a time when a political statement needs to be made and I make it."

"Sometimes I think the world is divided into those who have a comfortable relationship with power and those who have a naturally adversarial relationship with power."

"Another world is not only possible, she is on her way. On a quiet day, I can hear her breathing."

ARUNDHATI ROY has emerged as a leading voice in the worldwide anti-globalisation and peace movements today. From receiving the coveted Booker Prize in 1997 for her first novel *The God of Small Things*, to playing significant roles at the World Social Forum in Mumbai in 2004 and the World Tribunal on Iraq in Istanbul in 2005, this one-time architect and film professional has grown into a truth-telling, justice-seeking global citizen who has expressed solidarity with the dispossessed people of the world through her books, political essays and at numerous public forums across the world.

Protest was always a part of Arundhati's life. She grew up a misfit and a rebel in a caste-ridden Kerala village in south India, the daughter of a divorced mother who dared marry outside the community and later challenged its patriarchal inheritance laws in court. Arundhati learnt to revel in her womanhood like Mary Roy, her feisty mother, and drew strength from what seemed like disadvantages for those around her. "I had no father. . . . I didn't have a caste, and I didn't have a class, and I had no religion, no traditional blinkers, no traditional lenses on my spectacles, which are very hard to shrug off," she has said.

At a time when literary superstardom beckoned, Arundhati once again refused to conform. Turning away from writing poetic fiction, she immersed herself in social activism in India, which gradually widened into an international engagement with issues of social justice, equality, war and peace. About this turning point in her life, Arundhati says: "I think my eyes were knocked open and they don't close. I sometimes wish I could close them and look away. . . . But once you've seen certain things, you can't un-see them, and seeing nothing is as political an act as seeing something." Arundhati became involved with the Narmada Bachao Andolan (Save Narmada Movement) that was protesting against the Sardar Sarovar Project, a massive dam that would displace some 320,000 people and submerge 37,000 hectares of forest and agricultural land.

Arundhati had stumbled upon the reality of development work, and was astounded by the sheer injustice and inhumanity of it all. The result was a searing essay in 1999, 'The Greater Common Good', that exposed the myth of India as a welfare state.

Since then, Arundhati Roy has emerged as a powerful voice, unafraid to say it like it is. She has been able to skilfully use her celebrity status and formidable writing talents for highlighting the injustices of globalisation, neo-imperialism, and the 'war on terror'. Her recent books—*An Ordinary Person's Guide to the Empire, The Checkbook and the Cruise Missile, War Talk, Power Politics*—deal with these issues. She uses her incisive wit to expose the hypocrisy and propaganda of modern imperialist powers like the USA, and the anti-people policies of governments of developing nations that support them.

Arundhati Roy belongs to a growing fraternity of independent thinkers who make a connection between the exploitative policies of globalisation and the waging of wars in various parts of the world, including Iraq and Afghanistan. At the opening plenary of the World Social Forum in Mumbai, she said: "New Imperialism is already upon us. It's a remodelled, streamlined version of what we once knew. For the first time in history, a single empire with an arsenal of weapons that could obliterate the world in an afternoon has complete, unipolar, economic and military hegemony. It uses different weapons to break open different markets. There isn't a country on God's earth that is not caught in the cross-hairs of the American cruise missile and the IMF checkbook. Argentina's the model if you want to be the poster boy of neo-liberal capitalism, Iraq if you're the black sheep. Poor countries that are geopolitically of strategic value to Empire, or have a 'market' of any size, or infrastructure that can be privatised, or, God forbid, natural resources of value—oil, gold, diamonds, cobalt, coal—must do as they're told or become military targets."

As spokesperson for the jury of conscience of the World Tribunal on Iraq, which is a people's court of intellectuals, human rights campaigners and anti-war activists, Arundhati was scathing in her criticism of the war on Iraq. "The assault on Iraq is an assault on all of us: on our dignity, our intelligence, and our future," she said in her opening statement. "We recognise that the judgement of the World Tribunal on Iraq is not binding in international law. However, our ambitions far surpass that. The World Tribunal on Iraq places its faith in the consciences of millions of people across the world who do not wish to stand by and watch while the people of Iraq are being slaughtered, subjugated, and humiliated."

For her work with the global peace movement, Arundhati Roy was awarded the Lannan Cultural Freedom Prize by the Lannan Foundation, Santa Fe, New Mexico, in 2002 and the Sydney Peace Prize in 2004. As she continues on her self-chosen path of giving voice to the disenfranchised peoples of the world, and waging nonviolent war against the perpetrators of global injustice, Arundhati embodies our collective hope for the possibility of a better tomorrow.

Swati Chopra

ILYA PRIGOGINE
Dissipative Structures

"The fact that in chemistry and physics, past and present could play the same role, I found a little strange. It was so much in contradiction to ordinary experience. Everyone knows that tomorrow is not the same as today. Yet chemists and physicists described a universe where present and past were identical, timeless, and reversible."

"You cannot reverse the evolution of the universe, even theoretically. And you cannot predict its future, except in terms of scenarios that depend on never-ending series of crossroads in the chain of causality."

"The future is uncertain . . . but this uncertainty is at the very heart of human creativity."

A T THE END OF THE NINETEENTH century, two diametrically opposed views of evolutionary change had been formulated—one of a living world unfolding toward increasing order and complexity, the other of an engine running down, a world of ever-increasing disorder. The paradox of these two contradictory views of evolution was resolved in the 1970s by the Russian-born chemist and physicist, lIya Prigogine, who recognised that living systems are open systems, which maintain themselves in a state far from equilibrium that cannot be described by classical thermodynamics.

A living organism is characterised by continual flow and change in its metabolism, involving thousands of chemical reactions. Chemical and thermal equilibrium exists when all these processes come to a halt. In other words, an organism in equilibrium is a dead organism. Living organisms continually maintain themselves in a state far from equilibrium, which is the state of life. Although very different from equilibrium, this state is nevertheless stable: the same overall structure is maintained in spite of the ongoing flow and change of components. Prigogine called these systems far from equilibrium "dissipative structures", and he developed a new thermodynamics to describe them, for which he received the Nobel Prize.

Prigogine's theory of dissipative structures interlinks the main characteristics of living forms in a coherent conceptual and mathematical framework that implies a radical reconceptualisation of many fundamental ideas associated with structure—a shift of perception from stability to instability, from order to disorder, from equilibrium to non-equilibrium, from being to becoming.

While Prigogine developed his theory of dissipative structures, he was always intrigued by the more fundamental problem of the origin of irreversibility. Whereas in classical thermodynamics, irreversibility is associated with energy losses and waste, Prigogine's new thermodynamics shows the constructive role of irreversibility. He points out that all macroscopic processes in the real world, and in particular all chemical processes, are irreversible. Reversible processes always correspond to idealisations. We need to neglect friction in order to describe the swing of a pendulum as being reversible, as is customary in Newtonian mechanics.

From the beginning of thermodynamics, physicists had noticed a puzzling contradiction between classical mechanics and thermodynamics. Whereas the Newtonian equations of mechanics are completely time-symmetrical, so that all processes could run forward or backward in time without violating any known physical law, irreversibility, or the 'arrow of time', is a central feature of thermodynamics. The fundamental question is: How can the arrow of time, observable in all macroscopic phenomena, emerge from the microscopic world of particles to which classical mechanics attributes complete time-symmetry? Prigogine refers to this problem as the time paradox of classical physics.

After completing his theory of dissipative structures in the late seventies, Prigogine concentrated his attention fully on the time paradox of classical physics. Fifteen years later, he proposed a new formulation of classical mechanics (or "classical dynamics", as he prefers to call it) which solves the time paradox by making explicit that irreversibility—"the evolutionary character of the universe"—is contained in the structure of the fundamental laws of physics.

Prigogine's reformulation of classical dynamics resolves the conflict between the reversible time of classical physics and the oriented time of thermodynamics within the dynamics itself, without any need to introduce approximations or anthropocentric elements. This is achieved at the price of giving up a long-cherished scientific tradition, the notion of definite trajectories. For centuries, trajectories were considered the fundamental objects of classical physics. Now they are seen to play only a limited role, representing merely a special case. In general, Prigogine asserts, the laws of dynamics must be formulated in terms of probabilities.

Prigogine is well aware that going beyond definite trajectories amounts to a radical transformation of our description of nature: "I am aware that this extension breaks with a century-old tradition, a tradition in which the notion of a trajectory has become associated with common sense. . . . I have hesitated a long time before taking this radical step."

Fritjof Capra

MAUDE BARLOW
Campaigner against Globalisation

"I go crazy when I see certain things and I have to find out why they happen. And I have to tell people . . . I have to do something so that other people will also take action."

CANADA'S INSPIRATIONAL leader and celebrated global activist Maude Barlow's 2005 book *Too Close for Comfort* focussed on a dominant theme of Canadian reality over the last century: how not to be overpowered by its giant, pushy, dangerous neighbour, the United States. "Canada is not like the US," she says, "but it's a daily act of will to survive with our own culture, politics and spirit mostly intact," given a 3,000-mile border and a lot of heavy pressure. "Just singing the national anthem here is an act of resistance these days."

The US lobbied hard to get Canada to sign a new "US-Canada Prosperity and Security Partnership" which includes heavy economic, cultural and political sacrifices by Canada, and a new commitment to support the US militarisation of space. That this proposed deal lay below media radar, and that few activists were trying to block it, was the reason for her book. But it was only the latest iteration of a thirty-year activist career, which includes twenty books, leadership of Canada's most effective activist organisation, taking on only the toughest, cutting-edge issues—all too often, involving relations with its aggressive neighbour—awakening the Canadian public, and then the whole world about what is going on *sub rosa*.

Maude Barlow argued that the US-Canada Partnership would accelerate the loss of Canadian sovereignty and traditional Canadian social and environmental values, and lessen the distinction between the countries. "Canada's political and social system has been until recently one of the world's greatest and most successful experiments in applying government service to the public, democratic interest." She says, "The Canadian spirit has been collective and democratic, and we support a very strong social infrastructure. The private sector can never be counted upon to put people's real needs ahead of its own." In Canada, "we have always believed in sharing for survival; meanwhile the US still believes in survival of the fittest."

Despite the US pressure, and with the help of activists like Barlow, Canada has thus far maintained most of its universal health coverage, family allowances, progressive tax structure, good educational and public broadcast systems, good pension programmes, universal social assistance and unemployment insurance—all anathema to present US ideologies. Canada has also stood in opposition to the US in Iraq, on Kyoto, and on US demands for Canadian participation in its Star Wars programme for space domination. But all of this is under direct threat, and Canada's governing institutions show signs of yielding.

As usual, it falls to Maude Barlow, her colleagues and the 100,000-member Council of Canadians, which she founded and directs, to put out the first wave of opposition and organising, and then to carry the story abroad. The founding of the International Forum on Globalization (IFG) in 1993 [Barlow is also a Founding Board member of IFG] gave a big boost to their international collaborations, as it put them directly in touch with activists from all over the world, particularly from the Third World.

She has carried her local battles to a global audience, and vice versa. Maude was one of a small number of globalisation activists from IFG and other coalitions who travelled the world in the mid-1990s, systematically decrying the proposed Multilateral Agreement on Investment (MAI) which was being secretly hatched within the OECD and the WTO. Maude literally went from country to country, carrying her seminal book on the MAI (co-authored with her long-time colleague Tony Clarke), which detailed the draconian invasions that this new agreement would allow. Those efforts are widely credited with the ultimate defeat of the MAI.

For most people, such a victory over the MAI would be thought the crowning point of a career, but Maude has had many others. She began her highly eclectic activism in the 1970s and 80s, focussed on women's issues in Canada, and was Director of the government's Office of Equal Opportunity. There she earned the epithet, "the Gloria Steinem of Canada," and became Prime Minister Pierre Trudeau's Senior Adviser on Women's Issues during those turbulent years. Then it was on to other broad systemic issues— energy, labour and environment—and the forma-

tion in 1986 of Action Canada Network, which was a broad coalition active in all those subject areas.

It is Maude's habit to launch her campaigns with new books, and from 1990 to 2002 she wrote fourteen of them. They were on subjects ranging from the dangers of NAFTA and free trade (*Parcel of Rogues*), to the loss of Canadian sovereignty, the privatisation of Canada's schools, and the abandonment of a 'just society' (*Straight Through the Heart*); there was a fierce attack on the media empire of Conrad Black, her bestsellers on the MAI, and *Blue Gold: the Battle Against Corporate Theft of the World's Water* (also with Clarke).

In each case, as with the MAI, it is Maude's *modus operandi* to spend months travelling with her message across Canada to huge adoring audiences, where she has become so persuasive and popular a figure that she could, according to many people, successfully run for Prime Minister herself. Collaborating with activists abroad, she has helped form effective new coalitions and organisations on every continent. In late 2005 she was chosen for the coveted Right Livelihood Award, the 'alternative Nobel Prize' from Sweden.

I asked Maude Barlow how she saw the future, especially given recent military adventurism and the terrible environmental crisis we are in. "Of course the sensible thing is to worry," she said. "The weaponisation of space, the devastating development of Canada's tar sands as the most absurd response to the oil crisis, the still increasing use of cars, the continued trend toward bottled water, the advancing environmental catastrophe in China, the new Sino-soviet military pact to resist the US; I am very worried about all of these." But there are lots of positive developments too, she said, noting the many victories against the WTO, and now also against the FTAA (Free Trade Area of the Americas) led by a very impressive rising resistance in South America. "The world is emphatically rejecting globalisation. And I agree with what John Ralston Saul recently wrote: 'We are transitioning eras right now' and I think it could be in a positive direction. But in any case, hope is a moral imperative. We have no choice but to stay positive, keep fighting, and to have some fun doing it."

Jerry Mander

MAURICE ASH
Practical Philosopher

*"The values of the old order have all but run their course. . . .
Underneath, in the privacy of people's minds, the readiness
for change is growing. We must make sure that when it comes
it is well founded."*

MAURICE ASH PLAYED a large part in the lives of many people great and small. He had been a substantial player on the stage of public life, notably in his roles as Chairman of the Town and Country Planning Association (TCPA) and of the Green Alliance, which he helped to found. But he was also widely known and loved in the smaller world of two beautiful and innovative estates: those focussed on Dartington Hall and his own home, Sharpham House, on either side of Totnes in Devon. To all these spheres he brought an exceptional capacity to be a man of both ideas and action. As a thinker he was ahead of his time in recognising the extent of the damage that humans were wreaking on the environment, and in identifying Buddhist principles as a possible

corrective. As a pragmatist who believed in learning by doing, he helped the Dartington estate to renew itself, and at Sharpham created a flourishing community devoted to the production of milk, cheese and wine.

The slightly melancholy aura that sometimes hung about Maurice—though he could also be both convivial and entertaining—no doubt derived from his childhood, which he once described as "preternaturally lonely". His mother died soon after his birth; his father—Gilbert Ash, a successful building contractor—remarried, and for many years worked in India, where Maurice had been born. Although a natural athlete, he felt dependent for survival at his Norfolk boarding school on his then unremarkable intellect. This emphasis in turn led him to study economics at the London School of Economics, a decision he subsequently much regretted. It resulted, he believed, in a further suppression of his feelings by his intellect. The qualitative judgements of history would, he felt, have been more congenial and more liberating than the quantifications of economics.

The crucial event in Maurice's life was his marriage to Ruth Elmhirst, daughter of Leonard and Dorothy Elmhirst, founders in the 1920s of the multifaceted Dartington estate. It was the polymathic Michael Young, an alumnus of Dartington School and youthful Dartington trustee, who recommended that Maurice should write a report on the business side of the estate. Maurice was impressed to find that, although there was no measurable common denominator between the arts, industries, educational institutions that made up the totality, it was very much alive as an entity. Propagating the concept of wholeness was to become the central mission of his life.

His marriage to Ruth Elmhirst enabled Maurice to devote his life to clarifying and implementing his ideas, without the need to earn a living: Ruth's American mother Dorothy was a vastly wealthy and philanthropic Whitney heiress, while Leonard was a Yorkshire-born agricultural economist, a pragmatist with a keen interest in India, where he had worked and become a friend of the poet and philosopher Rabindranath Tagore. Leonard believed in learning by doing: at Dartington, head, heart and hand were to hold equal sway, and he was a great influence on Maurice.

At this early stage, Maurice and Ruth lived in semi-rural Essex, where Maurice farmed, rose to be Chairman of the TCPA, became a close friend of the sculptor Henry Moore, and founded the Harlow Arts Trust in order to endow the somewhat soulless nearby New Town with numerous sculptures. The TCPA's heavy involvement in lengthy public inquiries (Stansted Airport, Windscale and so on) brought Maurice into closer touch with the environmental lobby. In the fight against the degradation of the planet, the prodigal consumption of finite resources and the sheer inhumanity of free-market capitalism, Maurice found a cause that engaged his heart, his mind and his considerable energies. The upshot

was his emergence in 1978 as a co-founder and first Chairman of the Green Alliance, a pressure group set up to lobby for environmental causes across party-political barriers.

Maurice and Ruth moved back to Devon in 1962, to an austerely beautiful Palladian mansion with a substantial estate and superb views over the River Dart. Maurice soon became a Dartington trustee, and in 1972 succeeded Leonard Elmhirst as Chairman. A period of reanimation ensued, including the establishment of Dartington Glass in Torrington, of the Beaford Arts Centre seventy miles away in north Devon, and eventually of Schumacher College at Dartington, to propagate the 'new paradigm' (a favourite Maurice expression) of sustainable living. At Sharpham meanwhile he created a Buddhist-oriented community on the top floor of the house itself (later transmuted into a mini-college), and divided the estate proper into tenant-managed units. Those devoted to the production of Sharpham wine and cheese continue to be outstandingly successful. In their very different ways, his three daughters have followed in the same admirably practical tradition.

In Buddhism, Maurice found a belief system that sought to overcome the dualism (another favourite word) that separates the self from the world. Western man, he believed, following his beloved Wittgenstein, lives bewitched by the words with which he has defined the world, seeking to reduce his insignificance by the accumulation of knowledge, yet thus merely increasing his own isolation. That can best be overcome by reversing the hubris and self-absorption (Maurice favoured 'solipsism') that sets humans above the natural world; and by rebuilding local life with the aid of appropriate technology: he deplored the bias in 'green' attitudes in the West towards physical rather than social concerns.

Sadly, writing clear prose was not among Maurice's gifts. He will surely be remembered not so much for his brave attempts to define a philosophy of wholeness as for his success in living out his ideas in a life of rare integrity. He had the means to implement his vision, and to a large extent he succeeded in doing so.

Roger Berthoud

H. J. MASSINGHAM
Rural Writer

"In the present condition of society, in which mass production, cheapness and profit have submerged the older principles of use and beauty, the true task of the future is the conquest, not of nature, but of the machine which has been used as the instrument of that conquest."

"In my wanderings over the country, I could not but observe that our own culture, the latest and therefore the most advantaged in profiting from the examples of others, is the only one from BC onwards which has failed to enrich its mother-earth, whether under the soil by cultivation or above it by its buildings."

MASSINGHAM WAS WRITING at about the time that I was at agricultural college. I was being taught then of the complete supremacy of the scientific method and the complete inferiority of the tradition of good husbandry that had been built up in England since Neolithic times. What Massingham was writing was in direct opposition to this: what he was saying was heresy to the agricultural establishment of the day. But he went on, writing book after book, hammering away at the same theme.

He was saying things that nobody else was saying, and he was saying them so well and so forcibly that at least some people had to listen!

I wondered sometimes how he managed to get his writings printed in such establishment journals as *The Field, Country Life,* and *The Geographical Magazine.* But of course the reason was that he was the best country writer in England. His knowledge of every aspect of the English countryside was enormous, He would write you a piece on English vernacular architecture that no architect in the world could equal, and then go off into a dissertation on varieties of apples—or roses—or plums—or what you will that would put every pomologist or rosarian or prunologist completely in the shade. In every subject that he touched on he was the complete expert and therefore he had a following, always, among educated country people, and the sort of city people who wished they were country people too.

The readers of *The Field* and *Country Life* liked him because they had a misconception of him. They believed that he was nostalgic, a conservative, a reactionary even. They thought he yearned to go back into the past, a past that was very congenial to their class; a past of cheap domestic servants, underpaid farm labourers, overpaid and idle squires.

In this they completely misunderstood him. He did not want to go 'back' at all. He was nothing less than a revolutionary. He wanted to go forward; forward to an England where the countrymen and countrywomen would come into their own again; where the countryside would no longer suffer the weight and oppression of the city; where civilisation should be the flowering of a culture based on the soil. He realised that a human being is a creature of the soil—exactly the same as an earthworm is! That if we cut ourselves off from our origins, we are doomed to sterility and ultimately death.

Massingham was a highly literate man. His analyses of such English writers as Shakespeare, Kilvert, Vaughan, Cobbett and many another, are enormously perceptive. And the one thing that all our fine writers had in common, he realised, was that they were country people. They derived their inspiration from the English countryside. When the English became cut off from the soil of their country, as they did in the Industrial Revolution, they lost their genius, for it was a country genius. His analysis of Shakespeare particularly is penetrating. He points out that every image that Shakespeare used was a country image: Shakespeare was an English yeoman.

And the English yeoman was Massingham's ideal. The destruction of the yeomanry by the enclosures, and then the Industrial Revolution, was to him an unrelieved tragedy. He lived in time to see the last of village self-sufficiency, of the country craftsman, of the village mill, of true rural self-respect and self-reliance. He could scarcely contain his horror and anger at what was happening to his country.

No, he was not a reactionary in any sense. He did not yearn for an unobtainable past. His attitude to machinery, for example, was entirely practical and sensible: it was that the machine should serve 'Man' and not 'Man' the machine. In his book *This Plot of Earth*, when he has been talking about the moderate skilled use of simple machinery in the flax industry, he observes:

"This is surely the beginning of Man's mastery over the machine, without which no civilisation can or deserves to survive. It means putting the machine in its right place as the servant both of humanity and craftsmanship. To attempt to abolish the machine (even if it was desirable) is as Utopian as the paper-paradises of the mechanists. In the present condition of society, in which mass production, cheapness and profit have submerged the older principles of use and beauty, the true task of the future is the conquest, not of nature, but of the machine which has been used as the instrument of that conquest."

The machine then must be conquered, must be subjugated, but not necessarily abolished. The one thing Massingham knew was that the conquest of nature is impossible: for we are a part of Nature and therefore cannot conquer her. Everybody with any sense knows this now. The astounding thing about Massingham is that he knew it then. He knew it during the time when the whole world was boasting about human 'conquest of Nature'.

John Seymour

JERRY MANDER
Public Intellectual

"The glut of information was dulling awareness, not aiding it."

*"Globalisation is definitely doomed, but it can do
a hell of a lot of damage in the meantime.
The whole world is waking up to that."*

*"I don't spend a lot of time envisioning a future world.
I have pictures of what seems to work and what
doesn't seem to work; I know what I like."*

BACK IN THE MID-SIXTIES, I had a summer job at Freeman, Mander, and Gossage, a San Francisco ad agency where Jerry Mander was the rising star. Working with the witty, iconoclastic Howard Gossage, Mander's talent for 'seeing the zebra among the horses'—breaking through the prevailing paradigm to make something else visible—became mastery. He was proving himself to be a brilliant writer, working in a form—that of advertising—which can be as polished, compressed and potent as poetry.

Mander was glamorous and busy, yet always friendly and sympathetic to the college girl from Phoenix sitting behind the reception desk. That summer, he, Gossage and David Brower, then head of the Sierra Club, were creating a series of campaign ads for the hitherto staid organisation. One japed at a lame justification for damming the Grand Canyon with the headline, "Should We also Flood the Sistine Chapel so that Tourists Can Get Closer to the Ceiling?" Another called for the establishment of an "Earth National Park". The ads ran in the *New York Times* and several other American newspapers of record. They were provocative, text-rich, and helped stop the Grand Canyon travesty, build the Sierra Club into a political force, and give the ecology movement a bold presence.

David Brower was as persuasive a champion of the wild as ever lived. While working with him, Mander's early feelings for nature were rekindled. Then when the agency worked with Marshall McLuhan, Mander's gut-grasp that the medium is the message became a realisation that "commercial broadcast media alienate people from their own thought processes—from nature in ourselves."

After Gossage's death, Mander founded the Public Media Center, the world's first nonprofit advertising agency. Also about that time, he began work on his groundbreaking bestseller, *Four Arguments for the Elimination of Television* (1978), one of the first holistic critiques of any technology.

For years, Mander had worked with traditional American Indians who were struggling to protect not only their lands, but their own nature. After *Four Arguments*, writing about native issues took him from the far North to the Southwest and beyond to Hawaii. He wove strategic journalism together with memoir, manifesto, and essay to create *In the Absence of the Sacred: The Failure of Technology and the Survival of Indian Nations* (1991), a book that's still changing lives.

Meanwhile, Mander's friend Doug Tompkins, a highly successful businessman, and, like both Dave Brower and Arne Naess, a mountaineer, was having an ecological epiphany. Naess's philosophy and his own ascents of the wild prompted Tompkins to establish the Foundation for Deep Ecology (FDE). It would focus on "the power of ideas, the value of philosophical circles and the need for systemic analyses and critiques of the existing world-view". Naturally enough, Tompkins asked Mander, his "shadow teacher" to be the director.

For a heady decade the FDE engaged in some world-rocking intellectual community organising. Among its grantees were NGOs and authors in the vanguard of wilderness preservation, ecological agriculture and resistance to economic globalisation. On the latter front, with Mander's leadership the FDE launched an activist think-tank, the International Forum on Globalisation (IFG). A planet-spanning group of public intellectuals and seasoned campaigners—Helena Norberg-Hodge, Maude Barlow, Vandana Shiva, and Walden Bello among them—convened at teach-ins in cities around the world. The IFG helped build capacity internationally among groups to co-ordinate their efforts. "In Seattle," said Mander, "it all came together into this big noisy opposition."

When I spoke with Jerry at the IFG office near the Golden Gate, I rejoiced to see him, at seventy, trim as ever, still dressing with style, from his Einsteinian shock of bone-white hair to his festive socks, still working with ideas that matter. In addition to his ongoing action against globalisation, he's writing a book about the power of images.

Before we parted, I asked my old friend what he could foresee.

"I don't spend a lot of time envisioning a future world," he said. "I have pictures of what seems to work and what doesn't seem to work; I know what I like. I'm acting in the interest of people and cultures who are maintaining a way of being which we could call sustainable."

"Globalisation is definitely doomed," said Mander, "but it can do a hell of a lot of damage in the meantime. The whole world is waking up to that" (owing in no small measure to this apostate ad man's extraordinary work). For forty years Jerry Mander has been sounding the call to wake up and resist the forces of destruction and alienation, to "make yourself felt" for the good of Mother Earth. As native people in my bioregion say, Migwetch. Thank you.

Stephanie Mills

BUCKMINSTER FULLER
Future Designer

"A designer is an emerging synthesis of artist, inventor, mechanic, objective economist and evolutionary strategist."

"When I am working on a problem, I never think about beauty but when I have finished, if the solution is not beautiful, I know it is wrong."

"Everyone is born a genius, but the process of living de-geniuses them."

"Of course, our failures are a consequence of many factors, but possibly one of the most important is the fact that society operates on the theory that specialisation is the key to success, not realising that specialisation precludes comprehensive thinking."

RICHARD BUCKMINSTER FULLER was born in 1895 in a New England Transcendentalist culture. He died in 1983, well recognised as a prominent twentieth-century prophet—certainly a great moral teacher and a futurist, whose predictions proved most accurate, yet also an inventor, design scientist, and master geometer. Fuller discovered how to realise the ancient prophetic vision (*Isaiah* 2:4, *Mikha* 4:3): to "remake swords into ploughshares".

Fuller showed that, by calamity or by choice, humankind would either die out or reach a steady state with some ten billion people sharing the Earth. He also proposed a novel method of getting there by choice, through the 'World Game'. Trained as naval officer, 'Bucky' addressed the entire 'Spaceship Earth' (a term he invented): how to navigate humankind and our planet, with both love and precision, through their most critical passage ('navigate' seems the right word, for *Navi* means in Hebrew 'Prophet').

Fuller's basic insight was that historically, practically all human progress has been due to war. Not because there is anything admirable about war, but because only for winning victories were governments willing to make investments in research, and some of the discoveries of this research were then turned to peaceful uses. Computers, television, satellites and the internet are just some of the life-improving byproducts of military research. But, said Fuller, this need not be so: human improvement need not be just an accidental byproduct of military research. Fuller claimed we can be masters of our destiny: we can purposefully generate research that will improve human existence.

His strategy was to instigate a 'World Design Science Initiative' for the development of 'livingry' (as opposed to weaponry) tools. The Fuller design mottos included 'Reform the environment, not the humans' and 'Do more with less', well exemplified in his own Geodesic Dome and Tensegrity structures. The names of some of his many books spell well his stance: *Utopia or Oblivion*, *No more Secondhand God*, *Operating Manual for Spaceship Earth* and *The Critical Path*. New books about him keep coming.

Ironically, it was the military defence application of his best-known geometrical and civic invention that led to Bucky's fame. For many years he was a prophet calling in the wilderness, to whom no one listened. But when the North American anti-ballistic defence needed shelters for their radars, Fuller's patent of the Geodesic Dome seemed the answer. So after he got rich he became a global celebrity whose lecture tours circled the Earth more than twenty times over.

Fuller anticipated the creation of a world management system that would distribute material substances in a just way. His book *Critical Path* contains his visionary schemes for energy, economics, world management, trans-nationalism, city planning and more. His magnum opus, *Synergetics: Explorations in the Geometry of Thinking*, gets to the fundamentals.

His quest was to understand the principles of the Universe and "to discover human functioning therein, thereby to discover nature's governing complexes of generalised principles and to employ these principles in the development of specific artifacts that would benefit humanity's fulfilment of its essential functioning in the cosmic scheme". Fuller thoroughly explored the geometric design of nature, so that we should be able to organise humanity along similar patterns. In finding this cosmic, holistic perspective and working with it, instead of against it, we will attain the "conversion of all humanity into an integrated, omni-harmonious, economically successful, one-world family", where we all will "live comfortably and luxuriously on daily energy income from the Sun in its many derivative phases".

Yitzhaq Hayut-Man

ERICH FROMM
Liberator of the Mind

*"Man's main task in life is to give birth to himself,
to become what he potentially is. The most important
product of his effort is his own personality."*

*"Love is the only sane and satisfactory answer
to the problem of human existence."*

*"Both dreams and myths are important communications from
ourselves to ourselves. If we do not understand the language in
which they are written, we miss a great deal of what we know
and tell ourselves in those hours when we are not busy
manipulating the outside world."*

"MAN, THE MORE he gains freedom in the sense of emerging from the original oneness of man with nature and the more he becomes an 'individual', has no choice but to unite himself with the world in the spontaneity of love and productive work or else to seek a kind of security by such ties with the world as destroy his freedom and the integrity of his individual self." (*Fear of Freedom*, 1942, Chapter 1).

Fromm spent his life elucidating this paradox—that freedom from nature results in 'no choice' except between spontaneity and conformity, the one involving the discovery and fulfilment of the relational self, the latter involving the loss and degradation of that potential. His proposed spontaneity in love and work in the context of gritty struggle with evolutionary limitations, places him in the European tradition of moral philosophy, in his case informed by psychoanalysis. His rhetorical gifts contributed to the post-World War—especially 1960s—surge of individualist freedom and liberalisation.

Born in Frankfurt into a cultured Jewish milieu, as an adolescent he was attracted to the Messianic visions of universal peace and harmony in Jewish thought, and later belonged to the same circle as Martin Buber. He studied psychology and sociology, and trained as a psychoanalyst at the Berlin Psychoanalytic Institute. With other psychoanalysts (including Wilhelm Reich) he became interested in combining the insights of Freud and Marx, elaborated in the Freudo-Marxism of the Frankfurt School, where his colleagues included Adorno and Marcuse. One of his projects was an empirical study of workers' authority patterns based on psychoanalytic concepts. He emigrated to New York in 1934.

In America he embraced the new world idealism of freedom and individuality, but became a critic of conformist tendencies in the pursuit of money and power that masquerade as freedom. He taught that, just as a baby has to develop independence from mother as best it may, the human race has become subject to the painful loss of union with mother nature, a loss which we compensate against with compensatory pleasures of an alienating, schizoid and destructive variety. Hence the 'insane society', which he studied in *The Sane Society* (1956).

He remained a practising psychoanalyst all his life, developing his own voice, taking up what he had believed from his teens, that mankind has come to possess a fundamental free essence, a gift from evolution more precious than material possessions or temporal power.

He stood for true individuality against communist, capitalist, religious and consumerist conformities, and articulated insights that the insane forces of social collusion are invested in keeping obscure. For instance, that being is prior to doing and having; and that love is non-acquisitive, the basis for being open and welcoming. The insane (alienating) society, in which fundamental values are lost sight of, which he relentlessly exposed, has as its unconscious project to hide the destructiveness of Western and industrialised nations. Basing security on the arms trade and every kind of recklessly big business can only result in paranoia, terror and environmental degradation. Fromm wanted to lift the perceptual lid off all that horror, so that the presence of love as a socially cohesive, vitalising force, could be seen and realised.

In *The Anatomy of Human Destructiveness* (1973), he distinguishes benign forms of aggression necessary for generating and protecting life, from malignant forms of aggressive destructiveness. Having, as human beings, evolved beyond our basic animal nature, the issues we fight over are not only the animal needs for enough food, water, territory and procreative sex, but for more than enough—in pursuit of gratifications of every kind of power, hunger, material, sexual, and immaterial. We murder on inconceivably vast scales for the sake of symbolic causes, i.e. secular and religious ideologies and ideals, and in the process we rip up the earth upon which we are totally dependent.

In a late work, *To Have or To Be?* (1976), he again draws out the best in Judaism and Christianity, deferring to the prophets, the Shabbat, Jesus and his disciples and Meister Eckhart, and describes our loss of being and the processes of self-reification such that we want to have rather than to be, and how thus we sell ourselves. In this late work, when well into his seventies, he has one more heroic throw at making a difference. He declares that: "For the first time in history the physical survival of the human race depends on a radical change of the human heart." Having analysed the fundamental differences between the two modes of having and being, in the third part, in a spirit of urgent utopianism, he describes "The New Man and the New Society". He concludes that, though the "being orientation is a strong potential", the chances of survival are slim—but that the utopian goal is more realistic than the current corrupted realism.

Paul Zeal

LEOPOLD KOHR
Sage of Smallness

"Little states produce greater wisdom in their policies because they are weak. Their leaders could not get away with stupidity, not even in the short run. It is not by accident that the politically and socially most advanced countries of the world today are small states. Large powers, on the other hand, can get away with stupidity for prolonged periods. But who amongst us, if he feels that he can get away with stupidity, will ever take the trouble and pains of being wise?"

"It is always bigness, and only bigness, which is the problem of human existence. The problem is not to grow but to stop growing; the answer: not union but division."

"If a society grows beyond its optimum size, its problems must eventually outrun the growth of those human faculties which are necessary for dealing with them."

LEOPOLD KOHR

EOPOLD KOHR WAS BORN in the village of Oberndorf in the province of Salzburg, the village where the famous Christmas hymn *Silent Night* was created. He studied Law and Classics, Political Science, History and Economics at the Universities of Innsbruck, Paris, Vienna and the London School of Economics—a progression in which he collected two doctorates and which tells its own story of a student career of outstanding merit.

The Nazi takeover of his native land in 1938 prompted him to move to Canada where, after a spell as a lumberjack, he resumed academic work which in stages culminated in the Professorship of Economics in the University of Puerto Rico.

Despite the lifelong handicap of acute deafness, he was outstanding as a teacher, and his lecture notes on economics were models of their kind. On his retirement he became an extramural tutor at the University College of Wales in Aberystwyth. He later settled for the remainder of his life in Gloucestershire.

But all this time he was a ceaseless campaigner in the promotion of his theories of human scale, and was constantly in demand as a speaker or adviser by learned bodies and governments.

There was a deceptive simplicity about his writing which might lead the unwary reader to miss the significance of what he was expounding. The basic thrust of his ideas came from Aristotle: "To the size of a state there is a limit, as there is to plants, animals and implements, for none of these retains its natural facility when it is too large." In his *Breakdown of Nations* he wrote one chapter consisting of a single word. The heading was a question: Would governments act as he thought they should? His monosyllabic answer was "No"!

But in this he was surely mistaken. Recent decades have seen the collapse of the Soviet Union (such that today it is no longer a union), the Baltic states are free, there are discussions about cantonisation in Bosnia and South Africa, the Central African Federation has collapsed, Bangladesh has divided from Pakistan, Czechoslovakia has split in two, Singapore has hived-off from Malaysia; and this note of division into smaller and more democratically controllable units is an increasing *leitmotiv* of our times all over the world.

And the man who single-handedly provided the theoretical basis for all these developments and clearly of many more to come was Leopold Kohr. One of his books is subtitled *The Translucent Society*, but Leopold himself was a translucent spirit who illuminated our lives often in areas where darkness was most pronounced. When I told a friend that Leopold had died, he responded, "We have lost a star which shed a great light." And so we have. Schumacher said he was "the man from whom I have learnt more than from anyone else". His impact on public opinion was far less than Schumacher's, partly because he was writing before his time and partly, perhaps, because his sense of fun in impressing his ideas prompted people to assume he was not quite serious. But he was serious all right: serious enough for the city of Salzburg to confer on him the rare honour of the Golden Ring, and to found an institute in his name. For a change, a man was a prophet with honour in his own country. Nevertheless, it was a richly deserved tribute which many of his friends and students might echo: a fitting tribute indeed to one who initiated a revolution in human thought which will surely reverberate down the ages.

John Papworth

JOHN MAYNARD KEYNES
People's Economist

"The decadent international but individualistic capitalism in the hands of which we found ourselves after the war is not a success. It is not intelligent. It is not beautiful. It is not just. It is not virtuous. And it doesn't deliver the goods."

"Capitalism is the astounding belief that the most wickedest of men will do the most wickedest of things for the greatest good of everyone."

"A study of the history of opinion is a necessary preliminary to the emancipation of the mind."

SEVENTY YEARS AGO, John Maynard Keynes delivered one of his most important but most ignored texts, entitled 'National Self-Sufficiency'. This isn't a lecture that you'll find much reference to in modern economics textbooks: Keynes' economist followers have found it uncomfortable, and tend to brush it under the carpet. But actually it speaks to our problems today almost as dramatically and inspiringly as it did then.

The only paragraph that is widely quoted now in anti-globalisation circles is: "I sympathise, therefore, with those who would minimise, rather than with those who would maximise, economic entanglement between nations. Ideas, knowledge, art, hospitality, travel—these are things which should of their nature be international. But let goods be homespun whenever it is reasonably and conveniently possible; and, above all, let finance be primarily national."

This remains a powerful statement: Keynes is attacking a very specific kind of globalisation— the primacy of money over life, and as such, the rest of his forgotten lecture urgently deserves to be revived and studied again. "To say that a country cannot afford agriculture is to delude oneself about the meaning of the word 'afford'," he said in the lecture. "A country which cannot afford art or invention, agriculture or tradition, is a country in which one cannot afford to live." With today's agriculture shrivelling in the face of monopolistic global food conglomerates, this has dramatic relevance.

Keynes is not an obvious candidate for a eulogy inside a magazine like *Resurgence*. He was, after all, the creator of the concept of Gross National Product (GNP), which has done untold harm to people and planet by pretending that only things with money-value matter. He was the creator of the International Monetary Fund and the World Bank, though his original design was vetoed by the Americans. And he was, of course, the originator of what is now known as Keynesian economics: the idea of kick-starting depressed economies by borrowing and spending, which led to inflation, unrestricted growth and the consumer society.

On the other hand, he never swallowed the lies of economics that somehow everything in the world could be subsumed into it. He saw economic problems as moral crises based on people's fatal love of money. "The minds of this generation are still so beclouded by bogus calculations that they distrust conclusions which should be obvious, out of reliance on a system of financial accounting which casts doubt on whether such an operation will 'pay'," he said. "The same rule of self-destructive financial calculation governs every walk of life. We destroy the beauty of the countryside because the unappropriated splendours of nature have no 'economic' value. We are capable of shutting off the sun and stars because they pay no dividend. . . .

"Or again, we have until recently conceived it a moral duty to ruin the tillers of the soil and destroy the age-long human traditions attendant on husbandry if we could get a loaf of bread a tenth of a penny cheaper.

"There was nothing which it was not our 'duty' to sacrifice to this Moloch and Mammon in one; for we faithfully believed that the worship of these monsters would overcome the evil of poverty and lead the next generation safely and comfortably, on the back of compound interest, into economic peace." And we were wrong, he said— and now we have to do something about it.

We must be clear what this lecture isn't. It isn't, for example, a condemnation of the idea of trade in itself. It isn't a puritanical disapproval of luxury, or a nationalistic demand for self-sufficiency because we fear foreigners. Nor is it a plea to overthrow the financial system: Keynes is very clear about the dangers of haste or intolerance. It is a plea for what Rabbi Michael Lerner calls a "new kind of bottom line" for society. The bottom line, for Keynes, isn't money, despite his expertise and fascination. It's art and culture and beauty.

His plea is to be "disobedient to the test of an accountant's profit". Not simply unbalancing the budget, but finding ways to bend the economic system so that it doesn't just save the planet, but makes it a wonderful place. This is what I believe Keynes meant when he said this: "If I had the power today, I would surely set out to endow our capital cities with all the appurtenances of art and civilisation on the highest standards . . . convinced that what I could create I could afford." It's a vision of economics turned upside down, so that money is bent into the service of people, not the other way round.

Keynes died of a sudden heart attack at the age of sixty-two. Over the previous few years, he had been corresponding with a young economist called E. F. Schumacher, still thirty years away from writing *Small is Beautiful*. Keynes recognised in him a fellow magician. "If my mantle is to fall on anyone," he told a friend, "it could only be Otto Clarke or Fritz Schumacher. Clarke can do anything with figures, but Schumacher can make them sing."

David Boyle

CARLO PETRINI
Saint of Slow Food

"The relationship between gastronomy and ecology is very close. A gourmet who eats and eats and eats but does not appreciate where his food comes from is a fool."

"It is useless to force the rhythms of life. The art of living is about learning how to give time to each and every thing."

"Food history is an important as a baroque church. A cheese is as worthy of preserving as a sixteenth-century building."

"We all go to the same place, so let us go there slowly."

CARLO PETRINI WAS BORN in 1949 in the small market town of Bra, in the Piedmont region of north-west Italy. After studying sociology at the University of Trento, he returned home, and in the 1970s he and a group of friends first dabbled in the world of local radio, then founded the food and wine association, originally named Arcigola, that has since developed into the Slow Food international movement, now with over 80,000 members worldwide. At that time, 'Carlin' was also working as a food and wine writer for Italian periodicals and newspapers, such as *L'Espresso*, *L'Unità* and *Il Manifesto*, and in 1986 he and other journalist acquaintances in Milan came up with the Slow Food Manifesto, which formally stated their case. In November 1989, representatives of fifteen countries endorsed the document at a meeting at the Opéra Comique in Paris. The linchpin of Petrini's philosophy was the right to pleasure. "I came to understand," he said, "that those who suffer for others do more damage to humanity than those who enjoy themselves. Pleasure is a way of being at one with yourself and others."

Thanks to his untiring enthusiasm and creativity, Slow Food soon turned into a breeding ground for innovative ideas, many of which materialised into major events. The first was *Salone del Gusto* (Hall of Taste), a huge food fair/forum held every two years in Turin since 1996. One thing led to another, and Petrini used the *Salone* to launch the 'Ark of Taste', a project that aims to rescue quality food production from "the deluge of planetary standardisation", and the 'Presidia'—dedicated small-scale projects to save animal breeds, plant species and food products in danger of extinction. There are now as many as 600 food products on board the Ark of Taste and nearly 300 Presidia in thirty different countries. Two years ago the Slow Food Foundation for Biodiversity was created in Florence to co-ordinate the scheme.

In 1997, Carlo Petrini turned his native Bra into the 'world capital of cheese' with 'Cheese', a showcase for 'milk in all its shapes and forms'. He subsequently commenced work on one of the most ambitious projects in the history of Slow Food: the first University of Gastronomic Sciences with campuses in Pollenzo, near Bra, and Colorno, near Parma. It seemed an impossible dream, but the university is now in its second year and attracting students from all over the world.

A brilliant orator, Petrini has defined the movement as 'eco-gastronomic', for lovers of good food who are mindful of tradition and aware that the protection of agro-industrial heritage also presupposes protection of the environment. "Today a gastronome who is not an environmentalist too is an idiot," he likes to say, "and an environmentalist who is not a gastronome is a sad case!" Petrini argued that eating is a social event and, as such, demands the protection of local economies and eco-friendly consumerism committed to sustainability. Hence the birth of the revolutionary Terra Madre event and ongoing collaboration with food activists, environmentalists and agro-ecologists.

The first Terra Madre, a meeting of producers and workers in the world of food and agriculture, was held in October 2004 in Turin. It was attended by about 5,000 delegates from 131 countries organised into 1,250 'food communities', a new concept that identifies the extended production chain running from producers through processors to distributors. One of the guests at the conference was Prince Charles who, in his closing speech, defined Terra Madre as "a small but significant challenge to the massed forces of globalisation, the industrialisation of agriculture and the homogenisation of food . . . a great tribute to the unceasing energy of Dr Carlo Petrini." One of the subsequent outcomes has been the building of a 'lean' communications network interlinking the food communities, free of ideological connotations but conducive to solving common problems in diverse contexts. The second Terra Madre will be held in Turin in October 2006.

Since the 1990s, Petrini has used Slow Food Editore, the movement's publishing company, to produce magazines and books on wine and food culture. He still works as a journalist, writing weekly columns on Italian gastronomy, sustainable agriculture and rural development for *La Stampa* newspaper in Turin, and is also the author of a number of books. His latest offering, *Buon, pulito e giusto* (Good, Clean and Fair, Turin 2005), lists and explains his 'principles for a new gastronomy'.

In October 2000 Petrini was named the International Wine and Spirit Competition Communicator of the Year, and in 2003 he received an honorary degree in cultural anthropology from the University of Naples. In 2004, *Newsweek* named him among its 'European heroes' for the year. On that occasion, in a specially written appreciation, the internationally acclaimed French chef Alain Ducasse wittily described 'Carlin' Petrini as, "a seducer, the Don Juan of the food world. He has changed the way we think about eating."

John Irving

SULAK SIVARAKSA
Engaged Buddhist

"For all of us who are interested in freedom, justice, nonviolence, democracy and environmental sustainability, we should intensify our activism, criticisms, and analyses—not seal our lips, refuse to think and disengage ourselves from the sufferings in the world."

"Radical transformation of society requires personal and spiritual change first or at least simultaneously."

SULAK SIVARAKSA has been nominated as 'one of the ten most outstanding Siamese of this century'—men and women who have greatly affected the course of the nation's history in the last hundred years. Among these ten eminent names, he is the only person who is still living, and who continues to adamantly advocate the causes of the poor and destitute. He is an enigma of Thai society: feared by men in power—whether in the government, business circles, or even the religious hierar-

chy—but by and large admired by the impoverished masses.

Whether you love him or hate him, it is impossible not to take note of what he has to say, as he is the most outspoken voice and conscience of the nation. Fearless when it comes to the upholding of social justice, at times putting himself in danger of imprisonment on falsified and politically motivated charges, he was forced to flee across the border and then finally to Europe and the American continent for espousing democratic views, which were at the time judged as an act of subversion by the authorities.

Sulak Sivaraksa may be described by any of the following names: spiritual guru, thinker, intellectual, teacher, educator, pacifist and anti-war activist, social critic, radical, revolutionary, conservative or traditionalist. Although he was indicted for *lesé majesté* and high treason on more than one occasion (but won the court cases), he is certainly not an anti-monarchist. One has only to read his book *Loyalty Demands Dissent* to recognise how unequivocally he is dedicated to the royal institution—even to the extent of being damned disloyal.

When it comes down to personal integrity and the principles he holds, he rarely backs down, standing his ground against whatever forces oppose him, with the arrogance of a man who knows himself and what he stands for. This is in contrast to the way he leads his rather simple lifestyle, dressed in baggy traditional 'Mor Hom' trousers and shirts of faded blue, and sporting a pair of worn sandals. He is always ready to bend over to dirty his hands and feet to help those who have been wronged or maltreated; he is a gifted scholar who willingly makes use of his ability and vast knowledge to serve the less privileged, often with no hesitation about jumping into the mêlée when things turn rough.

He tirelessly travels all over the country and abroad to give public addresses, organise conferences, attend meetings, actively involve himself in grassroots movements, and to give his backing to local communities who want to have a voice in determining their destinies. His opposition to the laying of a gas pipeline from Myanmar to Thailand through the pristine forests of Khanchanaburi province, and the support he gave the Assembly of the Poor over the opening of the dam gates in Ubonrajthani province, have aroused the ire of government officials.

Despite an apparently frantic lifestyle, he is able to maintain a down-to-earth way of life, simple and unassuming, in complete contrast to his often perceived haughtily held high principles. His house, with a multitude of cats roaming freely in the tiny space of a compound he calls home, is open twenty-four hours a day. It is a gathering place of people from all walks of life, whether rich or poor, aristocrats or commoners, priests or laymen and laywomen, or even total strangers. They come to seek his advice, and in search of solace for their troubled souls, and he will often stay with them well past midnight, discussing and going over all sorts of subjects with the guests, solicited or unsolicited, slouched over a glass of wine, preferably French red. On these occasions he jokes and laughs at his own human frailties—things that not many men would dare to do. When proven wrong beyond doubt by the facts, he willingly turns around to make his apologies and correct his flawed views.

Young people seem to provide him with a constant source of strength and inspiration. They encourage him to forge ahead with new ideas and to uphold his convictions. He always finds time to work closely with the younger generations, listening patiently to their thoughts and ideals, and where necessary endeavouring to put them on the straight and narrow.

His insights into Tibetan Mahayana Buddhism have informed his perspective, giving him a deep understanding of Buddhism, and how it should be taught and applied to a world where materialism, greed, power, and wanton accumulation of wealth are rampant. It has brought him into the presence of His Holiness the Dalai Lama at Dharamsala in India on several occasions, who greatly influences his thoughts and writings. These meetings have taught him to take on and adapt Buddhist teachings to help to solve the current human crisis, and bring happiness and peace to the world. Mahatma Gandhi has been his icon from an early age; Gandhi's teaching of *ahimsa* (nonviolence) has become the mainstay of his belief in the possibility of peaceful co-existence among people of various races, creeds, religions and ethnicities. He is passionately against the use of force in solving social and political conflicts, whether in Afghanistan, Iraq, or at home in southern Thailand. His unwavering support of those campaigning for the release of Aung San Suu Kyi has kept him from setting foot on Myanmar soil—not to mention a few other countries as well.

Taken from Seeds of Peace journal

GREGORY BATESON
Systems Thinker

"There is a larger Mind of which the individual mind is only a sub-system. This larger Mind is comparable to God—a certain humility becomes appropriate, tempered by the dignity or joy of being part of something much bigger. A part—if you will—of God."

"If a man achieves or suffers change in premises which are deeply embedded in his mind, he will surely find that the results of that change will ramify throughout his whole universe."

"Every move we make in fear of the next war in fact hastens it."

GREGORY BATESON (1904-1980) was born into an academic family in Cambridge in England. His father, William Bateson, the famous biologist who invented 'genetics' and coined its name, became the first Professor of Genetics in the world and named his son after Gregor Mendel, the Austrian monk whose 'atomic theory' of heredity (his 'atoms' are now 'genes') was a seminal influence on his own work.

The young Bateson studied zoology, but side-stepped his father's prominence by taking up anthropology, studying tribal societies and their processes. He met (and later married) Margaret

Mead in New Guinea, became a US resident at the start of World War II, worked in (and was "sickened by") intelligence and propaganda, became a leading thinker in the new discipline of cybernetics (the study of circular or more complex informational systems of control), moved into psychology, developed the still famous double-bind theory of schizophrenia, made significant contributions to the development of family therapy, and then studied communication and learning in wolves, otters, octopuses and dolphins. In the mid-1960s he became aware of our growing ecological problems, and set up some major conferences, developing his central theory of 'mind' as existent in all the living systems of the world. He taught at Harvard, Stanford and UC Santa Cruz, married twice more, was appointed by Governor Jerry Brown as a very critical Regent of the University of California, became an outspoken opponent of nuclear weapons, collected many of his own papers and lectures into *Steps to an Ecology of Mind* (1972) and, still calling himself "a fourth generation atheist", came to see the totality of the 'mental' systems of the material, living Earth as "the sacred". Suffering from lung cancer, he spent his final years at the Esalen Institute, "coming round", to quote one of his Santa Cruz students, "to the view that it is important not only to propagate ideas but to act on them", working successfully against time to complete *Mind and Nature: a Necessary Unity*, but leaving *Angels Fear: towards an epistemology of the sacred* to be completed by his daughter, Mary Catherine Bateson, after his death.

It is important to recognise the unity of Bateson's thought. Some scholars see his progress through so many different fields as haphazard and contingent, but Bateson's great gift was to transcend disciplinary boundaries and to develop a body of thought which linked many areas of understanding. He did this by following and illuminating a few key themes within all the academic situations in which he found himself. The anthropological work he carried out in New Guinea raised questions in Bateson's mind which were later to illuminate other fields. Having asked what processes keep tribal behaviour within sustainable limits, during his war work he was able to

transfer this thinking to understanding national morale and our conceptions of other races. The post-war development of cybernetics enabled his recognition of positive and negative feedback in the New Guinea societies. Cybernetic ideas illuminated his work with schizophrenics and his study of the dynamics within families. Above all, he came to apply his understanding of 'mind' to all the living systems of the world. From the purposive reactions within an organic cell, through bodily sub-systems, organisms of all kinds, groups or societies of all species, to the vast ecosystems that enable the continuance of life on this planet— each of these systems is, for Bateson, a mind. Such minds are not necessarily conscious, but they are all capable of perceiving and responding to informational stimulus, 'news of difference' from their environment.

Bateson came to attach great importance to aesthetics. We have acquired, he believed, through our evolutionary experience, a 'more-than-conscious' way of recognising ecosystemic health. When we see a beautiful flower, animal, person or landscape, we are recognising a healthy ecosystem. Ugliness indicates disease, abuse, pollution or loss of health. When, says Bateson, we engage with the beautiful by singing, dancing, gardening, spending time in wild nature with trees and animals, painting, sculpting, appreciating poetry and metaphor— when we engage with the more-than-human world or any form of art—we can recover the grace of systemic wisdom: of knowing how to live sustainably within the living community of Earth.

Gregory Bateson came to recognise "the sacred" totality of all the mental processes of the living world as something very like God. His message is one of total integration. All the living world is the product of the great process-mind which is divinity. Hence, all of creation is divine, sacred, sacrosanct—it becomes a moral imperative that it be respected, honoured, revered. The living things are the product of this sacred system. Nothing is separated, nothing is other. It is the relating between all the living systems that is holy, divine, sacred. Bateson's wisdom is to be treasured, studied and acted upon, if we are to survive our present ecological extremity.

Noel Charlton

A. T. ARIYARATNE
The Awakening of All

"We who have been born Buddhist, Hindu, Christian, Muslim, or any other faith can be very comfortable in each other's temples, mosques and churches, praying or meditating together to create a spiritual mass of consciousness which can overcome our greed, hatred and illusions."

"When we try to bring about change in our societies, we are treated first with indifference, then with ridicule, then with abuse and then with oppression. And finally the greatest challenge is thrown at us. We are treated with respect. This is the most dangerous stage."

"Several million Sarvodaya adherents in Sri Lanka have proved that they can transcend racial, religious, linguistic and ethnic barriers to accept a common state of ideals, principles, and constructive programmes to build a new society as collectively envisioned by them."

A. T. ARIYARATNE

I S IT POSSIBLE to organise the power of love? Such is the question and lifelong meditation of Dr A. T. Ariyaratne, founder of the Sarvodaya Shramadana Movement in Sri Lanka.

"A soul force lies dormant in all of us," Dr Ari says, and "No human life is worth living if these inner treasures are not discovered and experienced."

Many spiritual leaders focus on the personal cultivation of love and self-enlightenment, and believe that society will take care of itself. Social activists, on the other hand, focus on external structures of domination, oppression, and injustice, and often put down religious or spiritual values as irrelevant. Dr Ari goes beyond these artificial distinctions and asks: Can we activate the interior life of human beings while at the same time transform social and economic structures of global civilisation?

His life's journey has led to a remarkable story of a two-fold awakening of self and society, building the world's largest spiritually-based development movement.

As a Westerner, I have had twenty-five years experience in social movements and also of the inner journey. My heart was lifted when I found out about Sarvodaya because it answered a deep schism and also a yearning within the Western psyche—how to combine the personal and the social in transformation.

Sarvodaya translates as "the Awakening of All through the sharing of energy" (labour, thought, energy, materials, etc). It is a powerful prescription for what ails us, not based on a naïve view of life, but one that takes into consideration all the forces within human beings and the society we inhabit.

Ari works in three spheres of life: consciousness, power and economics. These pillars are interwoven in the fabric of the Sarvodaya movement, and have led to practical success in mobilising millions to participate in their own development.

The sheer numbers are enough to make us take notice. Sarvodaya, under Ari's leadership, has mobilised more than 16,000 villages; energising them to build more than 5,000 schools, community health centres, libraries and cottage industries; establish thousands of village banks and more than one hundred thousand small businesses; dig thousands of wells and latrines; promote biodiversity, solar energy, rehabilitation . . . and peace.

Although Sarvodaya is rooted in Buddhism, Gandhian thought and Sri Lankan culture, the principles on which it is based are universally applicable. The primary thought is that consciousness and personal transformation are an integral ingredient in any effort to change society. Peace does begin at home. So Sarvodaya works to cultivate qualities that enable people to co-operate to improve their condition: kindness, compassion, equanimity, sharing, and joy in the joy of others.

Sarvodaya incorporates these qualities into practical efforts to transform people's day-to-day reality, working at the community level. Focussing on common issues that people face, it works to systematically build the infrastructure of community self-reliance and people's participation. We in the West should take notice of the simplicity in finding common projects that can bring everyone in a community together.

Transforming consciousness, community participation, building 'horizontal' people's power, promoting unity amongst a diverse population, self-reliance, and finding common projects to work on—these are the hallmarks of Sarvodaya, and are things we can learn from.

Dr Ari envisions a worldwide network of thousands of communities that are working internally to build up their capacity for cultivating the good within people as well as promoting self-reliance. Imagine thousands of villages, towns, and communities sharing ideas, experiences, and economically co-operating through trade, and building up a 'horizontal' people's power—a basis for lasting peace on Earth.

Richard Flyer

RIANE EISLER
Promoter of Partnership

"To heal ourselves we also have to heal society."

"Part of our higher destiny is to put love into action by challenging unjust authority, by truly caring for ourselves, for one another, and our Mother Earth."

PPLES FELL OFF TREES before Sir Isaac Newton defined gravity, but without name or explanation, the concept was hard to grasp. Riane Eisler uses this image to demonstrate how the domination and partnership social models, as described in her best known book, *The Chalice and The Blade: Our History, Our Future,* have inspired people all over the world to see their relationships more clearly. She is a researcher, social philosopher and passionate believer in the human race's ability to overcome the self-imposed destructiveness we have brought upon ourselves.

The Chalice and the Blade, translated into over twenty languages, is impeccably researched. In it Eisler traces the development of our species from Paleolithic times and lays out stark choices for our future. While she acknowledges that there are wild cards which could destroy us, she bristles at the suggestion that we have already sown the seeds of our destruction and become an evolutionary dead-end. In the last analysis, our future is up to us.

So who is this 'us'? Is it the 'partnership' people who acknowledge the gifts—intellectual, emotional, and spiritual—of both genders, or is 'us' the tough guys and their subservient women? Is it the dominators who believe in 'holy wars', or those who realise that in our age of nuclear and biological weapons, cultures of peace are a survival requisite? Who has the power to write the next chapter of the human race—or its final one?

Credibility comes from historical perspective, and *Chalice* has that. It presents a picture of humankind and how we got here. Some of it is not so pretty, but Eisler is quick to point out that what sets us apart from other species is our enormous capacity for caring, empathy, compassion and creativity. We have the capacity for killing and violence, traits which abound in nature, but it is our gentler side, deeply rooted in evolution, that makes us unique.

Eisler's motivation is simple and universal. She is a mother and grandmother who cares deeply about the world in which her descendants will grow up and live. Her commitment reflects that caring. Born in Vienna during the rise of the Nazis and a massive regression to the dominator model, she and her parents were hunted with licence to kill. They escaped by a hair's breadth. It is the search for an alternative to recurring violence and cruelty that has fuelled her passion.

But also, during the 1960s, she found herself a single mother of two, working as a lawyer, teaching at UCLA, active in the women's movement, feeling the need for a life's partner, grieving over the death of her parents and finding her health giving way. She realised changes were necessary. She quit her law practice, radically changed her lifestyle, and began the ten years of research which would result in *The Chalice and The Blade*.

The partnership and domination models are two basic social alternatives that go beyond religious vs. secular, capitalism vs. socialism, and so forth. Unlike conventional studies, Eisler's analysis gives importance to the relations between women and men and between parents and children—relations where people first learn either respect for human rights or acceptance of human rights violations.

When asked if it is not true that the dominators are in control worldwide, she points to nations where partnership prevails. The Nordic nations rank high in educational surveys and lead UN Human Development Reports. Finland is ahead of the much richer US in the World Economic Forum's economic competitiveness ratings. There aren't the huge gaps between haves and have-nots; there is more equal partnership between women and men, and stereotypically feminine traits are highly valued. These countries support care-giving, universal healthcare and quality childcare. They practise environmentally sound policies and laws prohibit corporal punishment of children. The men's movement defines 'real masculinity' quite apart from domination and violence.

Eisler acknowledges that in much of the world today we are seeing a regression to the dominator model—a growing gap between haves and have-nots, more violence, and a push to return women to their 'traditional' place in a punitive family. This kind of family, she notes, is foundational to violent, authoritarian cultures. She invokes modern history: "Just a few hundred years ago . . . speaking of human rights would end you up in an insane asylum—or worse—but it has changed because [partnership] people have worked for such change."

We are, Eisler says, co-creators of our own evolution. Once we diverged from our primate ancestors, we were on our own to evolve socially, to create societies in our own image. And we did that as a dichotomy: dominator/partner; one a formula for growth and success, the other a recipe for failure and doom as a species.

Can we do it? Yes! Eisler states firmly. When it is suggested that humanity has no future, that human nature has proven itself to be a benighted, aggressive presence on this Earth, she asks: "If human nature is incapable of finding enlightened survival, how could it be that millions of people are working toward partnership societies? Clearly it is within the scope of the human animal to make enlightened choices. The human yearning is for partnership. If we say it is hopeless, what is the point of anything?"

Dominator-raised people are frightened of change. They look to 'strong' leaders for security. But the old structures aren't working—which gives us a tremendous opportunity for change.

Eisler is President of the Center for Partnership Studies, www.partnershipway.org, and co-founder, with Nobel Peace Laureate Betty Williams, of the Spiritual Alliance to Stop Intimate Violence, www.saiv.net. She continues to work and to write, sometimes with David Loye, her partner in life and work.

Bob Lebensold

ARUNA ROY
People Power

"Poor people must be the agents of their own development and claim what is rightfully theirs by exercising their right to information."

"Leadership has to be redefined to include the collectives of ordinary people and the ideas they generate."

"We can't all be Gandhi or Mao. We have to work in a limited area. However, we have to understand how to relate our small work with big issues. Increasing this understanding is very important."

AS AN EFFECTER OF CHANGE and builder of grassroots movements, Aruna Roy has acquired a formidable reputation in India. Since 1990, with the setting up of the Mazdoor Kisan Shakti Sangathan (MKSS), a 'Labourer-Farmer Empowerment Organisation'

in Devdoongri, a village in the north-western state of Rajasthan, Aruna has led a people's movement for the right to information and the public's right to scrutinise official records. The wide public debate in India set in motion by her work, for which she also received the Ramon

Magsaysay Award in 2000, culminated in the Indian parliament adopting the Right to Information Act in October 2005.

As a former member of the Indian bureaucracy (she was an officer in the Indian Administrative Services), Aruna knows the ins and outs of the official 'system' like the back of her hand. Impatient with the ungainly system and frustrated by the rot that had set in deep, she quit the IAS and joined an experimental village livelihood project in Tilonia in Rajasthan.

Aruna soon became convinced that mere economic support was not sufficient to effect real change; it had to come through empowering people with knowledge. She and her colleagues at the MKSS, Shankar Singh and Nikhil Dey, began with the foundation of the 'Barefoot College', imparting the skills of rural self-sufficiency, and moved on to coach the people in the art of making their government work. By the mid-1990s, they were holding public hearings, known as *jan sunvai*, through which the people cross-checked bills, vouchers and employment rolls and thus exposed schoolhouses and health clinics paid for but never really constructed, or worse, famine and drought relief services recorded but never rendered.

"The *jan sunvai* offered a platform for open debate and demonstrated that freedom of information could curb the abuse of power. Many a wrongdoer paid back siphoned money after public humiliation, thus underlining the importance of public audit in stopping corruption," says Aruna of this radical way of shifting the focus from unresponsive officials back to the people themselves.

Through a decade-long struggle for what she calls the "basic right to know, the basis of all human rights", Aruna has been able to question the simplistic definition of democracy as merely a right to vote. "By casting a vote, we accept our share of the responsibility for shaping and controlling the system of governance," she says. "We cannot shrug off that responsibility for five years until the electoral process begins all over again. Questions need to be asked consistently, since accountability is a continuing process."

When the Right to Information Act came into effect, Aruna asked citizens around the country to begin asking questions of government departments. "It is the only way we can make our governments work," she said. Following her call, 'demand information' weeks were organised by non-governmental organisations to train people in the use of the Act.

Aruna has herself proven to be one of the foremost wielders of the right of citizens to obtain information about government work. Barely a month after the Act came into being, Aruna used it to request and obtain documents pertaining to a controversial World Bank-funded water supply and sewerage project in Delhi, which is part of the move to privatise water in the national capital region. Aruna's contention was that "in an area like water supply at least, commercial viability cannot be the hallmark of necessity and sustainability."

For Aruna, the fact that neither the people's opinions were taken into account nor were people made party to the many aspects of this matter which related to a basic necessity of life was unthinkable in a democratic society, as was the non-transparent attitude of the World Bank. When the Bank refused to attend a public hearing on this matter but invited Aruna for a closed-door meeting "over a cup of tea", Aruna turned it down, stressing the need for transparency in the Bank's functioning and for the government to take into account its citizens' views.

In 2004, Aruna Roy was inducted into the National Advisory Committee that advises the government of India on policy matters. This, however, has not dampened her belief in the value of constantly questioning the government and its various agencies and departments—a fundamental way in which people can make the governments they elected to act in their interests. In a country where common citizens often find themselves helpless in the face of rampant corruption and systematised lethargy, Aruna's efforts have provided them with a tool that can make the system work, or shake it up at any rate. In terms of sheer population, India may be the world's largest democracy. But it is people like Aruna who are showing how it can actually become a working democracy.

Swati Chopra

IVAN ILLICH
Culture of Conviviality

"In a consumer society there are inevitably two kinds of slaves: the prisoners of addiction and the prisoners of envy."

"Modern medicine is a negation of health. It isn't organised to serve human health, but only itself, as an institution. It makes more people sick than it heals."

"The compulsion to do good is an innate American trait. Only North Americans seem to believe that they always should, may, and actually can choose somebody with whom to share their blessings. Ultimately this attitude leads to bombing people into the acceptance of gifts."

IVAN ILLICH—a polymath, one-time Catholic priest, medieval historian and teacher on two continents—is best known as a critic of institutions, in particular of the counter-productive hypertrophy of profession-alised medicine and education: the way health care, at ever greater cost, may keep us not so much alive as excruciatingly moribund, and the sacrifice of our native ability to learn at the altar of institutionalised and certified knowledge. His ecological thinking—his piercing yet compassionate vision of the devastation being visited on the Earth and its inhabitants by industrialism—was always allied to a social and philosophic perspective, which celebrated the full richness of human potential.

Unlike many ecologists, Illich did not merely preach a gospel of impending catastrophe based on physical, 'scientific' limits. The catastrophe, for Illich, is already with us, not just in the destruction of nature but in the cultural devastation of impoverished language and the forgetting and atrophying of innate human capacities of caring, consoling, entertaining and creating. He saw the ecological crisis as a genuine turning-point, a once-in-a-generation opportunity to rediscover what he called conviviality: "the autonomous and creative intercourse among persons and of persons with their environment". Conviviality at root means 'living with', and the word's celebratory ring can connote not so much tipsy jollity as the realisation of the joyful potential in full living, with one another and with nature.

Conviviality, in this sense, could hardly be more opposed to the currently prevailing versions of sustainable development or sustainability: the idea that we can continue consuming at the same or even at a faster rate, while reducing the environmental impact of that consumption through ever-smarter technologies. Proponents of so-called sustainable development argue that only through an intensification of the processes of expropriation and marketing, conducted under the aegis of multinational corporations, can poverty and scarcity be combatted, especially in the developing world. Illich maintained quite the opposite: that these processes are impoverishing, at first quite literally, and ultimately culturally and spiritually. Rural Mexico was one of the parts of the world Illich knew especially well—he was partly based in Cuernavaca for the last forty years of his life—and where he was able to witness the physical and cultural losses associated with the industrial mode of development. He records, for instance, the disappearance from the village of Acatzingo of the "four groups of musicians—who played for a drink and served the population of 800"—replaced by radios hooked up to loudspeakers.

Perhaps Illich's most controversial claim is that nearly all people in the industrialised world suffer from what he called "modernised poverty". He defined this as "the experience of frustrating affluence that occurs in people mutilated by their reliance on the riches of industrial productivity". He went on to argue that "beyond a certain threshold, the multiplication of commodities induces impotence, the incapacity to grow food, to sing or to build." Clearly, sustainable development, in the industrial mode, can only intensify this type of frustration. Not only that, but the kind of sustainable development which stimulates infinite desire and needs—we read, for example, that today's children cannot survive without television—in a finite world, is a contradiction in terms, ultimately as unsustainable as it is unsustaining.

In its place Illich offers us his inspiring vision of conviviality. Conviviality starts from the paradoxical notion that 'less is more'. His point is not so much that we must reluctantly accept limits to growth, as that we should joyfully embrace the limits to unbridled exploitation which allow us to live in harmony with the natural world and with each other. A reduction in commodities could lead to an increase in creativity; a decrease in the speed of transportation could lead to everyone having more, not less time; restraint on the spiralling spending on health care, especially what Illich called "intensive care for the dying", might bring about a revival of true caring. Bicycles and libraries are two paradigms of what Illich called "convivial tools". But perhaps the ultimate, and the most threatened, convivial tool is poetry, defined by Illich as the "ability to endow the world with personal meaning".

Sceptics might argue that conviviality hardly amounts to a political programme, let alone a plausible electoral platform (who ever voted for reductions in services?). Illich would agree: conviviality is not a programme but a principle designed to sanction legal limits to the size and structure of institutions, countering what he called radical monopoly. Conviviality rests on a probable belief in the inherent creativity of human beings, gathered together in communities and polities of the right size and scale.

Harry Eyres

PATRICK GEDDES
Integrated Planning

"The age dawning in the twentieth century must have something better; it will have something better: a life-centered, folk-centered culture. It will have an instruction based not on the three R's but on the three H's: the vital education of Heart, Hand and Head."

"It can hardly be too strongly insisted that good teaching begins neither with knowledge nor discipline, but through delight."

SIR PATRICK GEDDES is often described as 'the founding father of modern town planning'. He was born in 1854 in Ballater, Scotland, and died in Montpellier in 1932 after a lifetime's work covering a vast range of activities, interests and passions. For me, he's one of those pioneers of what we now call sustainable development whose work, sadly, is almost entirely ignored.

I discovered his work by chance, more than ten years ago, when running a course at Schumacher College on the history of green ideas. One star in my galaxy of individuals involved was Lewis Mumford (a great American scholar, sociologist, urbanist and planner), and one star in Mumford's historical galaxy was Patrick Geddes. Mumford described Geddes as a man who "conveyed what it is to be fully alive, alive in every pore, at every moment, in every dimension".

Although it's true that a lot of Geddes' writing is pretty difficult, he was a dab hand at the odd sustainable development soundbite. I much enjoy pointing out to sustainable development activists that one of their favourite catchphrases, 'Think Global, Act Local', did not emerge from that crucible of catchphrases, the 1992 Earth Summit, but rather from Geddes' *Cities in Evolution* in 1915.

Beyond that, he was constantly seeking to provide snappy summaries of his ideas—often in the form of verbal troikas! Perhaps the best-known of these is 'Place, Work, Folk', to which I shall return in a moment. My own favourite, however, lies in his three S's: Sympathy (for all people and the natural world), Synthesis (of the different parts of the system), and Synergy (the combined co-operative actions of people working together to make their place a better place). It's clear that Geddes would have been a great champion of today's 'stakeholder' approach to getting things sorted out!

There are dozens of controversial issues exercising people's judgement today about which Geddes was expressing radical opinions more than a hundred years ago. At the heart of much of his thinking was this notion of 'Place, Work, Folk', which matches up intriguingly with our own rather emaciated notion of the Triple Bottom Line: Environment, Economy, Society. 'Place', it seems to me, is a much more empathetic way of talking about the environment, not least because it assumes humankind to be an embedded part of the environment, rather than as a species standing apart from the environment—as in that classically dualist form of words, 'humankind and the rest of the environment'.

Geddes was a real systems man and holistic thinker, believing that one can only make sense of things by seeing them as parts of a bigger system. As regards the concept of 'Place', he thought in terms of what might be described as 'nested layers', with each spatial layer critical in its own right, but only properly comprehensible (and therefore 'plannable', as it were) by reference to those other spatial layers nested in it or in which it was nested.

But there are some big questions as to how much influence his work still has. Indeed, there are some who have argued that there is now so little of the radicalism and holistic thinking of Geddes left in contemporary planning practice as to cause Geddes himself to disown it altogether were he still around to do so. One such critic, Michael Small, puts it thus: "Geddes has been hijacked by the planning fraternity, who have, in preserving his name from oblivion, also narrowed it into a space in which it cannot breathe. Gone is the pioneering ecology, the arguments for self-management, mutual aid and decentralisation, and in its place an insipid and technocratic paternalism. The glaring contradiction between Geddes' vision and the crimes that have been done by planners, who still claim Geddes is their inspiration, is breathtaking."

That, I suspect, would be considered by many planners today to be an excessively harsh viewpoint. But others would certainly concur with a less inflammatory viewpoint that one of the reasons why the standing of the planning profession as a whole would appear to have become somewhat shrunken is that it has lost that inspirational purpose that drove Geddes throughout his life.

At the heart of Geddes' anxiety about the direction the world was taking in the early part of the twentieth century was the phenomenon he described as "nature starvation". He despaired of one-off, piecemeal decisions that gradually stripped out nature from town and city centres, claiming on one occasion that, "since the Industrial Revolution, there has gone on an organised sacrifice of men to things, a large-scale subordination of life to machinery." He found it impossible to imagine sound educational systems that didn't constantly place children in nature, rather than reading about nature from afar or looking out on it from behind safe windows and walls: "The child's desire of seeing and hearing, touching and handling, of smelling and tasting are all true and healthy hungers, and it can hardly be too strongly insisted that good teaching begins neither with knowledge nor discipline, but through delight."

I would argue that most of us are still suffering from chronic nature starvation, and that this is as much a challenge to planners today as it was when Geddes was alive.

Jonathon Porritt

MARY HARRIS
Workers' Warrior

"Pray for the dead and fight like hell for the living."

"My address is like my shoes. It travels with me. I abide where there is a fight against wrong."

"Injustice boils in men's hearts as does steel in its cauldron, ready to pour forth, white hot, in the fullness of time."

"I'm not a humanitarian, I'm a hell-raiser."

"Whatever your fight, don't be ladylike."

I AM OFTEN ASKED, "Who inspires you?" It's this woman. The story of Mary Harris's life leaves me stunned and inspired. Oh, to be half of this woman! How can you lose all your children and your husband in one week and still find the fire within you to dedicate your life to action?

She worked with miners and took an early interest in the labour movement in America. Her radical politics led her to activism and she was, by all accounts, a superb orator. This minute woman would stride about the stage in a towering rage, or bring the audience to laughter or tears. Harris was the greatest woman agitator of her time. She was not simply a leader of a revolutionary labour movement in America, but a self-made symbol of that movement. She intentionally cast herself as a matronly old woman with a trademark black hat and lied about her age. (She routinely added a decade or two to enhance her motherly image.) Initially, she was disregarded by the establishment as harmless, but she was trusted by coalminers and textile-factory labourers as a mother figure.

Positioned in this way, Mother Jones, as she became better known, was able to defeat violent and unfair bosses and reform exploitative labour laws in the American East before the powers-that-be knew what had hit them. The movement she led eventually gave Americans the forty-hour working week, the minimum wage and workplace safety laws. Yet her name has practically disappeared from history books and popular memory, except as the title of a progressive magazine in America.

What drove Mother Jones was her Catholic faith, which she viewed as a mandate to stand up against injustice. If nothing else she was a survivor, and she discovered in herself a gift for leading others through the darkest times. Born Mary Harris in 1830, she was raised in poverty in Cork, Ireland, in a strict Catholic family. When she was only ten she witnessed the horrors of the potato famine, which drove her family from their homeland to Canada, where she trained as a teacher. She wanted to travel, and in her early adulthood she taught in many cities around America, until she met and married George Jones, a skilled foundry worker and a member of the International Iron Moulders Union. They had four children.

The first three decades of Mary's life were a desperate personal struggle marked by tragedy. In 1867, a yellow fever epidemic struck Memphis, killing her husband and their four children. Left a widow while still in her thirties, Jones went to Chicago and set up a small dressmaking shop, which was burned down in the Great Fire of Chicago in 1871. Luckily she escaped. Alone, and with every reason to be angry with her god, she searched for a purpose above her own trials.

By the turn of the century she had found a new voice. Strengthened and educated by her own tribulations, she fashioned herself as the matriarch of the working class in America. No-one called her Mary any more, but always 'Mother'. She emerged from nowhere in her antique black dresses and massive silk hats to lead the poor and exploited. This new role freed her. Most American women at that time devoted their lives to their families and their homes; they weren't supposed to have opinions, and certainly shouldn't have been speaking out publicly.

Mother Jones took to the road, and roamed America for twenty-five years; she had no home, but said, "My address is like my shoes; it travels with me wherever I go." She helped workers in the garment, steel and mining industries fight for better pay, better working conditions and twelve-hour days, and spoke out for labour activists imprisoned in California and Arizona.

One of her best-known actions was leading a 125-mile march (known as the March of the Mill Children) of child workers from Pennsylvania textile mills to President Theodore Roosevelt's vacation home on Long Island to publicise the cruelty of child labour. For those two months, Mother Jones and her street theatre and speeches made front-page news.

Mother Jones wasn't known for subtlety, but rather for her rousing speeches and a gift for what today we call the 'soundbite': "I'm not a humanitarian. I'm a hell-raiser!" Her weapons were her stories and her experiences of strikes she had led, the prisons and convict camps she had visited, her encounters with government officials and presidents. She became one of the most famous women in America, frequently appearing in magazines and newspapers. She was an icon and a legend in working-class America. A district attorney in West Virginia once called her "the most dangerous woman in America". She took it as a compliment.

Mother Jones died in 1930, shortly after celebrating her hundredth birthday. Her funeral was attended by more than 20,000 people. For me, her life offers a vivid reminder of what remains among the most under-acknowledged issues of our day: that we have become a class-driven society—and not just in America. The rich are getting richer and the poor are getting poorer. She embodies the activist spirit. She once said, "Pray for the dead, and fight like hell for the living."

Anita Roddick

J. C. KUMARAPPA
Economist of Permanence

"Often buyers are only concerned with satisfying their own requirements as near as possible and as cheaply as they can. This way of going about business is to shirk one's duties. What are the duties of an efficient consumer or buyer? When buying an article of everyday use one has to take account of the full repercussions of one's transaction."

KUMARAPPA WAS A MAN ahead of his time, and a seer who mostly walked alone. Scarcely remembered in his own country today, his contribution to ethical economic thought is monumental. Simply put, Kumarappa was Gandhi's economist. He advocated the village as the centre of economic affairs, the revival of village industries and rural technology, and agrarian reforms. The homespun *khadi* and *swadeshi*, or economic self-reliance, were institutions greatly enriched by Kumarappa.

Gandhi took great comfort in Kumarappa's confirmation of his own inner principles. Gandhi was intuitive, while Kumarappa was a pragmatic analyst. Together they made a great pair. At times Kumarappa went beyond his mentor. Kumarappa realised that Gandhi did not dwell much on agriculture (Gandhi admitted ignorance of the subject as the reason), and on his own account took steps to experiment with agricultural practices to orient them within the path of truth and nonviolence.

Kumarappa, like Gandhi, was the embodiment of sublime moral and spiritual values, living and practising all that he believed and preached. Throwing overboard flourishing career opportunities in India and the UK as a chartered accountant, he embraced austerity and lived a simple life until his end. Born in 1892 into a devout Christian family, he was provided with a good education, and went on to London and to the US for more advanced studies and to find work.

In 1929 he met the Mahatma. Gandhi had invited Kumarappa to discuss the latter's pamphlet, *Public Finance and our Poverty*. In it Kumarappa had explained how the British government was impoverishing India. This encounter would alter the course of Kumarappa's life in a decisive fashion. He became Gandhi's faithful follower.

In his books Kumarappa discussed how, when going down the prevailing economic path, wars are inevitable as nations vie with one another for raw materials and markets. As the modern transnational corporate-dominated economy breaks down national barriers and sovereign laws in its relentless pursuit of profit, the potential for conflict intensifies, further aggravating the situation.

Kumarappa elaborated on the kind of responsibility that hangs on us when we buy something. He wrote, "Moral values are always attached to every article for sale in the market. We cannot ignore such values and say 'business is business'. Goods produced under conditions of slavery or exploited labour are stained with the guilt of oppression." He was a critic of standardisation, viewing it as a bane that robbed goods of the finer qualities they should possess. Kumarappa also recognised the wisdom and care needed in dealing with renewable and non-renewable resources.

Kumarappa's knowledge of economics and statistical methods was formidable. His criticisms of conventional economics were well founded, and his observations incisive. While advocating decentralisation, he showed that the capital needed to provide full employment in a centralised model would be two thousand times the annual budget, whilst in stark contrast it would only be forty times in a decentralised scenario. He lamented that the government was intent on taking the suicidal centralisation route despite sound evidence to the contrary. For example, while proving the dangers of diverting land to cash crops, he drew a precise table of what could be grown on 77,000 acres of land to sustain, nourish and clothe a population of 100,000 people. The details were amazing in both depth and understanding.

In his book *Why the Village Movement?*, Kumarappa wrote: "Work is even more consequential than ceremonial religion. We may almost say that work is the practical side of religion. To deny man his opportunity to work is therefore to deny him the privilege of being a full-fledged human being . . ." Small wonder then that E. F. Schumacher, on whom Kumarappa's works had great influence, referred to him as "the Indian philosopher and economist".

In 1955, perhaps in the evening of his life, Kumarappa spoke at the T. Kallupatti Ashram to university students and delivered a powerful message on the ways of modern economics. He said, "Though the Lancashire mill is located in England, its ramifications extend the world over. To work it, therefore, we need worldwide control of the cotton-growing soils, farmers, the research institutes, and the railway rates, ports, steamships, ocean routes and bases like Singapore, Aden and Gibraltar, and markets too have to be controlled. Without such worldwide domination, the Lancashire mill cannot be worked for one day. Such complete and widespread political control necessitates the army, navy and the air force." In a similar vein, Kumarappa had warned that dependency on oil would lead to wars.

Thus we find in Kumarappa's writings and speeches every strand of thought that has come to constitute the voice of alternative philosophy. As the leading light behind the All India Village Industries Association (showing early awareness of appropriate technology!), Kumarappa sought to put these principles into practice. As a Gandhian he knew that unless something is put into practice it does not gain authenticity. He was a pioneer in ethical and ecological economic thought, and deserves a place amongst the pantheon of philosophers who have been offering us the sanity of alternative economics.

A. Rangarajan

THEODORE ROSZAK
Explorer of Counter Culture

"Technology has destroyed interrelations in the human community. . . . We are living among dispirited and agonised teenagers who can't find any hope."

"What do parents owe their young that is more important than a warm and trusting connection to the Earth?"

"It is indeed tragic that in a crisis that demands the tact and wisdom of maturity, everything that looks most hopeful in our culture should be building from scratch—as must be the case when the builders are absolute beginners."

THEODORE ROSZAK is perhaps still best known for coining the term 'counter culture' in his book *The Making of a Counter Culture* (1969), yet he remains one of the most astute analysts of the modern world. Twice nominated for the US National Book Award and a former Guggenheim fellow, Roszak's contributions to ecological thought have included the founding of ecopsychology, with his book *The Voice of the Earth* (1991), and writing the original introduction to the US edition of E. F. Schumacher's *Small is Beautiful* (1973), which may well have been a contributing factor to that book's success in America.

THEODORE ROSZAK

Roszak has been a prominent voice in the neo-Luddite movement, and his *The Cult of Information* (1986) continues to sell as one of the most sweeping critiques of computers and the 'information age'. In the 1990s Roszak established himself as a founding conceptualiser of the longevity revolution. Highlighting the positive aspects of ageing, he emphasises the 'ecology of wisdom' as a crucial factor for helping to humanise our industrial culture. Roszak has also been gaining increasing recognition for his novels which have included *Flicker* (a recent bestseller in France), *The Memoirs of Elizabeth Frankenstein* and *The Devil and Daniel Silverman* (a satirical novel dealing with evangelicals in the US).

Born in Chicago in 1933, Theodore Roszak gained his PhD in history from Princeton before beginning his academic career at Stanford University. In the late 1960s he helped set up the Anti-University of London and edited the pacifist-anarchist journal *Peace News* in London before continuing his teaching career as Professor of History at California State University, Hayward. One of the hallmarks of Roszak's non-fiction work—from his 1962 essay 'The historian as psychiatrist' to his most recent book, *World Beware: American Triumphalism in an Age of Terror* (2005)—has been the marrying of incisive scholarship to shrewd psychological insight into the problems of modernity.

Roszak's ecopsychology offers a radical challenge to mainstream psychological theory. Many of us recognise that there is something maniacal about our society's abuse of the non-human environment. When dire environmental warnings and problems have become the news of the day, our spontaneous response is often to say: "But that's crazy!" And yet, as Roszak points out, the dominant schools of psychotherapy have no theoretical category for pathology in our relations with the non-human. Ecopsychology addresses exactly this category of pathology and suggests that if psychosis is the attempt to live a lie, then the collective psychosis of our time is the lie of believing we have no ethical obligation to our planetary home. Ecopsychology also challenges the way many environmentalists have up until now gone about their task:

"Like all political activists busy with their mission, environmentalists often work from poor and short-sighted ideas about human motivation; they overlook the unreason, the perversity, the sick desire that lie at the core of the psyche. . . . It is one thing to have the Good clearly in view; it is another to find ways to make people want the Good."

Roszak insists that environmentalism must move beyond 'guilt-tripping' in order to find alternative and more persuasive means of reminding our fellows of their ethical obligation to the planet.

What had been crucial about the counter culture, for Roszak, was that it was counter to a dominant culture characterised by ecocidal industrialism, reductionist science and corporate regimentation. To be counter to that dominant culture, according to Roszak, meant asking searching questions about nature, knowledge, and human needs. The counter culture represented a deep critique of both our urban-industrial society and the scientific world-view that seemed to underpin it. For Roszak, the counter culture of the 1960s offered perhaps the most important post-industrial vision of society yet:

"I have always imagined it to be an Arcadian commonwealth much like the utopia William Morris envisioned in his *News from Nowhere*, but with the addition of a 'small is beautiful' technological base to relieve the drudgery. There the free flowering of personality, the ideal of organic community, the adventure of ethnic diversity, the exploration of the further reaches of human nature, life lived gently on the earth, an economics of permanence, a new biocentric contract between our species and the more than human world from which we draw our sustenance become the priorities of the day."

Roszak suggests that it is the scale and complexity of our globalised urban-industrial order which pose perhaps the greatest menace to persons and planet in our time. He therefore calls for a creative disintegration of industrial society. Ecopsychology, like the counter culture, counsels us to slow down, scale down, decentralise, and democratise—for the sake of both the planet and our own mental health.

Jonathan Coope

VINOBA BHAVE
Defender of the Poor

"All revolutions are spiritual at the source. All my activities have the sole purpose of achieving a union of hearts."

"A country should be defended not by arms, but by ethical behaviour."

THE NAME OF VINOBA BHAVE has resonated throughout India since the death of Mahatma Gandhi. As Gandhi introduced nonviolence to the struggle for India's political independence, Vinoba Bhave used the technique of compassion to bring about social and economic independence. For eighteen years he walked the length and breadth of that vast subcontinent. Every village, every town, every hill, every river, every valley he passed through vibrated with his love and laughter. His mission was to establish a kingdom of compassion and to abolish oppression. His method was to stay in touch with Mother Earth and so he walked on his two legs. His feet reached parts of India no other mode of transport could have reached.

Vinoba's movement was to make it possible for every man and woman to share the fruits and bounty of Mother Earth. What kind of family is that in which only some children get the loving care of their mother and others are deprived?, questioned Vinoba. The answer was obvious. Working on the land, with the soil, among plants, around trees and beside animals uplifts us physically, materially, economically and spiritually. Why on earth do only a few people own the land and the rest have no share in it? Land belongs to God, it belongs to all or to none. Nobody created the land, then why should anyone claim to possess it? Air, water, sunshine, forests, hills, rivers and the earth are part of our planetary heritage. No one group or individual has a right to own it, possess it, spoil it, pollute it or destroy it. We can receive the earth's fruits as God's gift and return what we do not need to God.

And so Vinoba knocked at every door, persuading landlords, capitalists and communists to establish a new relationship with the earth and its people. He won the hearts and minds of many millions. People relinquished some of their attachment to property and shared it with the poor and the peasantry. Vinoba collected five million acres of land in gifts to be distributed among the people. If you are rich, give; if you are poor, give. No one is a 'have not'. Some possess land, and others intellect and physical labour. Furthermore love and affection permeate the hearts of all human beings. We all have something to give, so give and give.

Through the campaign of giving gifts Vinoba inspired people to make a gift of land, gift of labour, gift of money, gift of tools, gift of knowledge. This was economics of the imagination. Hardly anybody refused this divine beggar. Vinoba's practice was never to antagonise the landlords, but to assist them to act rightly.

Vinoba himself was without personal ambition. For him life was a search for knowledge of God. He saw the problems of India not as political or economic problems, but as spiritual problems. He had immense faith: he believed that if the landlords were not converted today, they would be converted tomorrow. He was a saint, scholar, sage and servant of God all rolled into one. Because of these qualities Mahatma Gandhi chose him to be the first Satyagrahi (truthful campaigner) to end British Rule. In June 1916, Mahatma Gandhi wrote to Vinoba's father: "Your son is with me. He has acquired at so tender an age such high-spiritedness and asceticism as took me years of patient labour to do." To Vinoba Gandhi wrote: "I don't know what epithet to use in respect of you. Your love and character overwhelm me." Another time, Gandhi described Vinoba's qualities thus: "He is one of the few pearls in the Ashram. They do not come like others to be blessed by the Ashram, but to bless it, not to receive but to give!"

When Gandhi was assassinated in 1948 Vinoba was seen as a natural successor to his heritage. People looked to him to continue Gandhi's work of spiritual and social upliftment through pure means and simple living. Vinoba plunged into a new experiment of liberation from the money-economy. He started working in the fields for hours on end, digging the stony ground with the pick-axe and making the land fit for cultivation. He and his co-workers took a solemn pledge to eat only what they could grow on the Ashram land and to wear only what was spun and woven by themselves. All donations except in the form of labour were strictly ruled out. Vinoba started digging a well. Hundreds of volunteers and students from places nearby participated in this project and after the day's work assembled for community prayers at sunset. Vinoba, with his body besmeared with earth, used to conduct the prayers standing. While singing in a loud voice the devotional songs, he virtually danced with joy and exhilaration.

Living like the poor, loving the poor and seeing God in the poor does not mean accepting the domination and exploitation of the poor. Vinoba became a fearless defender of the poor. So many poor have nothing to live on because some of us have too much. We don't know when enough is enough and therefore we have a bottomless bog of greed. This kind of conviction carried such a power that successive prime ministers and presidents came to see Vinoba in the thatched huts or bamboo cottages where he camped during his long walks through the country.

At the age of seventy-five Vinoba decided to relinquish all action. He stopped his travels, took a vow of silence and spent his time in prayer, meditation and contemplation. At the age of eighty-seven he felt weak and unwell. He saw the Death God slowly approaching him. Doctors tried to protect him from the final departure, but Vinoba had no fear of death. If life was a celebration, death was the culmination of it. Vinoba stepped forward to embrace death. He renounced all food, drink and medicine. When he undertook this magnificent fast all his friends and followers knew that the great departure was imminent. In their thousands they gathered near Vinoba from all over India. After eight days Vinoba made his journey to the heavens in total peace.

Satish Kumar

ALBERT SCHWEITZER
Reverence for Life

"The purpose of human life is to serve, and to show compassion and the will to help others."

"A man is ethical only when life, as such, is sacred to him, that of plants and animals as that of his fellow men, and when he devotes himself helpfully to all life that is in need of help."

ALBERT SCHWEITZER'S achievements were manifold. Born in Alsace in 1875, his passionate intellectual curiosity, combined with huge physical energy, enabled him to win degrees in philosophy, theology and music at Strasbourg University, while earning a living as a Lutheran curate.

Two passions in particular ruled his thinking—a passion for the person of Jesus, and a passion for truth. In both fields he refused to accept ideas handed down by others that did not personally convince him. Thus he found himself in conflict with many of the thinkers of earlier times as well as his own, and was ruthless in his criticism. In his sermons as a pastor, by contrast, he was gentle and sensitive; but again refused to say anything that he had not tested on his own heart, mind and soul.

But he was driven by something more powerful than a striving for academic excellence: an insistent sense that he must pay something back for his happy childhood and his joy in university life. At the age of twenty-one this was so intense that it forced him to resolve that when he was thirty he would do something practical for humanity. But what? A missionary magazine article provided the solution. A doctor was urgently needed at a mission in the heart of the Equatorial Africa—at Lambarene, 150 miles up the Ogowe River in the Gabon. Instead of writing fat books for academics he would do something small "in the spirit of Jesus".

So he began to study for a fourth degree, in tropical medicine, while at the same time still lecturing on his degree subjects, preaching at his church and writing books on Bach, on organ-building, and, most importantly, on the ministry of Jesus.

In all these subjects he challenged conventional thinking, successfully overturning accepted views. In *The Mystery of the Kingdom of God* he laid out the proposition that Jesus's words and deeds cannot be understood unless we accept that Jesus was convinced that the present order of things was about to end. The Kingdom of God would dawn, and the world would be transformed. The lion would lie down with the lamb and there would be no more pain. But according to the prophets this demanded mass repentance from the people of Israel. When this failed to appear, he decided that he must die on their behalf in order to usher in the Kingdom, resurrecting after three days. But the transformation did not happen.

This, of course, was rank heresy, and as a result, when Schweitzer wanted the support of the Paris Missionary Society for his hospital at Lambarene, he was refused. All that they were prepared to give him was a piece of land at the mission. The money he needed for the medicines and equipment and their shipment to Africa he would have to raise himself.

The apparent paradox that Jesus's mistake did not lessen his admiration for him is solved when we realise that, to Schweitzer, none but the greatest soul in history could have brought in a new testament, with its astonishing new ethical principles, based simply on the two great commandments to love: "Thou shalt love the Lord thy God . . ." and "Thou shalt love thy neighbour as thyself." These positive commandments replace the negative commandments of the old testament. That was the Jesus that Schweitzer followed,

regardless of what the church might say.

So he and his wife raised the money, went to Africa, and found things much worse than they had imagined. The Africans had every imaginable disease. The climate was devastating, the work endless. The hospital expanded and had to be rebuilt twice, on better land, with money raised by his own concerts, to his own designs and built with his own hands. After World War I tuberculosis prevented his wife, Helena, from returning, but with various interruptions Schweitzer stayed there until his death at the age of ninety.

But there was a further, crucial step in his thinking. In his philosophical and theological studies he had sought endlessly for a concept that he felt must be there, but which he could not find anywhere. What he wanted was a philosophical proposition whose truth was unarguable and which at the same time could be the basis for a useful life: an ethic that was not life-negating. It was in that primeval forest, with the huge forces of life and death locked in endless struggle, that in 1915 the phrase came to him—"*Ehrfurcht vor dem Leben*"; not quite adequately translated as Reverence for Life. From then on, this was the foundation for all his thought and action.

"Every living thing, from an elephant to a blade of grass, deserves my reverence, for no other reason than that, like me, it lives and wants to go on living."

Schweitzer was a realist. He knew that, to live, a pelican must eat fish and a leopard must kill and eat its prey. Human beings are aware of the consequences of their actions, so must take responsibility for them, in the spirit of Reverence for Life. He ran his hospital in this spirit, and similarly, when he was awarded the Nobel Peace Prize in 1952, he used the opportunity to launch on the world stage the first major call to peace and nuclear disarmament.

He said "I made my life my argument"; and many who were there said that Reverence for Life worked. This, he claimed, was his legacy to the world, and it was undoubtedly one of the foundation stones for all the ecological movements of the twentieth century.

James Brabazon

OSCAR ARIAS SANCHEZ
President for Peace

"I want to see our children walking with books under their arms and not with machine-guns on their shoulders."

"The more freedom we enjoy, the greater the responsibility we bear, toward others as well as ourselves."

"Peace is a never-ending process. It cannot ignore our differences or overlook our common interests. It requires us to work and live together."

WHAT HAS BEEN your great motivator in life?
I should start by telling that my dream in life, since childhood, which I told my friends in school, was to become president of my country. The best way to express humility is to tell the truth. I was delighted and honoured to be the President of Costa Rica.

That must have been a very impressive moment.
Yes it was. At the time I was elected, it was evident that the basic need of the people was peace. Without peace, there is no economic and social development. You cannot raise the standard of living for the country if there is war. "I want to see our children walking with books under their arms and not with machine-guns on their shoul-

ders"—this was my cry. The essence of my plan was free elections as a prerequisite for peace. In order to have peace, we needed to become democratic. And we committed ourselves to consolidate democracies in the region.

In my view, Gandhi was not a leader, he was a coach. People got inspired by him. He had no state power to back him. The only authority he had was his moral authority. But I do believe that people need to be led. Gandhi led his people. If moral leaders have state power behind them, they can bring about a real change and lead the world toward peace.

But who is leading the leaders?

Principles, values and their own conscience. The people from Costa Rica did not want me to get involved in bringing peace to Central America. They had immediate problems; they did not want me to spend my time trying to pacify the whole region. It was a matter of my conscience. The role of leadership is to change reality, not to accommodate reality. It is the task of a leader to persuade people what has to be done. In a democracy I believe the public is also responsible, because they need to choose the right leaders.

How can people have power for themselves?

In today's world, the main purpose of so many political leaders is to remain in power. And in order to remain in power, they do whatever is needed—even if many decisions they take go against their own conscience or value system or principles.

I believe in leadership in the sense that only a morally strong leader can persuade people of the right way. There is a big difference between leadership and dictatorship. Leadership is compatible with democracy and moral values; dictatorship is not.

What is the most effective way to lead the people?

Education. Imagine what we could do if a proportion of military spending was redirected to invest in education. In 1995, world military spending totalled nearly 800 billion dollars. If we redirect-

ed just 40 billion dollars of those resources in the next ten years, all the people in the world would have basic social services such as education, health care, nutrition, clean water and sanitation. Another 40 billion dollars would provide all people of the planet with an income over the poverty line. But there is neither the political will nor moral leadership to achieve that.

How can we mobilise the people to realise that?

The non-governmental organisations must play a very important role. The reason I want to cut military spending is simply because I don't think we can survive in the twenty-first century with the antiques of the twentieth century. Eli Wiesel said that the opposite of love is indifference. He had the holocaust in mind. People and governments were indifferent. No one said anything at the right time. We shall have outlived the bloodiest century since the arrival of Christ. I keep telling my friends in Washington: "You are the only economic and military superpower. But the world expects from you a different kind of leadership. You also need to become a moral superpower. But all you do is put profits before principles." The United States has become the main exporter of arms in the world.

We live in a world where 1.3 billion people are living under the poverty line, where almost one billion people are illiterate, where more than one billion people have no access to water and where 60 per cent of the world population earn less than £1 per day. The gap between the richest and the poorest 20 per cent of the world population has rapidly increased. In this kind of world, with so much injustice, so much inequality, how can we have peace? The industrialised world does not understand that if you keep fuelling potential conflicts by selling arms, the twenty-first century will be just like the twentieth century. In armed conflicts, 90 per cent of the casualties are innocent civilians. Most of these conflicts take place in the poorer parts of the world. The more arms you sell, the more you perpetuate poverty.

Interview by Fred Matser

WINONA LADUKE
Voice of Native Cultures

*"We don't want a bigger piece of the pie.
We want a different pie."*

*"There is no social-change fairy. There is only change
made by the hands of individuals."*

*"We don't think scientists have the right to contaminate
the state grain—and it could happen through cross-pollination,
if they develop a genetically enhanced wild rice and
plant it in Minnesota."*

*"Rice is our most important grain, as a people.
It's used to tell the story of our migration."*

WINONA LADUKE was born in Los Angeles, and grew up in Oregon. After graduating from Harvard, and a year's study at Massachusetts Institute of Technology, she decided it was time to move back home to rural Ponsford, Minnesota, which sits in one of the poorer counties of the state, at least a hundred miles away from the nearest cappuccino bar or feminist bookshop. She has continued living there, even after gaining national acclaim as Ralph Nader's vice-presidential candidate on the 1996 Green Party ticket.

"The thing about being an Indian person," Winona explains, "is that you feel most at home with your own people. I'm best suited for Indian country. Sure, I could go out and get a job in a boardroom. But that's not going to help anyone else on my reservation."

While growing up on the West Coast, with an Anishinabe father who worked as an actor in Hollywood westerns and later became an author and lecturer on native spirituality, and a Jewish mother, who taught art and was involved in the civil rights movement, Winona always felt a strong tug from the direction of White Earth, the ancestral lands of the Anishinabe people. She revelled in stories about the forests and lakes, about ceremonies and feasts, about gathering wild rice and preparing herbal medicines, about how most of their land was stolen and the struggles to win it back. "People back there kept asking me when I was going to come home."

So in 1983, after finishing school and working for a while on the Navajo and Pine Ridge reservations, Winona moved to White Earth. She quickly found herself involved with a lawsuit to recover lands promised to the Anishinabe people by an 1867 federal treaty. When the case was dismissed in court four years later, she founded the White Earth Land Recovery Project to continue the effort to regain the lost lands. Over ninety per cent of the original 830,000 acres is now in the hands of non-Indians. Using foundation grants and a $20,000 human rights prize awarded to Winona by the Reebok company, the group has bought back 1,000 acres and hopes to acquire 30,000 more in the next fifteen years through purchases, gifts and by legal process.

Besides her work on White Earth, Winona is involved in an array of other native issues. "If you beat a uranium mine, dam project or timber company here, they're just going to move on to Saskatchewan or James Bay or somewhere else. You have no choice but to work on the international level. But in order to do that," she notes, "you have to have sound footing in one place. If you work on the international level but your community doesn't know what you're doing, then what's the point? The more you're an isolated intellectual, the more you're out of touch."

Winona LaDuke's commitment to White Earth extends beyond the length of her life. "When I go speak at Rotary Clubs in towns around here," she says, "I tell them that 150 years from now native people are going to get back most of the land here on White Earth. It took eighty years for things to get this bad on White Earth, and it will take time for things to get better."

"Americans want a victory in fifty-four minutes," she observes. "Activists in this country have won some victories, but we have to acknowledge the magnitude of what we're trying to change. South Africa is the perfect example. Those people waited a long time. Mandela wasn't in jail for just six months."

Winona, who has a daughter and a son, cites the intergenerational nature of native people's struggles as a key element that nurtures people through long years of political adversity. "We tell our stories to the children. It's incumbent on us to offer oral history because no one else will. At our ceremonies we have an elder who prays for us all. We make sure the kids are part of everything."

Traditional practices are the other source of power and sustenance for Winona. "Spirituality is the foundation of all my political work. Just yesterday we had the changing of the seasons feast. The land, the water and all that is around me, ceremony and community—these are the things that restore me. I go to every single pow-wow I can. I dance as much as I can. What we all need to do is find the wellspring that keeps us going, that gives us the strength and patience to keep up this struggle for a long time."

Jay Walljasper

MANFRED MAX-NEEF
Barefoot Economist

"The forms of social, economic and political organisations currently in force in the world are essentially antagonistic to the achievement of a tripartite harmony between Nature, Humans and Technology."

MANFRED MAX-NEEF earned his nickname 'the barefoot economist' for his work with groups of people who existed below the radar screens of the dominant economic paradigm. He recognised that although these people were financially and materially poor, they were rich in many other ways. Hence began a critique of mainstream development economics and a journey of searching for a new language that could truly articulate people's experience of the quality of their lives, which also along the way led to him becoming one of the early winners of the Right Livelihood Award, in 1983.

His personal journey, of course, began much earlier. He was born in Valparaiso on the coast of Chile in 1933, to parents of German origin. His

mother became one of his most powerful early influences. She could recite from memory stories from the Odyssey and the Iliad, and the young Manfred would sit on her lap listening to these archetypal tales for hours. He recounts that he would always ask her to re-tell the story of the battle between Achilles and Hector, and when she asked him why always, he replied that he kept hoping that Hector would win! Reflecting on this, he said that it always annoyed him how invincible Achilles was, and that he wanted the little guy to win despite the odds being stacked against him. In a sense this became a theme for his life.

Manfred followed his father's career by becoming an economist. After graduating, his first job was for the Shell oil company in Chile, where he quickly rose to become a regional director. However, one day he came to a sudden realisation that whilst he would become successful in the business world, he would ultimately feel unfulfilled, and within a week he handed in his notice. Instead he returned to university to teach and study economics.

His dissertation for his PhD was on the social structure of economic development, which soon got him into trouble, as no decent economist in Latin America considered sociology to be worthy of attention. So he found it hard to get a teaching post in Chile, but eventually he was offered a job at the University of Berkeley in California. It was now the mid 1960s—a time of great social upheaval amongst the student population in the States—and Manfred became closely associated with many of the activists. After Berkeley he obtained a job with the UN development programmes and returned to Latin America on field work. It was now that he started to put some of his radical ideas into practice.

In his book *From the Outside Looking In: experiences in barefoot economics*, published in 1982, he recounts and reflects on the impact of his interventions. He was instrumental in the mobilisation of over 300,000 Indian and black peasants living in misery conditions in the Sierra and coastal regions of Ecuador, in a project that promoted their ability to become self-reliant. This radical practice of Schumacher's idea of "economics as if people mattered" ultimately proved far too successful and threatening to the military elite. Manfred became *persona non grata*, and finally was given a week to leave the country. In due course he went to Argentina, and worked closely with Carlos Mallmann, a renowned sociologist. It is from here that Manfred started to formulate ideas about the understanding of human needs, which later formed the theoretical background to his articulation of the idea of Human Scale Development and a set of fundamental human needs.

As well as recalling his fieldwork, *From the Outside Looking In* is remarkable for its philosophical interludes: remarkable in the sense that many of his speculative ideas or visions predate later ecological and economic thought. For instance, he notes that it is not just population

figures that are an environmental threat but also resource usage—not such a radical idea—but he goes on to to suggest that a new unit of measurement should be devised: an 'ecoson'. An ecoson would be calculation of how many people a country had in terms of a fair share of global ecological resources. This idea was a forerunner to the now well-established and increasingly politically accepted notion of the ecological footprint.

In a way it is Manfred's playful ideas, or flights of fancy, which most clearly demonstrate his visionary thinking. One lecture that he gave in London in 1989, hosted by the Gaia Foundation, literally changed my life. What caught my attention that evening was his insight that the West was trapped in an economic language that was incongruent with the environmental crisis that it faced, and that the issue of primary importance was to create a new language to address the crisis. These ideas were later published as two essays, 'About the pruning of language' and 'A stupid way of life'.

Manfred's way of addressing his own questions was to think in terms of people having a set of universal fundamental needs, and seeing that cultures had different particular ways of seeking to satisfy these needs. This idea opens a myriad of possibilities for societal structures that could address these underlying human needs—a refreshing challenge to the single mantra of 'more economic growth'. Indeed, his set of needs (subsistence, protection, affection, understanding, participation, idleness, creativity, identity and freedom) allows us to think in terms of different kinds of human poverty and wealth. In Western (so-called developed) countries we may have financial wealth but we also have many other types of poverty such as identity, idleness or even affection. In fact Manfred went as far as to describe many Western nations as un-developing countries, in that a threshold between development and economic growth had been reached and that now these concepts were de-linked.

Whilst Manfred has not published much in the last decade, and his theory of needs has not been nearly as influential as in my opinion it should be, his reputation as fearless and creative thinker remains.

Nic Marks

PETER BROOK
Authentic Theatre

"We are aware that the conductor is not really making the music, it is making him.... If he is relaxed, open and attuned, then the invisible will take possession of him; through him, it will reach us."

"Everything is possible but you must find your own way. So, if you look at my work and think 'Ah, there is an example, I will start by what he's done,' you are bound to go wrong. Because the work that I do today is the result of all the work that I've done through trial and error, in changing times."

I N ANY POLL of British theatre directors, the odds-on favourite for the title of greatest post-war director would be Peter Brook. And yet, if he had never directed any of his landmark productions, if there had been no *Marat-Sade* (1964), no *King Lear* (1969), no *Midsummer Night's Dream* (1970) no *Mahabharata* (1985) and no *The Man Who* (1992), Peter Brook would still rank as one of the most influential voices in post-war theatre.

That claim would rest on a slim volume he wrote in 1968. The opening lines of *The Empty Space* are justifiably famous: "I can take any empty space and call it a bare stage. A man walks across this empty space whilst someone else is watching him, and this is all that is needed for an act of theatre to be engaged."

Generations of actors, directors and students absorbed the lessons of *The Empty Space*. Brook had divided theatre into four types: 'Deadly

Theatre', 'Holy Theatre', 'Rough Theatre' and 'Immediate Theatre'. The first was the most prevalent. "When we say deadly," Brook wrote, "we never mean dead: we mean depressingly active, but for this very reason capable of change."

The Empty Space was a manifesto for simplicity and authenticity in theatre. In other words, truth. But, as Brook was the first to acknowledge, "Truth in the theatre is always on the move." It was this quest for truth that took this acclaimed director, who had been working with stars of the calibre of Rex Harrison, Paul Scofield and Vivien Leigh, on a thirty-year journey from ancient ruins in Persia to a new home in a derelict opera house in Paris.

On the way he systematically took apart the key elements of theatre: language, narrative, design and performance. Inspired by abstract painting, he did so to discover what was essential, what could be eliminated, and what new things came to light once the inessentials had gone. It is a journey he is still on.

Brook was born in West London in 1925. His parents were Russian emigrés who had arrived in England in 1914 with only a pound. (His father had supported the Mensheviks and been imprisoned for two months.) At their home in Chiswick his parents continued to speak Russian. Brook was a talkative and precocious child. At the age of eight, he possessed a miniature Victorian toy theatre. At the age of ten, he owned a movie camera.

Brook failed to share the ethos of the private schools he went to—with their passion for sport and inter-house rivalries. The important thing, it was soon made clear to him, was to know your place and not get above your station. "I wanted to be an individual," Brook told his biographer Michael Kustow. "I was endlessly saying, 'Why should I support the house?'"

He went up to Oxford in 1942. "It was as if he'd come up by public request," wrote the drama critic Kenneth Tynan, "Rather like a high-pressure executive arriving to take over a dying business." At Oxford he directed a stage version of *Dr Faustus* and a film version of Laurence Sterne's *A Sentimental Journey*. Soon after leaving Oxford, at the age of twenty, Brook went to the Birmingham Rep, to direct Paul Scofield in three plays. The theatre's founder, Sir Barry Jackson, described Brook as "the youngest earthquake I've known".

During the fifties Brook was directing three or four shows a year. His career might have fallen into a routine of doing "one play after another" had he not set himself two major challenges. The first was to find an adequate dramatic response to contemporary events. At the Royal Shakespeare Company, he brought together a group of actors, writers and musicians to collaborate on a production about the United States' policy in Vietnam and their own outraged reaction to it.

When he was challenged that the play, 'US' (1966), would do nothing to help stop the war, Brook compared the theatre's responsibility to that of a restaurant serving good food to its customers. "There is only one test: do the spectators leave the playhouse with slightly more courage, more strength than when they came in?"

His desire to explore the basic building blocks of theatre led to his collaboration with Ted Hughes on *Orghast* (1971). For this production, which was staged at the Shiraz/Persepolis festival, Hughes invented an entirely new language. The idea was that there would be a connection between actors and audience that took place at a deeper level than a linguistic one. "One can hardly imagine," wrote Tom Stoppard at the time, "a bolder challenge to the limits of narrative."

In 1974 Brook moved to a derelict opera house, the Bouffes du Nord in Paris, a venue he altered as little as possible. It has been his base for thirty years. Here he assembled a troupe of actors drawn from all over the world. The cast for his epic eleven-hour production of *The Mahabharata*, for instance, came from eighteen countries.

To a remarkable degree, Brook's later productions have combined a seriousness and authority, which is rare in British theatre, with lightness, colour and grace. Brook compared this style to that of telling a bedtime story to a child. He had arrived at a wise naïveté. As he wrote at the end of *The Empty Space*, "To play needs much work. But when we experience the work as play, then it is not work any more."

Robert Butler

D. H. LAWRENCE
Priest of Love

"Be still when you have nothing to say; when genuine passion moves you, say what you've got to say, and say it hot."

"If I take my whole, passionate, spiritual and physical love to the woman who in returns loves me, that is how I serve God. And my hymn and my game of joy is my work."

DAVID HERBERT LAWRENCE was born in 1885 in Eastwood, a mining village on the Nottinghamshire/Derbyshire border. The mines were hideous 'blots on the landscape', the air stank of sulphur, and rang with the din of pit machinery. Human life was here entirely subjected to the demands of the mining industry. Few men escaped injury, and their wives fought a constant battle against poverty and dirt. But between the mines there survived some farms and woods, beautiful remnants of the old Sherwood Forest, and on his way to work at Brinsley pit, Lawrence's father might gather mushrooms or catch a rabbit.

It was from his father that he inherited his love of the natural world and learned his knowl-

edge of it. His young friends recorded how Bert could bring alive for them, make them see for the first time, the flora and fauna they passed every day. In later life *Birds, Beasts and Flowers*, a collection of some of his finest poems, revealed an amazing awareness of the otherness and sacredness of the non-human world. He saw creatures as 'little living myths', as tokens of our own inner lives and psychic energies, the 'honourable beasts of our being'.

The new Education Act enabled Lawrence, pushed by his mother (who worshipped "the great Goddess of Getting-On"), to go to grammar school and college, to escape first into teaching, then into writing. The fiercely independent spirit of non-conformism was so thoroughly absorbed by Lawrence (and so closely fitted his temperament) that by the time he was twenty-two he was refusing to conform to any organised religion, writing to the Eastwood Congregational minister that every man had an obligation to formulate his own religion, slowly and painfully, subjecting it to constant modification. He remained true to that belief throughout his life. His works are that process of constant modification.

Lawrence completed his escape by eloping to the continent with Frieda Weekley, a married German aristocrat and free spirit, who encouraged him to sever all his bonds. Their love became the bedrock of his life. In Italy his work blossomed. There he was able to develop his acute sensitivity to the spirit of place, a gift which produced not only several splendid travel books, but which made place far more than background in his fiction. He saw how human life had been shaped by place, and each place had its own quite different gods. Lawrence's ceaseless travelling was what he called his "savage pilgrimage" in search of a mode of life in harmony with nature. He came to understand and admire the Indians of the American south-west, but felt that their way was not his. Finally his search brought him back to Italy, to the Etruscan tombs. It seemed to him that for a short time the ancient Etruscans had found a perfect balance between themselves, their immediate environment, and 'the wheeling cosmos'.

It was his third novel, the autobiographical *Sons and Lovers*, which first brought Lawrence to the notice of the literary world, and his last, *Lady Chatterley's Lover*, which earned him lasting notoriety. But his finest novels are *The Rainbow* and *Women in Love*. Wiggiston in *The Rainbow* and Beldover in *Women in Love* are industrial hells, where life is mechanised and degraded. His protagonists, Ursula and Birkin, must learn through trial and error how the life that is in them needs to be lived. The rainbow for Lawrence symbolised all the varied potentialities of life working in harmony, a spiritual life grounded in the earth and the body.

Lawrence defined pornography as that which does dirt on sex. He wanted to rescue sex from the puritans and 'censor-morons' who spoke for majority opinion in England at that time. Lovemaking seemed to him almost the only experience left to us in which we could escape from the hard shell of ego and become one with the rhythms of our essential nature. He called himself "a priest of love", and his choice of that term implied that he saw his erotic life with Frieda and Connie's with Mellors in *Lady Chatterley's Lover* as religious experiences. The woods of Wragby in that novel are a remnant of an unfallen world briefly reclaimed from the Moloch of industry, represented by Connie's husband, the mine-owner Sir Clifford.

Lawrence died of tuberculosis at the age of forty-four. He had produced an enormous body of work in all genres. It was as though his very life flowed through his pen. The last years brought his final fiction, *The Escaped Cock*, in which he daringly marries the risen Christ and a priestess of Isis, many lovely poems ("new blossoms of me") which are seemingly effortless epiphanies, and his major philosophical work, *Apocalypse*:

"The magnificent here and now of life in the flesh is ours, and ours alone, and ours only for a time. We ought to dance with rapture that we should be alive and in the flesh, and part of the living, incarnate cosmos. I am part of the sun as my eye is part of me. That I am part of the earth my feet know perfectly, and my blood is part of the sea. My soul knows that I am part of the human race, my soul is an organic part of the great human soul, as my spirit is part of my nation. In my own very self, I am part of my family. There is nothing of me that is alone and absolute except my mind, and we shall find that the mind has no existence by itself, it is only the glitter of the sun on the surface of the waters. So that my individualism is really an illusion. I am part of the great whole, and I can never escape. But I can deny my connections, break them, and become a fragment. Then I am wretched. What we want is to destroy our false, inorganic connections, especially those related to money, and re-establish the living organic connections, with the cosmos, the sun and earth, with mankind and nation and family."

Keith Sagar

OREN LYONS
Wisdom Keeper

*"When we walk upon Mother Earth, we always plant our feet
carefully because we know the faces of our future generations
are looking up at us from beneath the ground.
We never forget them."*

*"We can't afford, now, to have these national borders.
We can't afford to have racism. We can't afford apartheid.
We cannot—it's one of those luxuries that we can't have
any more as human beings. We've got to think now, in real
terms, for that seventh generation."*

OREN LYONS HAS BEEN an uncompromising fighter since boy-hood. In the eighth grade, he was taken to a truant officer who informed him, "Indians are all alike—dumb." Lyons recalls that he nearly lashed out at the officer, "But I told myself, 'I'll learn my way, so some day I can shove it down his throat!'"

He quit school for good, and spent his time hunting, fishing, and playing lacrosse—the Iroquois' national game, played long before Columbus's arrival. "But first of all," says Lyons, "it's a medicine game for the health and the welfare of the community."

Lyons got an athletic scholarship to Syracuse University and was given the Orange Key for athletic and academic achievement. In order to try out his artistic talents, he moved to New York to design cards for the Norcross Greeting Card Company. But he began to feel impelled towards the Red Power movement, which was so inspiring in the 1960s.

He became involved in a Unity Caravan of various nations, which moved around the country talking to Indians about their traditions. In 1972 Lyons became a leader in 'Trail of Broken Treaties' national caravan, which converged on Washington to confront the BIA (Bureau of Indian Affairs). This action woke many white people to the bitterness of the Indians' resentment, and stimulated Lyons and others to join in the bloody conflict at Wounded Knee.

Lyons was also becoming convinced that the Red Power movement had broad implications in the world. He helped organise a national walk protesting at ongoing violations of Indian treaties, in which many black people joined. In 1977 he participated in the Haudenosaunee delegation to the first International Conference on Racism, and in 1980 was invited to the Bertrand Russell Tribunal, which focussed on the rights of indigenous peoples.

Since then Lyons has spoken at numerous international gatherings, including the Earth Summit at Rio, and used every opportunity to form networks of indigenous peoples. He has frequently spoken with the United Nations Conference on Environment and Development (UNCED), particularly to emphasise that indigenous peoples should not be expected to speak at the UN as non-governmental organisations. "Peoples without nation-state status are treated as part of the flora and fauna!" says Lyons.

"At first, I wanted to defend the Iroquois. Then my sights broadened to embrace other Indians. Then I saw this had to include defending indigenous peoples all over the world. And now I look even further, to the 'Human Family', which includes animals, birds, trees, mountains—the family of all beings."

Over the years, Lyons has become increasingly conscious of the connections among the many 'cancers' which beset the planet. "Racism is entwined with imperialism," he says. "So much, that Americans aren't even aware of their own behaviour. The language of American soldiers and generals is full of it. Vietnam was 'Indian country'. Iraq—'Indian country'."

"The way [indigenous people] are treated is a kind of cultural imperialism. Some tribes are dying off, taking with them, forever, secrets of traditional medicine. And every year, more and more indigenous peoples realise that their problems are similar. We need coalitions to stop this colonisation of our cultures."

The concept of the natural law is implicit among all indigenous peoples, and the disregard for this law among modern societies will have dire consequences. "The power structure of the Pentagon and the multinationals goes on. These power structures forget the natural law. They think they have real power. The reality is, we are all governed by the natural law."

"What does the law tell us?"

"If you poison the air, the water, the earth, you will die. Your children will die. The law tells us no single entity can grow unchecked without damaging itself and the environment. We consume too much. We breed too much. Humans cannot grow unchecked. It goes back to the natural law. Which is also a spiritual law. We could go on a while longer violating it. But not much. There will be a sudden crash and then the deterioration will go faster than we think. There is no forgiveness under the natural law. Western peoples—Americans, especially—are used to buying their way out, but that won't happen this time."

It is a struggle for this Iroquois faithkeeper to retain hope these days. "Sometimes I think the environment crisis will be a catalyst to make more people aware of what's wrong with our values. On the other hand, resources are getting scarcer, and there are going to be more and more resource wars, inside and outside the country.

"And yet, people are so unpredictable. Sometimes they do rise to the occasion. What we really have to learn is that we belong to community. We humans are part of the natural cycle—being born, coming to maturity, dropping back into earth again, the way trees and birds do. We're all of the land."

Marjorie Hope and James Young

FRANK LLOYD WRIGHT
Green Architect

"A great architect is not made by way of a brain nearly so much as he is made by way of a cultivated, enriched heart."

"There is nothing more uncommon than common sense."

"Freedom is from within."

TO UNDERSTAND THE VISION of Frank Lloyd Wright, you should first make a visit to Taliesin, the home and workshop he built for himself near Spring Green, Wisconsin. In *An Autobiography*, Wright described how the Villa Medici at Fiesole inspired him to build Taliesin: "I saw the hill-crown back of the house as one mass of apple trees in bloom . . . I saw plum trees, fragrant drifts of snow-white in the spring . . . I saw thickly-pendant clusters of rubies like tassels in the dark leaves of the currant bushes . . . I saw the vineyard . . . Yes, Taliesin should be a garden and a farm behind a real workshop and a good home."

Taliesin was the name of an early Welsh poet, whose birth is a tale of transformation, of witchcraft and of magic. Wright's mother was Welsh, and he changed his middle name from Lincoln to Lloyd to acknowledge his Celtic ancestry. In Welsh, Taliesin means 'radiant brow', and the house wraps itself round the brow of a hill overlooking the valley in Wisconsin where Wright had grown up. He said, "I knew well that no house should ever be put on a hill, or on anything. It should be of the hill. Belonging to it. Hill and house should live together each the happier for the other." Wright believed in Henry Thoreau's maxim that "we are but a sojourner in nature".

Pavilions and pergolas surround courtyard and garden, in an informal asymmetric design. The flat building stones for the fireplaces and piers came from the hillside itself, and from the beds of local streams, in accordance with the principles of English Arts and Crafts architects such as E. S. Prior and Ernest Gimson. The stucco which covered the wood-framed walls was made of yellow sand from the Wisconsin River running through the valley below, and the hipped roofs were covered with cedar shingle. Wright described it as "low and wide and snug, a broad shelter seeking fellowship with its surroundings. . . . Its countenance beamed, wore a happy smile of well-being and welcome for all. It was intensely human, I believe."

This piece of anthropomorphism says much about Wright's approach to architecture. He was seeking not so much a style as an ethical approach to life. His buildings were organic because he wanted to be as one with the ground on which they stood. "The land is the simplest form of architecture," he wrote. "It is man in possession of his earth. It is the only true record of him where his possession of earth is concerned. While he was true to earth his architecture was creative."

In his richly researched account, *Frank Lloyd Wright*, Robert McCarter draws attention to the influence that Victor Hugo had on the young architect. There is a chapter on architecture in *The Hunchback of Notre Dame* in which Hugo proposes that architecture was the chief form of human expression before the invention of the printing press. "From the sixteenth century on," he writes, "architecture turned miserably into a classical art; once it had been Gallic, European, indigenous, now it became Greek and Roman; once it had been true and modern, now it became pseudo-antique." Frank Lloyd Wright was seeking to establish in America an architecture that was both indigenous and modern.

Wright's ideas began to be developed in his Prairie Houses (which in spite of their romantic name are situated in the suburbs of Chicago). Although symmetrical from the outside, they were beginning to exhibit in their interiors some of the characteristics of his later buildings—open spaces, asymmetry, the movement from dark to light, and, through his cruciform plans which allowed rooms with windows on three walls, the integration of the surrounding landscape with the living area. Rooms flowed into one another, as Wright developed his ideas for an open-plan house, "a broad shelter in the open, related to vista, vista without and vista within".

By the time he came to build his most famous house, Fallingwater, some forty years later, these burgeoning ideas had developed into a fully realised organic architecture, in which the natural setting is the inspiration for the building. "At Fallingwater," Wright wrote, "nature and art were made to complement one another." Cantilevered terraces stretch out over the rocks and the waterfall, like the branches of the trees that surround it. Holes were left in the structure for existing trees to continue growing up through the building. And of course the waterfall itself rushes below the structure, and the sound of the water and the way the light is reflected from it are part of the experience of being in the house, as much as the vistas from windows stretching the whole length of the living room. Stairs from this room descend to the waterfall itself. Wright told his client, Edgar J. Kaufmann Sr, "I want you to live with the waterfall, not just to look at it, for it to become an integral part of your lives."

Frank Lloyd Wright's vision emerged from America's greatest contribution to human ideas, the transcendentalism expressed by Thoreau and Emerson. It was a response to the landscape in which they found themselves. Wright's buildings showed how man could be a part of the natural world, and for him the design of buildings had an ethical and spiritual meaning. His influence on the way we articulate space in our buildings is profound, and as one of the pioneers of organic architecture he is making his presence felt even today. But perhaps we need him most for his very approach to the way in which we create the buildings in which we live. "A great architect is not made by way of a brain," he said towards the end of his life, "nearly so much as he is made by way of a cultivated, enriched heart. It is the love of the thing he does that really qualifies him in the end. And I believe the quality of love is the quality of great intelligence, great perception, deep feeling."

Harland Walshaw

SPIRITUAL VISIONARIES

"I slept and dreamt that life was joy.
I awoke and saw that life was service.
I acted, and behold—service was joy."

—Rabindranath Tagore

THE DALAI LAMA
Ocean of Compassion

"My religion is very simple. My religion is kindness."

"Love and compassion are necessities, not luxuries. Without them humanity cannot survive."

"Happiness is not something ready-made. It comes from your own actions."

"If you want others to be happy, practice compassion. If you want to be happy, practice compassion."

"In the practice of tolerance, one's enemy is the best teacher."

"Old friends pass away, new friends appear. It is just like the days. An old day passes, a new day arrives. The important thing is to make it meaningful; a meaningful friend—or a meaningful day."

THE DALAI LAMA

ONE HOT SUMMER DAY in Japan, a country whose roots are still deeply, if invisibly, steeped in Buddhism, I found myself thinking again about His Holiness the 14th Dalai Lama. Everywhere I go these days, I seem to run into his words, his image, pictures of him, stories of him.

It is hard to believe that fifteen years ago, when I'd mention his name in New York, few people even knew who he was (and some people I arranged to have lunch with him cancelled because of lack of interest). And with all the exposure and admiration has, inevitably, come a shadow side: people eager to look for bad in him, or to read all or many of his actions in a sceptical light.

I wondered: what is the real nature of his charisma, his appeal? And on this particular day, the answer that came to me was: he's suffered. To an almost incomprehensible degree. He's seen more suffering in this incarnation than most of us will see in a thousand lifetimes. If there's one major theme in his life, it's the central Buddhist theme of loss.

At the age of two, he was wrenched out of his quiet life by a group of travelling monks from Lhasa and put through a quite ferocious scholarly and monastic training. By the time he was fifteen—when most of us are just trying to deal with adolescence—he was a head of state, up against Mao Zedong and the largest nation in the world.

He was forced to leave the country he loves and serves, he's seen hundreds of thousands of Tibetan people die, often in his service, and he's seen almost every diplomatic advance of forty years rejected. As Dalai Lama, he accepts all this as his responsibility, his destiny, but there's a human side, too, that can only feel the pain.

His mother dies, his closest brother dies, and he's away trying to rescue Tibet at the time. His teacher dies. Refugees come to his room daily, weeping uncontrollably. Meanwhile, as more and more of the world comes clamouring to him with its problems, more and more of the young people in his community start rising up, saying: "What's he done in forty years? All this talk of forgiveness and conciliation, and all that's happening is that China's wiping out our country and more of our people are dying in vain."

And in the middle of all this, what is the man famous for? Pure optimism. Happiness, calm and an invincible sense of peace. His smile, his warmth, all the things that make him what one friend of mine calls "the happiest man alive". It makes you humble, in a way; it also causes you to think.

If someone who has seen and lost all that he has seen and lost—forty years of waiting to go back to a home that is slowly, systematically, being destroyed—can look at the light in things, what right do any of us have to feel sorry for ourselves? If he can find hope, how can the rest of us not do so?

It's the same spirit you see in all of history's affirmers, and not only the ones, like Mandela or Gandhi or Aung San Suu Kyi, who have served time in different kinds of prison. The story of Emerson's life is a chronicle of loss.

Some people would say, and I think with justice, that the Dalai Lama's message, on one level, is a rigorous optimism. Others would just point to his kindness—the equivalent of the Buddha holding up a flower and saying nothing.

Pico Iyer

JIDDU KRISHNAMURTI
Free Spirit

"In oneself lies the whole world and if you know how to look and learn, the door is there and the key is in your hand. Nobody on Earth can give you either the key or the door to open, except yourself."

"You must understand the whole of life, not just one little part of it. That is why you must read, that is why you must look at the skies, that is why you must sing and dance, and write poems and suffer and understand, for all that is life."

"A man who is not afraid is not aggressive, a man who has no sense of fear of any kind is really a free, a peaceful man."

"Freedom from the desire for an answer is essential to the understanding of a problem."

JIDDU KRISHNAMURTI

KRISHNAMURTI IS universally renowned as the Master who renounced the role of Master, refused to countenance a devout following, gave no teaching or rule of life, and proclaimed that truth and reality are to be found, always and only, within each of us for ourselves. The responsibility, which from time immemorial humanity has loved to lay on some saviour-figure—the Lord Buddha, the Lord Jesus, the Prophet Muhammad, and a religious body of doctrine and organisation arising therefrom—Krishnamurti declared lies within ourselves alone. Doctrines and institutions he abjured; perhaps his rejection of tradition was too absolute for the greater part of humankind to emulate.

Many are perhaps not ready to abandon the security of religious props, organisations, 'Masters'. Krishnamurti said "My purpose is to make men unconditionally free, for I maintain that the only spirituality is the incorruptibility of the self which is eternal, is the harmony between reason and love." But how many are ready to assume the burden of such freedom? In 1929, in renouncing the role of world-teacher for which he had been prepared from boyhood by Mrs Besant and the Theosophical Society, Krishnamurti declared, "I maintain that Truth is a pathless land, and you cannot approach it by any path whatsoever, by any religion, by any sect. . . . Truth, being limitless, unconditioned, unapproachable by any path whatsoever, cannot be organised."

Nevertheless, the life of Krishnamurti was, from beginning to end, that of a great world-teacher. The strange story of Mrs Besant's 'discovery' of a young Brahmin boy from southern India, singled out to be an avatar—the Buddha-to-be, perhaps—and educated for the part he was to play, is well known. His mother's early death (and later that of his much-loved brother), loneliness, intensive education for his role, the grandeur of the Theosophical Society's vast grounds (and later an aristocratic ambience in England) may have contributed to the awakening of psychic powers in the boy Krishnamurti, but do not account for his remarkable intellectual gifts as manifested in his subsequent life.

Early in life he underwent, over a number of years, a progressive spiritual opening and expanding of consciousness accompanied by intense pain, mental and physical. As a young man he nevertheless enjoyed fun and fast cars, and throughout his life retained this alternation of a playful and an inspired presence. Beautiful outwardly and inwardly alike, he attracted multitudes; and uniting as he did an Indian and a Western education, he was, like Sri Aurobindo, a world-figure. Yet his teaching was a ruthless destructuring not only of received teachings and beliefs, systems and attitudes, but of being and consciousness itself. His method was Socratic dialogue and evocation from those groups or individuals who participated, of the answers—or rather non-answers—to their questions. It is important, he insisted, to ask questions to which there are no answers.

His teaching has been likened to that of Gautama Buddha (who also offered no consoling doctrines), but Krishnamurti offered no rule of life to be followed by his disciples. Others see his teaching as akin to the *advaita* (non-dual) Vedantic tradition. Others again might see his mission as being, above all, to the modern West and to Westernised India; he was fascinated by scientific theories of the brain (sometimes he seems to make no distinction between 'brain' and 'mind' in the way that, for example, Sir John Eccles distinguishes the brain as simply an organ used by the mind, not itself a creator of thought). Computers and artificial 'brains' also fascinated him. He was deeply concerned with the predicament of the modern world, and believed that only some 'mutation' of the brain—which he nevertheless insisted must come from within individuals—could avail. Without some such transformation he saw little hope.

What can remain of a teaching that so radically rejected tradition and the traditional role of the teacher? Perhaps the schools he founded in India, Ceylon, England and the United States? Who can say where the thought of a great mind begins and ends?

Kathleen Raine

DEEPAK CHOPRA
Holistic Healer

"When you live your life with an appreciation of coincidences and their meanings, you connect with the underlying field of infinite possibilities."

"Whatever relationships you have attracted in your life at this moment, are precisely the ones you need in your life at this moment. There is a hidden meaning behind all events, and this hidden meaning is serving your own evolution."

"In the midst of movement and chaos, keep stillness inside of you."

"There are no extra places in the universe. Everyone is here because he or she has a place to fill, and every piece must fit itself into the big jigsaw puzzle."

"The less you open your heart to others, the more your heart suffers."

DEEPAK CHOPRA

DEEPAK CHOPRA WAS HERALDED as "one of the top 100 heroes of the twentieth century" by *Time* magazine in 1999, and as "one of the most lucid and inspired philosophers of our time", by Mikhail Gorbachev that same year.

The first time I became aware of Deepak Chopra was on the eve of an important business meeting which, looking back now, was a major turning point in my life. Knowing that the outcome of the meeting would have a far-reaching effect on both my business and personal life, I was anxious and couldn't sleep. I went downstairs to the hotel newsstand, to find some distraction in the rows of books and magazines. Thumbing through the pages of Deepak's *The Seven Spiritual Laws of Success*, I caught some words and phrases that struck a chord, so I purchased the book and spent the next hours reading it cover to cover.

As I was reading the book, I felt a certain calm take over that could only come from a higher perspective. Deepak's words refocussed my attention, from the outer world—the outcome of the meeting—to my inner world, the values and principles that had guided my life. His message of the unity of all, of non-attachment, of joyful existence in the face of fear, had so inspired my thinking that it altered my course.

The meeting flowed easily from the moment it began, and all present were struck by how relaxed I seemed, especially given the circumstances and stakes. By releasing my attachment to a specific outcome, I was able to access a higher creativity, and secure a positive result.

Afterwards, I sought to meet him, and to thank him for the wonderful gift that he had given me. Within a year our paths had crossed, and I found myself sitting with him. Deepak relaxed deeply into his seat, his eyes twinkling to match his smile. His being conveyed the deep serenity that comes from one who lives a life of service; one who knows well the joy to be found in helping others. At the same time, his smile marked a connection, and the beginning of a lasting friendship.

Deepak is a blessed being, one of our world's great treasures. He'll tell you that what he has to say has been said by others. He'll laugh, and quote—at length and easily—from the sages of all time, and remain humble. His words and actions spring forth from our common Source, yet he carries them so differently. He radiates the joy of creation.

Deepak sees himself as a vessel, not a prophet—as a tool in the hands of a divine artist. I think it is this quality that makes his work so approachable. He has been able to find the place in which Eastern knowledge and traditions can meet, and bring understanding to, the findings of Western science and culture. On both sides of the divide, there are many people who work for civic and social change, and many others who work in the area of personal development and transformation. Deepak bridges both. His work takes the position that meaningful, sustainable, change will never take place without reflecting the balance of inner and outer work; that personal transformation ultimately leads to social and civic transformation.

Deepak has said that the remainder of his life will be spent working toward global peace and unity. As written in *Asia Times Online*, "Chopra's personalised *practicum* to attaining a peaceful conscience runs as follows: free up emotions to feel the anguish of (others); relate to others non-violently and bond with mutual trust; love and respect the environment with awareness; give up outworn . . . ways and encourage evolutionary impulses; relinquish grievances and send out forgiveness; and offer help without expecting gratitude or recognition." To help further this message throughout the world, Deepak accepted the Presidency of the Alliance for a New Humanity (www.anhglobal.org) in 2004. This organisation is dedicated to connecting people who are committed to creating a just, peaceful, and sustainable world, in order to accelerate a cohesive global movement of personal and social transformation, reflecting the unity of humanity and human relationship with the Earth.

Deepak Chopra's influence will be felt in our world for a long time to come. Deepak's legacy is one of inspiration—the inspiration that encourages us to be more, to stretch our minds in understanding, to open our hearts in compassion, and to free our spirits to dance among the stars.

Sheryl Leach

KATHLEEN RAINE
Creative Spirit

*"Meanings, moods, the whole scale of our inner experience
finds in nature the 'correspondence' through which
we may know our boundless selves."*

*"I couldn't claim that I have never felt the urge to explore evil,
but when you descend into hell you have to be very careful."*

*"Is there any child who does not wonder how human beings
could ever wish to do otherwise than live in the forest
with the creatures and the trees and flowers and sun
and rain and winds and storms and clouds?"*

KATHLEEN RAINE MADE an extraordinary contribution to the life of literature and holistic thinking. Her work is best viewed as a complex whole. She did not follow one discipline. She was not a careerist. She was not an academic. Rather like Carl Jung, whom she greatly admired, she followed the life of her own inner daimon and the invitations of the creative spirit. When in the early days of running her journal *The Temenos Review* she ran into financial straits, she told me how she would simply sell one of her own cherished paintings—a David Jones, a Cecil Collins—to meet the bill. She was a free spirit, and lived by intuitive insight and not by pragmatic calculations or collective codes. In a similar way, following the path of inner intellectual passion and imaginative need, she turned from one literary form to another, from one creative activity to another, ever trying to give expression to her sense of metaphysical connection and divine unity.

First of all, she was a poet. At the heart of her poetry there is a profound commitment to direct truth-telling, a truth-telling that bypasses completely the strategies and vanities of the ego. For Kathleen Raine a good poem has to emerge directly from the primordial sources, of life. It has to speak its own life. In 'The Poet Answers the Accuser' she writes:

A note struck by the stars I am,
A memory trace of sun and moon and
 moving waters,
A voice of the unnumbered dead,
 fleeting as they are—
What matter who I am?

In her life Kathleen published eleven volumes of poetry, continuously exploring and embodying this notion of the poet's work. It was her most constant way of staying true to the divine vision in a time of spiritual betrayal. Tellingly, she was to write in the last decade of her life: "All I have known and been / I bequeath to whoever / can decipher my poem."

But her poetry does not stand apart from her other work. It has to be related to her four volumes of autobiography. Significantly, the journey of her life is presented as an archetypal one, beginning in the Eden of childhood experience, moving out into the ambivalent currents of adolescent and adult life and ending—in the final volume of her quartet of publications—with a profound sense of belonging to eternity. The vision of eternity—of Eden regained—is identified with the country of India, which she discovered late in life with a conviction of absolute homecoming.

The third aspect of her work is critical and philosophical. In our metaphysically ungrounded age all serious poets have to find a tradition in which to anchor their work. In Kathleen, as with Carl Jung, it led to the search for spiritual ancestors. She found these in the poets Yeats, Coleridge, Shelley and, most of all, in the poet, painter and visionary, William Blake. Her greatest contribution here was to demonstrate in an impressive number of scholarly books and essays the traditional learning of Blake. She reversed the idea that he was a crazy genius, a nomadic isolate, and showed that, in fact, he was part of a perennial tradition running back into the alchemists, the Neoplatonic thinkers and the gnostics. In the careful mapping of this long tradition of symbolic thinking, she was also, in effect, locating the deep geography of her own creative work. Once again, one discerns the holistic nature of her enterprise, the unity in the diversity, the inner gestalt of her imaginative needs.

Finally, Kathleen must also be seen as an educator of great tenacity. She achieved this in her dual role as editor of *The Temenos Review* and as founder of the Temenos Academy, an institution in London devoted to keeping alive the notion of perennial wisdom outlined in her critical writing. Her aim was two-fold: first, to draw together all those committed to what she named the learning of the imagination and, second, to ensure that the learning of the imagination was kept alive and actively disseminated. As both the journal and the Academy survive her death, one can only regard these as educational triumphs of the spirit in an age when education has become all but instrumental.

In her letters and in her conversations with me Kathleen talked often of fighting what she called "the Great Battle". There can be no doubt that she not only engaged brilliantly in the cultural battle for the best part of a very long productive life, but also in the heat of the collisions forged many of the weapons needed for keeping spiritual energy bright.

Peter Abbs

RABINDRANATH TAGORE
Cosmic Poet

"I slept and dreamt that life was joy. I awoke and saw that life was service. I acted, and behold—service was joy."

"A mind all logic is like a knife—all blade. It makes the hand bleed that uses it."

"Clouds come floating into my life, no longer to carry rain or usher storm, but to add colour to my sunset sky."

"Emancipation from the bondage of the soil is no freedom for the tree."

"POWER IN ALL ITS FORMS is irrational; it is like the horse that drags the cart blindfolded." Thus wrote Rabindranath Tagore in a letter to Mahatma Gandhi. Suspicious all his life of political power, of nation states, even of Gandhi's own anti-imperialist *satyagraha* campaigns if they whipped up dangerous mass feelings, Tagore might be expected to come out with a statement like that. On deeper reflection, the statement becomes more puzzling. Here was a man possessed with phenomenal creative power—endlessly prolific as a poet, song-writer, fiction-writer, playwright, essayist, letter-writer, even in his latter years as a painter—and who also had enormous personal charisma. On winning the Nobel Prize for literature in 1913, he added to his unrivalled standing in Bengal fame throughout India and indeed throughout the world.

He was the world's first intercontinental literary superstar: on his lecture tours throughout Europe, the Americas, South-East Asia and the Far East he attracted huge crowds and lavish press attention. His robes (not a traditional Indian form of dress at all, but his own pan-Asian design), his beard and locks and noble deportment had the look of a prophet. Even now in Bengal and India and in surprising countries such as Latvia or Hungary where his lifetime image has been lovingly preserved, Tagore as face, as icon, still reigns. The icon keeps his memory alive—as one of the great figures of his time who cannot be ignored—but is also a hindrance to efforts to understand and appreciate him fully as a man, artist and thinker.

Tagore had a name for his own, unceasing, mysterious creative power, which he felt (as many creative artists have felt) came from outside, from forces larger than himself. He called it his *jivan-devata*, or 'life-god': a force that relentlessly drove him forward along difficult paths. In his last poem of all, written just a week before he died, he gently rebukes his *jivan-devata* for setting many snares along the way, for being *chalanamayi* (full of deception), and asks at least if he can now claim his "indestructible right to peace". What were those snares? A fondness for posing for photographs? Enjoying his Western fame when his rivals in Bengal had been so jealous and scathing? Over-ambition in his experiments in education and rural development and efforts for international peace?

It is a mark of Tagore's greatness that he should have ended his life in so humble and bewildered a spirit, so shorn of all certainty or complacency. In some ways he seems too hard on himself, for it is difficult to think of any creative artist more giving, more self-sacrificing, more unselfish than Tagore. Yes, occasionally his composure snapped: most famously when a large deputation of people from Calcutta who had previously scoffed at him arrived by train at Santiniketan to congratulate him on his Nobel Prize, and he furiously sent them all packing. But much more typical was what he wrote in a letter to William Rothenstein: "I am doomed to be unrelentingly good to humanity and remain harnessed to a cause."

For some—and maybe, if they are honest, all—readers of Tagore, whether those who can read him in his endless rich and beautiful Bengali, or in translation, Tagore's dedication to goodness can be a problem. "There's a lack of grossness in Tagore," a Bangladeshi poet complained to me once, and, yes, one thinks with relief of the coarseness and grossness of Shakespeare. Does that lack stop Tagore from being, as his countrymen would so dearly like him to be, as great as Shakespeare?

In answer to that one can, if one knows Tagore's range as a writer, point to the sexual complexity of his novellas, the modernist experimentalism of his plays and paintings, the acerbic irony of his essays and polemics. But a surer way of recognising him as a fully achieved artist and visionary is to sense the heroism of his efforts to harness, rationally and morally, his unruly creative power. For one who loved solitude, what an effort it must have been to work with others—in Bengal's punishing climate—to create a school and university and centre for rural reconstruction. For one who was at his most natural and free in the elusive symbolism of his songs, what a struggle it must have been, in his stories and novels, to pin himself down to realistic characters and plots. For one who repeatedly warned his audiences that he was "not a philosopher", what a task it must have been to apply his reason and humanism to the hardest religious, ethical and political questions.

What in Tagore was most visionary? His Upanishadic spirituality? His belief in imaginative education in tune with the natural environment? His sense—expressed in the Indian national anthem—of India's 'unity in diversity'? His love—expressed in the national anthem of Bangladesh—for a *sonar bangla* (Golden Bengal) of ever-changing rivers, skies and seasons? The greatest visionaries are those who are most deeply loved, and no poet is loved by his countrymen—and by many others across the world dependent on translations—more than Tagore.

William Radice

THICH NHAT HANH

The Monk and the Mountain

"Life can be found only in the present moment. The past is gone, the future is not yet here, and if we do not go back to ourselves in the present moment, we cannot be in touch with life."

MOUNTAINS, REMOVED FROM the hustle and bustle of urban life, have historically been the location for Buddhist monasteries and practice centres. But for Thich Nhat Hanh, affectionately known at 'Thay', mountains have a most special significance. In his native Vietnam, at the age of eleven, this world-renowned Zen monk went for a school picnic on the mountain of Na Son where, he'd heard, a hermit practising to become a Buddha had taken up residence. Secretly hoping for an encounter, he climbed the mountain and searched for the Buddha-to-be, but the hermit eluded him. Finally the boy gave up and began to appreciate the sheer physical beauty that was all around him. After hiking in awe for some time he came upon the sound of water dripping in a well. He knelt and drank from the crystal-pure sparkling water. "This was", Thay later wrote, "as if I were meeting the hermit face to face." It was at that moment he made the decision to devote his life to being a monk.

Now at almost eighty, and nearing the end of a forty-year exile from Vietnam, Thay frequently uses mountains as a metaphor in his teachings. At Plum Village, his main practice centre in southern France, and at retreats around the world, he will often bring his fingertips together to form a mountain, and softly sing, "I am solid as the mountain, I am firm as the earth, I am free."

During a retreat at Green Mountain Dharma Center, the place his American students have established in Vermont, Thay talked about recognising the qualities of a mountain in oneself: inner strength, stability, the ability to weather the inevitable ups and downs of life. Mountains are sacred symbols of abiding presence and stillness, he said. The sun moves and the seasons change, the light and colour on the side of the mountain continually shift, but the mountain itself never moves. He tells young people to make good use of the mountain within so they are not as affected by what other people say and do to them, and they can be more true to themselves. In his book *Teachings On Love*, he uses the image of a mountain to illustrate the fourth of the foundations of true love: equanimity or *upeksha*. "*Upa* means 'over', and *iksh* means 'to look'. You climb the mountain to be able to look over the whole situation, not bound by one side or the other. If your love has attachment, discrimination, prejudice, or clinging in it, it is not true love."

Since he fled Vietnam in 1972 as a political refugee who demonstrated against the war (the CIA thought he was Communist, and the Vietcong thought he was CIA), Thay has written over seventy-five books. He is best known for bringing mindfulness meditation out from the secluded Buddhist monasteries on the tops of mountains and into the lives of urban Westerners. Yet the Buddhism that interests him most is what he calls "the living Dharma". This is, as he puts it, "the Dharma that lives within a person's actual experience". "When you practise mindful breathing," he says, "you are generating the living Dharma, the Dharma that does not need words. When you practise mindfulness of breathing or walking, you become yourself the living Dharma."

Thus, according to Thay, true teachers of the Dharma do not teach with their mouths, but with their body, their breath, and their steps. "The living Dharma", he adds, "is not something abstract. It's very real and available. You can have it any time you want, twenty-four hours a day!" He goes on to explain that mountains are themselves temples of living Dharma.

At his practice centre near San Diego, Deer Park Monastery, I visited Thay and Sister Chan Khong, his associate of many years. A long winter retreat had just ended, so they were both exhausted, but they nevertheless invited me to climb the mountain around which their centre is located. "Climbing the mountain does not make us tired," Thay explained. "It refreshes us," added Sister Chan Khong.

Up we went, and although he and she were at least twenty years my senior, I marvelled at how robustly they climbed the jagged rocks. Thay moved slowly but deliberately, choosing his steps carefully while I rushed over those rocks trying to keep up with him. When we finally reached the peak, I was huffing and puffing but Thay was calmly smiling. "We are at the summit of a lotus with a thousand rock petals," he announced happily.

Thay reflected on the challenge of being a leader in Buddhism. "The temptation to use the robes as a badge of importance, or to let it build the ego is always there. The key is to avoid being in conflict with the path of selflessness. You can distinguish the real teachers from the others fairly easily," he went on. "You don't see any joy . . . The happiness born of real practice is missing from their faces."

Thay's wide smile was infectious, his happiness evident. He told me about Chia Tao, a Zen monk who became a poet during China's Tang dynasty (777-841), and in his poetry recorded the lives of the sages, masters, immortals, and hermits who were responsible for establishing the great spiritual tradition of Zen Buddhism in China. Thay's favourite poem is called 'On Looking for a Hermit and not Finding Him':

I questioned a boy under the pine trees.
"My Master went herb-gathering" he says,
"He is still somewhere on the mountain-side,
So deep in the clouds I can't tell where."

We sat silently, contemplating the birds and the breeze, and even the very faint sound of freeway traffic far below. The swiftly falling sun cast a crimson glow on Thay's countenance. A line from a poem by another major Chinese poet in the Tang Dynasty, Li Po (701-762), came to mind: "We sit together, the mountain and me, until only the mountain remains."

Allan Hunt Badiner

DESMOND TUTU
Limitless Love

"I am not interested in picking up crumbs of compassion thrown from the table of someone who considers himself my master. I want the full menu of rights."

"I don't preach a social gospel; I preach the Gospel, period. The gospel of our Lord Jesus is concerned for the whole person. When people are hungry, Jesus didn't say 'Now, is that political or social?'. He said 'I feed you.' Because the good news to a hungry person is bread."

"BEWARE THE ANIMAL that eats your dreams" is a saying of the Indians of Costa Rica, which is indigenous vernacular for "Without vision, the people perish."

Like Martin Luther King in America and Mahatma Gandhi in South Africa and India,

Desmond Tutu had a dream—the same dream—of racial equality, justice and peace in his own native land. In the face of increasing militancy, the abandoning of key civil liberties, and most painfully, the post-1953 policy to impose government control on black South African education,

Tutu discarded his first career as a teacher and went into the Church.

From his ordination in 1961 in South Africa, 'Father Tutu' became the symbol of conflict between the established Anglican Church and the South African Government, not only over apartheid but the very meaning of Christianity. He was the most vociferous voice of the voiceless. Tutu had a vision: a vision of an unstoppable but united people of South Africa. Against all possible odds, and in the face of continual outbreaks of violence from all quarters and threatening political and personal hostility, Tutu continued to address vast political meetings and rallies.

After his ordination Desmond Tutu served as a curate in the Diocese of Johannesburg and was rapidly sent to England to read for a degree in theology at King's College, London. He followed his degree surprisingly with an MA in Islamic studies whilst serving as curate, first in Golders Green and then in the improbable setting of a Surrey village.

Tutu's rise through the ranks of the Anglican Church was meteoric. He returned to South Africa in 1967 to lecture, in 1976 was elected Bishop of Lesotho and ten years later became Archbishop of Cape Town and Primate of South Africa. He won the Nobel Peace Prize in 1984, and collected endless international awards in between. Yet despite his combined skills as a theologian and political tactician, the language of his persistent exhortations to his South African brothers and sisters was always simple, direct and focussed on the immediate practicalities of working together to abolish apartheid whilst completely renouncing all forms of violence. His sensitivity lay in appealing to the hearts of a flock derived from the widest possible ethnic and cultural backgrounds, many with little or no formal education. At the same time Tutu demonstrated tremendous personal courage and diplomacy. He was constantly negotiating with the most intransigent hard-line Afrikaner politicians, secret police, and overseas diplomats, realising that he was treading a minefield laid by people, many of whom would have wished him a rapid promotion to the celestial choirs!

Time and again Tutu's condemnation of apartheid and his appeal to the world community to apply economic sanctions to South Africa (supported by over 70 per cent of blacks) was balanced by his personal intervention to diffuse explosive and volatile situations, and his exhortations to put aside bitterness and the theology of retaliation, in the hope of finding positive and practical solutions. "White South Africans are not demons. They are ordinary people, mostly scared. Wouldn't you be if you were outnumbered five to one? If I was white, I would need a lot of grace to resist a system that provided me with such substantial privileges. Hence the whites who oppose apartheid should be praised to the skies. There are many of them and they have paid a heavy price for that opposition."

Through the rhetoric, the pain and sometimes the nadir of despair there emerges a picture of a very human 'man of God' who is also a man of his people. Tutu was not afraid to put his own safety at risk (he has been arrested and gaoled overnight along with other church leaders and his cathedral church has been stormed by police). Nevertheless, he used the pulpit to give sermons and proclaim vigils when public meetings and rallies were banned by government and police. The international press and his 1984 Nobel Lecture, 'Apartheid's Final Solution', were used to draw the world's attention to the plight of South Africa.

When Nelson Mandela was released from prison in 1990, Tutu admitted in an interview that he would now be taking a lower profile, as he had only stood in as a politician "while our real leaders were either in gaol or in exile". But he said, "I am a church person who believes that religion does not just deal with a certain compartment of life. Religion has a relevance for the whole of life and we have to say whether a particular policy is consistent with the policy of Jesus Christ or not."

Diana Schumacher

SRI ANANDAMAYI
Enchanted Spirit

"Try to treat with equal love all the people with whom you have relations. Thus the abyss between 'myself' and 'yourself' will be filled in, which is the goal of all religious worship."

"I find one vast garden spread out all over the universe. All plants, all human beings, all higher mind bodies are about in this garden in various ways, each has his own uniqueness and beauty."

EACH OF THE MAJOR INDIAN spiritual figures to emerge in our time had a highly distinctive, often energetic and active personality. Ramakrishna, Gandhi, Tagore, Aurobindo and Ramana Maharshi—one can see how remarkably varied these men were, refuting all attempts at generalisation. Sri Anandamayi likewise was unique, and not just because she was a lone woman in a field dominated by men. Her qualities as a public figure, and her enigmatic yet highly influential role through the grace and subtlety of her personality have a significance beyond the limits of India's ashram enthusiasts.

There are two related issues to examine when we try to comprehend the qualities of this remarkable woman: how did a person so girt about with the trappings of tradition and seemingly confined within the trammels of Hindu orthodoxy appeal to so wide, varied and numerous a following, in an age of secularism and lost faith; and how is it that this woman counted among her following quite a number of distinguished people who, in their official capacities, would otherwise need to preserve their distance from individuals connected with religious bodies?

Of course we can never know what transpired

behind closed doors between Sri Anandamayi and these people who, in a different dimension of their lives, bore the burdens of high office. Yet we can be sure that, whatever the topic of conversation may have been, it would have revolved around the problem of how to reconcile and balance the intrinsic secularism of our lives with our hunger for a deeper spiritual dimension. Implicit too would have been the risks attendant upon politics becoming entangled with religion. It is in her role as private counsellor on such matters that the extent of Sri Anandamayi's 'unseen' influence on her times was based, even though the predominant activity for which she is best known to the public is that of spiritual inspiration and guidance at the individual and family level.

Besides such pastoral care to the public at large, there was quite a large number of permanent inmates in her ashrams who led a life of strict monasticism and rigorous discipline under her instruction. Sri Anandamayi was also an administrator of great energy and skill, surrounded by senior monks and female attendants who accompanied her wherever she went and stayed beside her for a great many years. She remained outside all denominational categories and affiliations. It is difficult to imagine the degree of this freedom, and how it could be achieved with such modest means in a culture so intricately entwined in particularistic allegiances.

She was not, strictly speaking, a guru. "I am whatever you take me to be" was as far as she went in self-definition. She would often refer to scripture and to standard Hindu views on spiritual matters, but she would juxtapose differing viewpoints and leave the issue open. Whatever tradition she drew upon (her range of reference was enormous) she reformulated it all in her own distinctive style. One of the titles of Krishna is Supreme Poet; Sri Anandamayi was a living exemplar of a tradition which recognises verbal grace and metaphor in spiritual utterance as the highest level of poetry attainable. In discussion with the learned and the intellectually brilliant it was they who sounded dry and academic while she eluded all crabbed pronouncements through the language of metaphor.

Orthodox routines were strictly adhered to in her ashrams, no doubt an astute means to insulate inmates from the vulgarisation of the secular world and the touristic publicity that has now flooded the ashram scene. Ritual played a prominent part in daily routine, along with chanting; festivals were celebrated with great fervour. There was something unpretentious in her manner, an unusual mixture of the simple country woman and a lady of the highest refinement with varied and mobile features, a softly musical voice endlessly breaking into alliterative punning and an enchanting laugh.

Being a woman was enough in itself to detach Sri Anandamayi from the normal status hierarchy of the religious infrastructure. A formidably empowered woman without substantive social validation, unelected, without official position or function save as the guiding spirit of a *sangha* (community) reveals a kind of independent interdependence in sympathy with, but completely outside, any current feminist criteria. While it might well be said that, no matter what their gender, spiritual persons of a certain kind had reached "the strength made perfect through weakness"—Gandhi is a notable exponent of such a course—this very strength is embodied in a specifically feminine way by Sri Anandamayi.

With the passing of time we are gaining a perspective on Sri Anandamayi's significance in both an Indian and a universal context. We could say that it was her model disinterestedness that lifted her 'above it all'—above the conflicting vested interests of denominational religion, beyond the reach of quasi-political organisations and quasi-religious politicians. Through her model disinterestedness she was directly and openly accessible to allcomers, no matter what their caste, creed, nationality or race. By the same token of disinterestedness, the eminent as much as the lowly could not only enjoy this freedom of access, but also emulate that purity of spirit which is disinterestedness and apply it in their lives and in their dealings with the world.

While toleration is the essence of democracy, disinterestedness adds a spiritual depth. By unadorned simplicity, adamantine strength and luminosity of being, Sri Anandamayi has offered the world a century of inspiration.

Richard Lanoy

PETER REDGROVE
Shamanic Poet

"Obviously, few of us are in a position to restore the forests. . . . But tens of millions of us have gardens, or access to open spaces such as industrial wastelands, where trees can be planted, and if full advantage can be taken of the potentialities that are available even in heavily built-up areas, new 'city forests' can arise."

PETER REDGROVE WAS BORN in 1932. He had a conventional education at Taunton School, and went to Queen's College, Cambridge with a scholarship in Natural Sciences. From the outset his gifts required him to work with an exceptional range of seemingly competing capacities: an intellect able to engage with the revolutionary developments in science, a turbulent and compelling imagination, and huge reserves of psychic and physical energy (incidentally a judo black belt). Finding a way to 'keep together' the various strains of his energy would soon become not just a creative but increasingly a survival necessity. Writing, particularly poetry, emerged as the most compelling but also unifying form of expression, and he was able from the outset to bring to this work an instinctive and magical command of language, language that reflected the sum of his energies—his language.

At Cambridge he was in freak collision with a number of outstandingly gifted contemporaries, and with a group of them he attended the dynamic workshops of Philip Hobsbaum. It is apparent now that the language used since the thirties by the mainstream of English poets had become unresponsive to the cutting-edge concerns of the most deeply engaged and incisive of these young poets. It seems that they (I'm thinking of, among others, Ted Hughes, Rosemary Tonks, Sylvia Plath and Redgrove himself) were driven, each in their own way, to come up with a new deeper-rooted language of the senses. In what could be seen as a kind of shamanic undertaking they were alive to the unprecedented tensions of the times—the threat of nuclear wipe-out, the unresolved aftermath of wars and inhumanities that without a new capacity of language even the imagination could not express. Tensions, individual and of the collective, which until they could find expression would hold deeply frozen any possibility of a new consciousness emerging.

Within the competing strains of his energy this tension was so powerful in Redgrove that it brought him to his own point of breakdown—and it was the work of analysis that he now undertook with the inspirational Jungian John Layard that set him on the life-long path to integration. The work introduced him to alchemy and the power of its myth to guide and transform. In the living of it alchemy (and ultimately what he would refer to as 'wise wound alchemy') became the metaphor source and clearing-house for the main body of his writing—poems, novels, plays and radical psychology.

Alchemy is above all the celebration and ordinance of fundamental balance. The ultimate realisation of this balance is imaged as the Marriage in the Heart, the *Mysterium Coniunctionis*—and the proof to the individual of this 'estate of marriage' is the miraculous appearance of the Child in the cradle-centre of the psyche. The inner work under Layard's guidance indicated a practice that would draw the seemingly irreconcilable strains of his energy into single expression: became, so to say, the Child. The language began to speak—a new command able to contain the rationality of the scientist, the connective and imaginative gift of the poet, and the drive of the psychic explorer. As the exploration continued, so this empiric language became the vehicle for his finest poetry.

Where the psychic field is this much alive, materialisation and synchronicity are part of every operation. Not surprising then that at some given moment he should meet his life-work collaborator, Penelope Shuttle. A poet working a similar deep vein, and with the authority of her own 'off-limits' inner venturing, she could become, in alchemy's parlance, *soror mystica*, integral to the entire opus. A supporting role? That could occur only to someone who'd not read either Shuttle's own work or that which she and Redgrove co-authored (the seminal *The Wise Wound*, for instance). Hearing Redgrove so often allude to Shuttle and her judgement, and to that of Zoe, their daughter, was amazing to anyone who remembered the male categoricality with which when younger he stated his own views. The feminine, though, had always been in him a powerful determinant—at length he came to accept it fully, in fact to champion it in just about everything he did.

As with his two major contemporaries, Kathleen Raine and Ted Hughes, Peter Redgrove seems to have accepted that being a teacher (or guide or psychopomp) was an aspect of his vocation that he would never think to question. For all three an overall concern was to testify to the guiding role of Imagination in achieving the fulfilment of the individual, and so of society, and ultimately of human consciousness itself. Redgrove extended his commitment by becoming a lay-analyst. Here, as with all his work, his insight was grounded in his ever-questioning experience of himself. And maybe his most precious gift to others—writers, students, friends, clients—was in his fortifying them to face the shadow precincts of their own psyche, and so confront aspects of themselves their convention-ridden consciousness tended to recoil from, but which had to be encountered on the path to integration, on the way to 'making their gold'.

Peter Redgrove died in 2003. He left an immense store of imaginative writing—unsettling, gnomic, often humorous, always powerful and illuminating. Re-reading it today it is difficult, certainly from a *Resurgence* standpoint that has so many radical concerns in common, to argue with Philip Hobsbaum who described him as "the great poet of our time".

John Moat

THOMAS MOORE
Carer of the Soul

"Soul is different from spirit—the deep soul is the way we live everyday, our longings and our fears."

"I think that as you really let the other person be 'other', you have an opportunity to allow yourself to be 'different'. It's about two different people sharing a life, and the richness is in the difference."

BORN IN THE USA into a Catholic family of Irish ancestry, Thomas Moore grew up steeped in the Catholic tradition. At the age of thirteen he went to live and study in a seminary, and there followed twelve years of religious life. When he was twenty-four he realised that he did not want to become a priest, so he went to university and studied musicology, theology and religion. Nowadays he lectures extensively, practises psychotherapy and writes.

Thomas Moore draws his influences from painters, poets, alchemists, philosophers and psychologists; two of his most important influences have been Marsilio Ficino (fifteenth centu-ry) and Carl Jung, and among his contemporaries James Hillman has been his mentor.

Thomas Moore revives an ancient practice which has been falling out of use, that of caring for the soul. With this idea, he develops a counter-culture psychology, which looks not to answers but to 'living the questions'. He constantly points us away from the search for a panacea. Rather than attempting to rid ourselves of difficult symptoms, we are encouraged to build a relationship with them, to allow them to have meaning. In such soul work, we are encouraged to give up the search for sanity, emotional health, or a 'better' version of ourselves, because soul care is a purpose in itself.

Our relationship with money, with power, with illness, with love and with family conflicts, as well as our needs, our weaknesses, our obsessions, our impulses and curious habits; all can be understood as expressions of soul. So we could stop condemning our apparently 'problematic' or eccentric behaviours and begin to listen, recognising that the very richness of life is found in the particular. This is explored at greater depth by Moore in *Dark Nights of the Soul*, a book which enters into the profoundly difficult experiences of life, the suffering brought about by grief, loss, cruelty, meaninglessness and despair. Our society's fear of these dark states means that we tend to avoid or defuse this powerful aspect of existence, and try to distract, cheer up, cure, or drug ourselves out and away from the crisis.

But according to Moore, here in the darkness important processes are taking place. If we are able to listen to soul's communication at such times, and care for our soul as for a garden in a drought, or animals in winter—weather the storm, not deny it—then we can create rich compost from the rotting waste. A compost which will nourish the next phase of our lives. The soul's search in the darkness, or the underworld, is part of its instinct to deepen and mature.

Moore believes that soul is present in a way of living which sees the sacred in daily life, in the keeping of a home, in cooking, in the sensuality of the body, in music, painting, all arts and crafts which are personal, rather than technically virtuose. The presence of beauty, in nature as in art, plays upon the strings of our soul, and our aesthetic liveliness is part of our very core. Staying true to that deep thirst for beauty is a powerful way of connecting with soul.

Appreciating and nurturing soul is thus a profound response to meaninglessness, depression, disillusionment and a host of other 'problems' that come from our search for external solutions. Paying attention to soul qualities and soul needs reminds us that life is in the living, in the details, not in the ideals.

Moore always works from within the sphere of the soul, not tinkering from the outside, so that his work itself expresses soul, and connects the reader to soul. He tells us that the presence of Mercury—"god of fictions and fabrications"—helps us avoid excessive sincerity and literalism, that the imaginative, the changeable, the trickery, are all ways for the soul to find form. He considers his work a 'fiction' of self-help. And so his books are full of stories, biblical characters, Greek myths, stories from his own life and those of some of his patients. Through these we have images of the soul which are more allegorical than literal, stories which show the soul on a journey.

In his love of paradox, of living with things unresolved, Moore presents a strong challenge to the cleanliness of much scientific thinking, where things are always sorted, defined and ultimately closed off into boxes. He embraces paradox at a time when most intellectual thought looks for consistency, coherence and logic—a world under the endless shine of a laboratory lamp, a world without a dark side. But this is not true to our experience of life, which includes night and day, sun and stars, light and shadow, colour and depth. It is this encounter with the reality of things that makes Moore's work truly visionary.

When Moore speaks of religion he sees an opportunity to reawaken the soul within many practices, enabling a new lease of life and power within our religions. At the heart of religion there is always mystery, and this is where soul can find the space it needs. At the same time religion offers us rituals and traditions, whose symbolism is a rich language for the soul. In our modern world we can observe a split between mind and body, spirituality and materialism, ongoing dualisms which entice us to one extreme or another. But soul can be found in the middle, "holding together ideas and life". Thus soul work is vital in the effort to rebalance the radical consequences of the spiritual/material split, which we see on a global scale.

Moore is deeply concerned with the state of the world. In his work he links care of a person's soul with care of world soul. Soul is present in all things, so the more we are in touch with soul the more appropriately we will act. Connecting with soul in nature enables us to experience the natural world as sacred, rather than as a useful resource. It is also a tremendous gift from soul to soul.

Maya Kumar Mitchell

BEDE GRIFFITHS
Modern Mystic

"If Christianity cannot recover its mystical tradition and teach it, it should just fold up and go out of business. It has nothing to offer."

"God has graced every tradition with insight into the divine mystery, from the most primitive to the most sophisticated— each has a gift to bring to the world."

"God has brought me to my knees and made me acknowledge my own nothingness, and out of that knowledge I have been reborn. I was no longer the centre of my own life and therefore I could see God in everything."

BEDE GRIFFITHS' first spiritual experience, when he was seventeen, arose directly from nature. He saw some hawthorn trees in full bloom and "hardly dared to look on the face of the sky, because it seemed as though it was but a veil before the face of God". As an undergraduate he was painfully aware of the conflict between the ugliness of the modern industrial city and his ideal of a life in harmony with nature. After he came down from Oxford he lived in a small experimental community, rejecting modern civilisation and refusing to use anything made during or after the Industrial Revolution: this was in 1930, long before such words as ecology, environment and conservation were part of our everyday vocabulary.

He was to become known as a prophet, a man ahead of his time.

He was born on 17 December 1906 in Surrey, and when he was four years old his father, a manufacturing chemist, lost all his money. Alan, as he was then called, won a place at Christ's Hospital, a charitable foundation for the poor, and it was there that he had the mystical experience in which he glimpsed the unfathomable mystery behind creation. This was to be the catalyst to the rest of his life, colouring his time as an undergraduate at Magdalen College, Oxford and leading to his becoming a Benedictine monk. Before taking this step he endured spiritual and psychological crises, becoming a Roman Catholic in January 1932 and entering the Benedictine Abbey of Prinknash only weeks later.

For the next twenty-three years he led the normal life of a Benedictine monk. He was highly regarded as the guest master at Prinknash and seen as a natural leader, so it was no surprise when in 1947 he was sent to St Michael's Abbey, Farnborough, as Superior; but this was not a success, and after four years he was sent to Pluscarden, the most northerly Benedictine Abbey in the world. There he was regarded as a holy man with outstanding pastoral gifts, becoming both Novice Master and Master of Studies. It was there too that his interest in eastern spirituality, which began by reading Yeats' translation of the Upanishads, led to a longing to go to India.

Eventually his dreams were realised, and in 1955 he went to India. He felt something lacking in both the Western world and the Western Church, and wanted to experience "the marriage of these two dimensions of human existence, the rational and intuitive, the conscious and unconscious, the masculine and feminine. I wanted to find the marriage of East and West." He was going to India to "find the other half of my soul".

Immediately he felt at one with the Indian people, entranced by the sheer beauty and vitality of the human form. The reconciliation of East and West was to continue for the rest of his life, but it began immediately, with the realisation that here were people who lived not from the conscious mind but from the unconscious, not from the mind but from the body.

After an unsuccessful attempt to set up a monastic community near Bangalore, Father Bede moved to Kerala with a Cistercian monk who also wanted to make a foundation in India. On 20 March 1958 the two monks began life high on the holy mountain of Kurisumala. They lived a Cistercian interpretation of the Benedictine Rule, practised the liturgy of the Syrian Church, and honoured the tradition of the Indian *sannyasi*. It was a monastic experiment, and it was successful.

During Father Bede's ten years at Kurisumala he became increasingly well known and respected through his writings and appearances at conferences. In 1963 he went to America, and from then on he travelled frequently giving public talks and interviews on themes such as the Christian-Hindu Dialogue, the nature of consciousness, meditation, duality and the integration of mind, body and spirit.

He also wrote several books and contributed articles to the religious press.

In 1968 Abhishiktananda, one of the founders of Saccidananda Ashram in Tamil Nadu (also known as Shantivanam) retired to the Himalayas, and Father Bede took over as monastic Superior. He was to stay there until his death twenty-five years later. Under his aegis Shantivanam became a magnet to people of all ages and nationalities. The way he bridged Hinduism and Christianity, experiencing all religions as complementary rather than in competition, made Shantivanam a place where people of different religious traditions could meet in an atmosphere of prayer.

Bede's years at Shantivanam coincided with the spiritual revival he called a "New Age of Consciousness", which he felt had its roots in the new understanding of physics, such as Fritjof Capra's *The Tao of Physics*, and in transpersonal psychology. People were beginning to share the vision he had first glimpsed thirty years earlier— a vision which embraced spirituality, science, environmental concerns, evolution and a deep acceptance of the feminine. It was Bede's ability to make Christianity acceptable to people who had wandered from its embrace that was perhaps his greatest single contribution to twentieth-century spirituality.

Shirley du Boulay

CHOGYAM TRUNGPA
Unmasking the Mind

"Too often, people think that solving the world's problems is based on conquering the earth, rather than touching the earth, touching ground."

"Any perception can connect us to reality properly and fully. What we see doesn't have to be particularly pretty; we can appreciate anything that exists. There is some principle of magic in everything, some living quality. Something living, something real, is taking place in everything."

"Compassion automatically invites you to relate with people because you no longer regard people as a drain on your energy."

"Hope and fear cannot alter the season."

CHOGYAM TRUNGPA

CHOGYAM TRUNGPA WAS BORN in 1939 in remote north-eastern Tibet. He was less than a year old when the village was visited by monks, who identified him as the person they were looking for, the incarnate 11th Trungpa tulku, abbot to the important Surmang Monastery. His enthronement took place that same year.

In his memoir *Born in Tibet*, written in his early twenties and soon after his arrival in the West, Trungpa gives us a startlingly vivid account of his upbringing in the monastery, and the rigours of his training in the teachings and practices of the Kagyu line of Buddhism—the school of what he himself referred to as Crazy Wisdom, whose great adepts included Naropa, Marpa and Milarepa. At the age of eighteen he was formally installed as Abbot, and assumed immense responsibility as leader, celebrant and teacher. In addition, he was always drawn to the arts, poetry and painting, and tells how from the outset he dreamed of restoring Tibet to its former mastery of imaginative expression. This was never to be, for before he was twenty Tibet had been invaded and its culture ruthlessly proscribed by the Chinese.

The second part of *Born in Tibet* tells of Trungpa's agonising decision to follow the Dalai Lama into exile, and the four-month ordeal of escaping through seemingly impassable mountains into India. The book ends with a description of him in an aeroplane for the first time, flying from the high Himalaya down to the vast sweltering and crowded plains. It reads like an image both of Trungpa's own destiny, and also of the moment when the hidden store of Tibetan wisdom and practice would at last be be made available to the world at large.

In 1963 he received a Spaulding Award, and came to study at Oxford. There he was exposed to the student secular life of the sixties, and before long, to the dismay of some of his advisers, he renounced his monkhood.

This upheaval culminated in what he recognised as a moment of *abhisheka*: he lost control of a car and crashed into a building. When he came to, he saw that it was a joke shop. He was left partially disabled, but with a clear determination to make the power of his spiritual background available to people in the West.

In 1967 he co-founded Samye-Ling Tibetan Centre in Scotland, and that same year he married. In 1970 he moved to North America, and there soon founded Vajradhatu, an umbrella organisation which would comprise more than sixty-five meditation and study centres in the United States, Canada and Europe. In 1974 he established the Nalanda Foundation, a non-sectarian educational organisation, and the Naropa Institute, an innovative liberal arts college. Boulder, Colorado was home to the Institute and the nerve-centre of all these initiatives— and it was here at the foot of the Rocky Mountains, reminding of the landscapes of his upbringing, that Trungpa evidently felt most at home. Like some of his great Kagyu forebears, Trungpa mystified, and from some quarters drew cynicism, with the seemingly spectacular paradox of his way of life. There have been colourful accounts of his engagement with Western-style 'Samsara', and the alcohol that is said to have been responsible for his death at the age of forty-eight. A constructive view suggests that a teacher come from the isolated and intensely rarefied Tibetan way of life might feel his wisdom could have little relevance if he himself had not been fully exposed to the Western individual's predicament and its inherent temptations. But in any case, what will, along with his art work, endure as his unique and indelible gift are the vitality and immediacy of his teaching. And it is worth noting that this was something that was acknowledged at the time by other leading Buddhist teachers.

Not only is this teaching powerfully focussed on the practicalities and challenges of living today when planetary consciousness is felt to be in such crisis, it is informed by Trungpa's own lightness of touch, humanity and redoubtable but never-imposing intellectual grasp. Perhaps above all the teaching expresses life-affirming and profoundly purposeful common sense. At the core of this is always his focus on meditation, not as the mystical, devotional trip that, he suggests, so often draws on the Western aptitude for 'spiritual materialism', but as the practice of being fully involved, and down to earth.

John Moat

THOMAS MERTON
Activist Monk

"What can we gain by sailing to the Moon if we are not able to cross the abyss that separates us from ourselves? This is the most important of all voyages of discovery, and without it, all the rest are not only useless, but disastrous."

"A life is either all spiritual or not spiritual at all. No man can serve two masters. Your life is shaped by the end you live for. You are made in the image of what you desire."

"Art enables us to find ourselves and lose ourselves at the same time."

"By reading the scriptures I am so renewed that all nature seems renewed around me and with me. The sky seems to be a pure, a cooler blue, the trees a deeper green. The whole world is charged with the glory of God and I feel fire and music under my feet."

THOMAS MERTON WAS A MONK *extraordinaire*, who became a Trappist at the age of twenty-six and remained so for the rest of his life. He was born in Prades, France on 31 January 1915, the son of a New Zealander father and American mother, both of whom were artists. Sadly, Merton's mother died when he was only six, and he went to live with his father in the medieval French city of St Antonin. The city, dominated by its church steeple, was to create a tremendous impression on him.

It is clear that writing was always in Merton's blood, but increasingly it became the fruit of the deep contemplative life he lived at the Abbey of Gethsemani in Kentucky. On entering the Abbey he had decided that the 'writer' must be left behind and replaced by the contemplative. "There was this shadow, this double, this writer who had followed me into the cloister. He is still on my track. I cannot lose him. He still bears the name of Thomas Merton. Is it the name of an enemy? He is supposed to be dead. . . . He generates books in the silence that ought to be sweet with the infinitely productive darkness of contemplation."

Esther de Waal, one of Merton's biographers, has written, "Perhaps the biggest contradiction for Merton, as for so many of us, was the holding together of a life of prayer with a life of activity so that the one may flow smoothly into the other and the two can be held together as a dynamic unity."

Later in life Merton became increasingly interested in Eastern thought, developing great respect for Zen Buddhism and Taoist philosophy. In Merton's *The Way of Chuang Tzu* he expresses a strong appreciation for the simplicity and beauty of Taoism. Merton's love of solitude found a kindred spirit in Chuang Tzu, who "shared the climate and peace of his own kind of solitude and who was his own kind of person".

In October 1968 Merton set out on a longed-for pilgrimage to the East. During his travels he kept a diary, which was later published as *The Asian Journal*. His trip took him to Calcutta, Delhi, Madras, the Himalayas, Sri Lanka and Bangkok, and he was privileged to meet with many holy men, including the Dalai Lama and Chatral Rinpoche, to whom he felt especially close.

Merton's words to himself at the outset were: "May I not come back without having settled the great affair." One gets an insight into this "great affair" when he meets with Chatral Rinpoche on 16 November 1968. He says "The unspoken or half-spoken message of the talk was our complete understanding of each other as people who were somehow on the edge of great realisation and knew it and were trying, somehow or other to get lost in it."

As the journey unfolded, it seems that Merton came closer and closer to the realisation of "That" which he had so diligently sought. Just days before he died, in December 1968, the Heavens opened and an interior revelation unfolded within him. This was during a trip to the stone Buddhas at Polonnaruwa in Sri Lanka. "I was knocked over with a rush of relief and thankfulness at the obvious clarity of the figures. . . . Looking at these figures I was suddenly, almost forcibly, jerked clean out of the habitual, half-tied vision of things and an inner clearness, as if exploding from the rocks themselves, became evident. . . . The thing about all this is that there is no puzzle, no problem, and really no 'mystery'. All problems are resolved and everything is clear, simply because what matters is clear . . . everything is emptiness and compassion. Surely with Mahabalipuram and Polonnaruwa my Asian pilgrimage has come clear and purified itself. I mean, I know and have seen what I was obscurely looking for. I don't know what else remains but I have now seen and have pierced through the surface and have got beyond the shadow and the disguise."

On the morning of 10 December 1968 Merton delivered a paper to a meeting of Benedictine and Cistercian abbots. Questions were to await an evening session, but that session never came as Merton died after stepping out of a shower to turn off a faulty electric fan. It was twenty-seven years to the day that he had entered the Abbey in Kentucky as a postulant. His purpose on Earth was complete.

Liz Medler

MATTHEW FOX
Religious Revolutionary

"Beauty saves. Beauty heals. Beauty motivates. Beauty unites. Beauty returns us to our origins, and here lies the ultimate act of saving, of healing, of overcoming dualism."

"To connect with the great river we all need a path, but when you get down there there's only one river."

"Do not confuse beauty with beautiful. Beautiful is a human judgement. Beauty is All. The difference is everything."

"Creation is all space, all time— all things past, present, and future."

MATTHEW FOX, A PRIEST when I first met him, was trying to make religion relevant for the young, trying to revive a sense of spirituality in our lives, and the response of his church was to excommunicate him. Well, if the Pope thought he was a dangerous man, that was all the recommendation I needed.

Of course, it wasn't quite that glib, but the kinship I felt when Matthew and I met for the first time in 1993 definitely had an immediacy that sprang from our reputations as sacred cow butchers in our chosen vocations. His speciality was the spirit; mine, as founder of a global cosmetics company, was clearly the flesh. Still, we were both good at making connections between things that might seem opposed. Like the Catholic church and young people. Or science and spirituality. Or cosmetics and social activism. We shared a quest: to seek and honour the soul of life.

The first time I heard Matthew talk about the soul's geographic location in the body, I was floored. There was no pussyfooting around the subject. His declaration struck me as so unambiguous that it was daring. I've heard him talk a number of times since then and every time he has the same effect. He compels you to take on board the most provocative notions. In fact, if I close my eyes and think about Matthew, the strongest impression I have is his voice. Like a born orator, he captures his audience with sound.

My most startling memory of Matthew is the time he came to talk to the staff at The Body Shop at our head office in Littlehampton. It was around the same time that he was in the news as the mentor of a priest labelled "the rave vicar" by the English tabloids because of the kind of services for young people he'd been holding in his parish. Among the staff who jammed into our corporate cinema for the talk were a certain number of born-again Christians. I think they half-expected to be greeted by a minion of Satan. Instead, they got Matthew talking about the great mystics and how they saw God in everything. It was a lyrical, loving address and the audience was mute with admiration.

The danger with most public lovefests is that there is no tension. Without tension, there's no drama and—for me at least—without drama, there's no interest. In a public arena, that means I'm probably happier going head-on hammer and tongs with the president of the WTO than indulging in a mutual admiration society. Yet I don't feel that way about Matthew at all. I always learn from him when we talk together. His knowledge base is so vast that he stitches ideas together effortlessly and arrives at new perspectives. This has been specially valuable for me in my focus on alternative business practices.

Work and play have always been inextricably intertwined in my world but, when I see the joylessness of so much human labour, I realise I'm a fortunate exception. I have always appreciated how essential it was that one's work was an expression of one's values. That's what The Body Shop was built on. In his book *The Reinvention of Work*, Matthew claims the reinvention begins when a values system is attached to work. It's the kind of redefinition that the ethical business movement has been promoting for decades, but what Matthew brings to the debate is spirituality as an active, energising principle running through every aspect of daily life. He redefines wealth and success in a way I find particularly meaningful, having experienced a fair degree of both, along with the usual reactions, from guilt to freedom to an overwhelming urge to give it all away.

I can see perfectly well why an institution as hidebound as the Vatican would find Matthew a threat. His brand of pragmatism could never sit well with the self-interests of the church hierarchy. If it weren't so predictable, their intransigence would be tragic, because Matthew's message is their way forward. At the root of his faith is a reverence for the idea of community. As he has pointed out, even science has recognised that participation is part of the way we interact with the world. That recognition has shattered the so-called 'value-free' objectivity of the scientific world.

Confronted by the harsh evidence of the impact of globalisation on the majority world, big business can hardly hide behind objectivity any longer either. A sense of community will grab you in the end. Maybe it's something as elementary as the fact that every human being ultimately shares a heart and soul. You can't escape from interconnectedness, a point which is underlined by the 'new model for learning in the twenty-first century' which Matthew has established with the University of Creation Spirituality based in Oakland, California. The institute is remarkable for its pragmatic approach, embracing the body as it enhances the soul.

But it's not only the young who need their faith reactivated. The same challenge faces hordes of us at this moment in human history. That is the mission of people like Matthew.

Anita Roddick

RAIMON PANIKKAR
Builder of Bridges

"Western Christian tradition seems to be exhausted ... when it tries to express the Christian message in a meaningful way for our times. Only by cross-fertilisation and mutual fecundation may the present state of affairs be overcome; only by stepping over present cultural and philosophical boundaries can Christian life again become creative and dynamic."

"When man breaks his connection with Earth, wanting to fulfil himself, he becomes a monster who destroys himself. When man breaks his connection with heaven, wanting to lead himself on his own, he becomes an automaton that destroys others."

ARNOLD TOYNBEE ONCE remarked that the West's encounter with the East would be regarded as the most significant event of the twentieth century. Raimon Panikkar has devoted his life and his work to building bridges of mutual understanding between cultures and religions. Born in Barcelona in 1918, his calling was partly triggered by the fact of being the eldest son of a Hindu Indian father and a Catholic Catalan mother. For several decades he lived with a foot in each of two very different worlds: half of the year leading an ashram-like life in Varanasi, India, the other half being a Professor at the University of California.

Panikkar has always insisted that a culture cannot be properly known until you make an existential (not just intellectual) crossing of its waters, and until you come to see the world from the viewpoint of that culture. That implies accepting that every culture, and indeed every person, is a valid source of self-understanding. It also implies realising that there are no absolute truths, no final theories or views from nowhere: every view belongs to a context, to a time and a place, to a language and to a given way of experiencing the world. This is no post-modern relativism, but an attitude close to what Jains and many Indians have over the centuries called *anekantavada*, non-absolutism, a deep awareness of the diversity dwelling at the core of reality.

Panikkar claims to be at the same time a Christian, a Hindu, a Buddhist and a secular man of the twenty-first century—in the challenging sense of fully embracing each of those identities. As for his Christian identity, he is a well-respected theologian: Archbishop Rowan Williams devotes a whole chapter of his book *On Christian Theology* to what he calls Panikkar's "radical cultural pluralism", thoroughly praising his "exceptional service to authentic engagement between traditions in their particularity". But this is only one side of Panikkar's work. Author of more than fifty books and more than 1,000 articles, originally written in six languages, Panikkar is also a scholar of Hinduism and Buddhism and an intercultural philosopher.

His command of languages has helped him to shed new light on old words. "Philosophy" has been defined since Plato as the "love (*philia*) of wisdom (*sophia*)", and we all know how it has turned into a dry, academic pursuit. Panikkar enlivens the word by upturning its meaning, while respecting the Greek etymology: "philosophy" as the "wisdom of love", the wisdom that emerges from cultivating a loving attitude to the world, the Earth and all of her beings. One word coined by Panikkar in the early seventies (and independently coined, at the very same time, by Arne Naess) is "ecosophy". For Panikkar, ecosophy is a reminder that we not only need ecological science and technology, but ecological wisdom. Ecosophy means for him both our budding "wisdom about the Earth" and "the wisdom of the Earth herself"—a wisdom we may learn to listen to as we become more receptive.

St Bernard of Clairvaux wrote in the twelfth century that "the woods and stones teach you what can't be heard from the masters". Panikkar has learnt from woods and stones, mountains and rivers; he has realised, as he writes, that "everything is alive and the Earth herself has a soul, a life of her own. Life, anima, psyche, is not an accident of reality, an epiphenomenon in one tiny corner of the universe; it is an essential attribute of the real."

Another side to Panikkar is his radical critique of all contemporary forms of colonialism. For Panikkar, the essence of colonialism is monoculturalism, the belief that one culture is above all others, and that therefore the values and viewpoints of that culture must be applied everywhere. Panikkar not only applies this to mainstream 'development' and globalisation (aptly described by Arundhati Roy as "a mutant variety of colonialism") but to what he sees as the Trojan Horse of Westernisation: modern science. In his secular identity, Panikkar is well acquainted with science (he earned a doctorate degree in Chemistry, as well as in Theology and Philosophy), but underlying modern science he sees "a set of beliefs, assumptions, postulates or principles" that are incompatible with the experience of indigenous peoples and traditional cultures. This includes our modern notions of matter, energy, life, space and time. Therefore "modern science is neither neutral nor universal" — and indeed he sees science as "intrinsically compelled to technocracy", geared towards the rule of technology and machinery over people and planet.

It is part of Panikkar's teaching that we should dwell more fully in the present. "True hope can't be of the future; it has to be of the invisible, of another dimension that makes life worth living." He calls us "to share the wisdom of the Earth and the mysteries of the real", and invites us to "a full participation in the adventure of reality".

Jordi Pigem

STARHAWK
Sacred Earth

"The symbolism of the Goddess is not a parallel structure to the symbolism of God the Father. The Goddess does not rule the world. She is the world, manifest in each of us. She can be known internally by every individual, in all her magnificent diversity."

"Spirituality leaps where science cannot yet follow, because science must always test and measure, and much of reality and human experience is immeasurable."

"Any ritual is an opportunity for transformation."

WHEN I MET STARHAWK in San Francisco in 1977, she was finishing the manuscript for *The Spiral Dance*. In 1978, our coven celebrated her publication of *The Spiral Dance* by creating a Samhain (Halloween) ritual of the same name. The results were dazzling, a synergy of spirit, music, art, and poetry. The ritual, honouring who and what had died, tapped into the power of grief, then transformed that power into joyfully celebrating what grows out of death—new life.

Starhawk's special gift for ritual transported us with her that night to the timeless place of mysteries, where all good rituals lead. The first Spiral Dance was so appealing and empowering that it has now been celebrated annually for the last twenty-five years. I think that is when we understood that the world needed to hear what Star had to say.

This was our first big project as a coven. We were mainly in our mid-twenties, and already long-time political activists. We had all felt different from our peers. This was a time when political people eschewed spirituality as part of the discredited old order, and spiritual people felt that politics polluted their transcendent endeavours.

But our coven had found each other. We felt political action grew from our faith. Starhawk embodied this confluence as she began to speak and teach after *The Spiral Dance*'s publication, and co-founding the teaching collective, 'Reclaiming'. Eventually, this became distinct enough to become the 'Reclaiming Tradition'.

Starhawk is where social activism and spirit merged, nourishing and renewing both. Traditionally, culture tended to split politics and religion. Activists rejected spirit along with monotheistic religions which seemed authoritarian and disconnected, estranged from the natural world. Others feared spirituality as internal or transcendent, something that would separate them from caring about the physical world.

Starhawk articulates the clear connection between experiencing the Earth as sacred and taking action to honour this sacredness. Just as no religion would tolerate the desecration of what they hold as holy, Starhawk shows that working to stop the desecration of our planet is a sacred responsibility. Starhawk's work conveys the vision of the time when nations' decisions are made based on the interconnectedness of all life, when the criteria for what is good is not what will pay, but what will endure.

Another of her distinctive contributions is bringing the elements of ritual to political actions. By being rooted and connected, demonstrations become imbued with the ineffable ingredient of divinity, the whole becomes greater than the sum of the parts. In other words, Starhawk makes magic real, and the magic is working.

When we met in 1977, Star was a neighbourhood person, keeping house, gardening, writing at her desk, watching her community's street life out of the bay window. She still does that, but more rarely these days. Now, she travels far and wide, inspiring and instructing around the world.

Starhawk has written and co-written ten books, including *The Spiral Dance: A Rebirth of the Ancient Religion of the Great Goddess*, the now-classic ecotopian novel *The Fifth Sacred Thing*, and more recently, *The Earth Path: Grounding Your Spirit in the Rhythms of Nature*.

Her main focus for the last several years has been the global justice movement. Starhawk has taken part in many of the major actions, including those in Seattle, Washington DC, Quebec City, Genoa, New York City, Cancun, Mexico, and Miami. She co-founded RANT (Root Activists' Network of Trainers, www.rant.org), and teaches nonviolent direct action trainings for these demonstrations, as well as for groups throughout the US, Canada, Mexico, Europe, Palestine and South America. She is active in the revived American peace movement, and contributes her time to countless environmental and land use issues. Together with Penny Livingston-Stark and Erik Ohlsen, she co-teaches EAT (Earth Activist Training), intensive seminars that combine permaculture design, effective activism, and earth-based spirituality (www.earthactivisttraining.org).

Starhawk is a cofounder of Reclaiming, an activist branch of modern Pagan religion. She consulted on and contributed to the popular trio of films known as the Women's Spirituality series directed by Donna Read. Starhawk and Donna Read recently formed their own film company, Belili Productions. Their first release is Signs Out of Time (2004), a documentary on the life of archaeologist Marija Gimbutas, the scholar whose discoveries sparked the Goddess movement (www.belili.org). Starhawk and Donna are at work on their next film, an introduction to permaculture.

Starhawk's lesser-known accomplishments include creating art; she has created some remarkable embroidered landscapes, and now works in watercolour when she can. She's a passionate gardener who loves cooking what she and her friends grow, especially recipes with apples. She aspires to growing and pressing her own olive oil. Her passion for gardening led her to study permaculture, which she now practises and teaches on her land in northern California.

Diane Baker

JOSEPH CAMPBELL
Master of Mythology

*"Follow your Bliss and doors will open
where there were no doors before."*

*"We must let go of the life we have planned,
so as to accept the one that is waiting for us."*

*"The goal of life is to make your heartbeat match the beat
of the universe, to match your nature with Nature."*

*"A hero is someone who has given his or her life
to something bigger than oneself."*

*"God is a metaphor for that which transcends all levels
of intellectual thought. It's as simple as that."*

"I don't have to have faith, I have experience."

"Myths are public dreams, dreams are private myths."

IT WAS THE POLICY of the all-women's college, Sarah Lawrence, where the scholar Joseph Campbell taught, not only for the teachers to be guided by the students' interests, but for the teachers actively to find out what these interests were. For thirty-eight years Campbell taught comparative mythology, not in terms of 'facts and footnotes', but in terms of how the subject connected to the students' lives. It was a discipline that would make him one of the most influential teachers of his time.

Politicians and broadcasters often use the word 'myth' as a synonym for 'mistake'. For Campbell, a myth was a profound truth. He knew that within a few years of leaving Sarah Lawrence many of his students would find their lives radically altered as they became wives and mothers. What could he pass on to them that would remain of value?

Anyone who has come across the four-volume *The Masks of God* (1959-1968), *Myths to Live By* (1972) or *The Mythic Image* (1974) will know the answer. Campbell believed myths, fairy tales and religious texts, ranging across thousands of years and five continents, related directly to the life-journey his students were on. Whoever or wherever people were, the same stories would apply. "The latest incarnation of Oedipus," he wrote, "the continued romance of Beauty and the Beast, stands this afternoon on the corner of 42nd Street and Fifth Avenue, waiting for the traffic light to change."

In 1949 Campbell wrote the book that expressed his central idea about 'the monomyth'. (The phrase had been coined by one of his heroes, James Joyce.) Originally titled *How To Read A Myth*, it was published as *The Hero With A Thousand Faces*. Its influence was remarkable. The movie director George Lucas came across a copy in the early seventies. With the assistance of this book, Lucas said, he went on to write *Star Wars*. Another reader was Richard Adams, who said he used it to create the inner structure of *Watership Down*. The book influenced the choreographer Martha Graham, the director Steven Spielberg and the band The Grateful Dead, who invited Campbell to attend his first-ever rock concert. "What it is," said Campbell summing up the book's content, "is my first lecture to my students at Sarah Lawrence."

Campbell was born in New York in 1904. His parents were Roman Catholic; his father was a travelling salesman. When he was seven, Campbell was taken to see Buffalo Bill's Wild West Show. He was captivated by the sight of "a naked American Indian, with his ear to the ground, a bow and arrow in his hand, and a look of special knowledge in his eyes". Campbell became fascinated by American Indian culture. Later, while still a boy, he went to see a Western, and stood up and berated the audience for cheering the cowboys. "You don't know what you're doing. You wouldn't cheer if you knew!"

As he read the American Indian myths he recognised the same motifs he was being taught by the nuns at his Catholic school: creation, death, resurrection, ascension to heaven and virgin births. The idea that cultures share a pattern of motifs and symbols would dominate his work. Campbell believed that cultures were shaped, literally and imaginatively, by geography, soil and climate. But it was essential to understand individual myths in poetic terms—as metaphors— and not to get trapped by literal or dogmatic thinking. The most urgent task facing society, he believed, was to help religion outgrow its "local inflection".

In 1987 Campbell gave a series of TV interviews to the American channel PBS. These were recorded at George Lucas's Skywalker ranch and transmitted shortly before Campbell's death. Viewers learnt that the journey of the hero involved the conquering of the individual ego and an awakening to the surrounding world. "What all myths have to deal with," Campbell said, "is a transformation of consciousness. You have been thinking one way, you now have to think in a different way." The interviewer Bill Moyers, asked how this occurred. "Trials and revelations are what it's all about."

Campbell was making ancient stories relevant to modern people. The TV series was a hit. The book of the series, *The Power of Myth* (1988), became a bestseller. The number of people taking his comparative mythology class had widened to millions.

Robert Butler

C. G. JUNG
Insight into the Unconscious

"Who looks outside, dreams; who looks inside, awakes."

"The more one sees of human fate and the more one examines its secret springs of action, the more one is impressed by the strength of unconscious motives and by the limitations of free choice."

"All the works of man have their origin in creative fantasy. What right have we then to depreciate imagination?"

"Children are educated by what the grown-up is and not by his talk."

"MATTER IN THE WRONG PLACE is dirt. People got dirty through too much civilisation. Whenever we touch nature, we get clean." You may not associate such sentiments with Swiss psychiatrist C. G. Jung, but they do appear throughout his writings, speeches, letters and interviews. So central to him was a living connection with nature that he claimed, "Without my piece of earth, my life's work would not have come into being."

Jung grew up in the Swiss countryside, and attributed his close connection with nature to this background. His autobiography, *Memories, Dreams, Reflections*, describes his early experiences: "Nature seemed to me full of wonders, and I wanted to steep myself in them. Every stone, every plant, every single thing seemed alive and indescribably marvellous. I immersed myself in nature, crawled, as it were, into the very essence of nature."

His background in the rural countryside provided a foundation that served Jung well later, as he explored the far reaches of the human psyche. An active connection with a natural life flowered again when Jung built by hand a stone cottage beside Lake Zurich, which he used as a retreat throughout his professional life. Photos show him in a workman's apron carving on huge stone blocks or holding a stick, moving pebbles from a stream so it could flow more freely. This, he said, is what his work was all about—helping to move aside obstacles to life's natural flow.

Jung was deeply concerned about the loss of connection with nature which was such a part of the development of modern society. He considered consciousness, as it had developed in the West, to be a Janus-faced achievement, a blessing and a curse, since the type of consciousness we've achieved seems bent on repressing nature. In earlier times, Jung reminds us, nature was "fully as much spirit as matter". Now, we approach nature only from the material side; as if nature is solely the external physical world.

After travelling in various tribal countries, Jung remarked that tribal people did not glorify human powers or place themselves above other animals, and were still able to converse with a bush-soul. In a poetic voice, Jung lamented that "modern man" has lost his emotional participation in natural events and thus feels isolated in the cosmos: "Thunder is no longer the voice of a god. . . . No river contains a spirit, no tree a man's life, no smoke is the embodiment of wisdom, and no mountain still harbours a great demon. Neither do things speak to him [modern man], nor can he speak to things like stones, springs, plants, animals."

Jung's concern reached a high point in the 1950s and 1960s. When he was interviewed for the Houston Films in 1957, he said, "Look at the rebellion of modern youth . . . The real, natural man is just in open rebellion against the utterly inhuman form of life. You are absolutely divorced from nature, and that accounts for the drug problem."

So what did he recommend? Was a re-connection with Nature possible? Jung noted that often, when we make the effort, we merely "cultivate" nature in a domesticated way. "Nature is an incomparable guide if you know how to follow her. . . . Modern man needs to return to nature, not to Nature in the manner of Rousseau, but to his own nature. His task is to find the natural man again."

In an excellent essay, 'Analytical Psychology and Weltanschauung', Jung outlines how a dialogue with the deep unconscious could contribute to a new paradigm, or Weltanschauung. His prescription was that we hold onto the level of reason we have achieved and then enrich it "with a knowledge of man's psychic foundation".

To experience both the modern mind and the primal (original) mind will entail a conflict of major proportions. Jung encouraged us not to shake off or avoid the conflict, but to hold it in consciousness so that a new synthesis could emerge. "We should test the two possibilities against each other . . . the life we live and the one we have forgotten." Establishing a living bridge between the primal and the modern may be the evolutionary task of our time.

To help the instincts come back to life, Jung recommended that we work a four-hour day and have a small plot of land where the rest of the time could be spent. He recommended the sparest use of radio, television, newspapers, and all supposed time-saving devices, "which do not, paradoxically, save time but merely cram our time so full we have no time for anything." And he advocated reforms "by retrogression", which are less expensive and return to the simpler, tried and tested ways of the past.

In an interview with Hans Carol, Jung said, "I am fully committed to the idea that human existence should be rooted in the earth. . . . Nature, the psyche and life appear to me like divinity unfolded—what more could I wish for?"

Meredith Sabini

G. K. CHESTERTON
Founder of Distributism

"When men have come to the edge of a precipice, it is the lover of life who has the spirit to leap backwards, and only the pessimist who continues to believe in progress."

"How you think when you lose determines how long it will be until you win."

"I believe in getting into hot water; it keeps you clean."

"Fallacies do not cease to be fallacies because they become fashions."

"The machine would be our master, for the machine would produce our food, and most of us could have no notion of how it was really being produced." Made in 1925, this accurate prediction about the food industry alone should have singled out G. K.

Chesterton as a voice worth listening to, yet despite many other accurate prophecies, he remains an unsung hero.

Born the son of an estate agent in 1874 and educated at St Paul's in London, he attended the Slade School of Art, where he was drawn more to writing than to drawing or painting. He became a professional writer in his twenties, his prolific energy leading him to cover a huge number of topics in essays, poems and novels. However, it was in the enormous number of reflective and provocative essays he wrote for magazines such as *New Witness* and his own *G.K.'s Weekly* that he developed his more radical ideas.

Many of his passions—workers' co-operatives, concern for the environment, smallholdings for every family—were before their time. Although now considered by many to be desirable and practical solutions to today's problems, it is surprising to learn that they were initially inspired by Chesterton's deep commitment to orthodox Catholicism. As a Christian, the command to love one another was central to his faith, and yet he was realistic about the difficulties of putting this into practice. For, as he wittily remarked, "We make our friends; we make our enemies; but God makes our neighbours."

Chesterton would have relished this apparent paradox, yet seen no need to explain it, for he believed paradox to be the pattern of the world, of our existence. He recognised early on that what we value often destroys us and what we chase so often eludes us.

Seeing this tendency towards the paradoxical in all human activity, he was able to see that our inventions in the name of progress were likely to ensnare us later, and that the very steps we make towards material comfort might fulfil us temporarily but ultimately destroy the environment for later generations.

At the heart of Chesterton's life was a humble acceptance of our ability to get things wrong at almost every turn. He confidently held, however, that this is paradoxically our greatest asset. For without the freedom to make mistakes for ourselves, to reflect on where we go wrong, we would be unable to develop or learn.

In the early 1930s, Chesterton, together with Hilaire Belloc, founded a movement that came to be known as Distributism. Conceived in part as an alternative to the soulless offerings of Socialism, Distributism shared a commitment to the universal rights of humanity but, derived that legitimacy from our shared divine origin. No one,

they argued, needs more than they can consume themselves, for the right and proper purpose of life is learning how to love the divine, for which material wealth has little benefit.

Chesterton wrote: "The aim of Distributism is family ownership of land, workshops, stores, transport, trades, professions, and so on. Family ownership of the means of production so widely distributed as to be the mark of the economic life of the community—this is the Distributist's desire."

For the Distributist, family ownership was the obvious choice: it is the smallest unit of social organisation which accurately reflects both our relationship to God (parent to child) and to society (sibling to sibling). As we have all learned the hard way, families are indeed both divine and maddeningly human and, as such, are the best places to learn the lessons of love. Small-scale, co-operative ownership of the means of production and distribution allows the flowering of individual self-knowledge, which can then be sustained by the deep roots of a close-knit community.

Though thoroughly urban and of incredible appetite, Chesterton was blessed with the imagination to see the commonplace afresh, rattle it around and see if it didn't yield an unexpected flash of light. "Upon the whole", he wrote in an aside on an essay about patriotism in the thirties, "I came to the conclusion that the optimist thought everything good except the pessimist, and the pessimist thought everything bad except himself." Chesterton turns things on their head and then asks us to sympathise with those he pokes fun at, rather than attacking them or scornfully dismissing them like our tabloid culture does today.

It is ironic that his obsession with paradox gave him the insight to develop his most influential prophecies, yet remains the greatest barrier to his gaining a wider audience. For the sense of his prose is often in danger of getting lost in his sometimes exaggerated and bombastic style. However, maddening as his prose can be, he has much to teach us about prejudice and thoughtful questioning of the status quo, not to mention grace, wit and friendship.

Ben Jolliffe

SEYYED HOSSEIN NASR

Philosopher of the Sacred

"To express the truth is in fact the most important of all acts, and we should take every opportunity to do so even if we are not able to perceive its effect."

"It is hopeless to expect to live in harmony with that grand theophany which is virgin nature while remaining oblivious and indifferent to the Source of that theophany both beyond nature and at the centre of man's being."

SEYYED HOSSEIN NASR was born in the East (if one may use such a phrase) and sent to the West at an early age to be educated. This resulted in a great good fortune for the world today, since, combined with his penetrating intelligence and discernment, it has given him a remarkable understanding of the Western mentality while at the same time remaining true to the traditional point of view. Thus he has become the most important bridge between the timeless outlook of the East and the ever-changing outlook of the West, offering—we believe—

the most valid path for the contemporary world.

In the USA the highest honour for a philosopher is to be included in the Library of Living Philosophers. The comparable honour in theology is to deliver the annual Gifford Lectures at Edinburgh University, and only two people have ever been awarded both of these honours: Alfred North Whitehead and Seyyed Hossein Nasr. His Gifford lectures were published under the title *Knowledge and the Sacred*, the title of a book by Nasr which he considers to be his magnum opus. His extraordinary insight into the relationship between knowledge and the sacred, together with the importance of tradition, mark him out as the philosopher of our times. At the heart of Nasr's philosophical outlook is a profound belief in the transcendent unity of all religions, and the transformation of the soul being the essence of human development. However, what he insists upon is that this transformation take place from within one of the great revealed traditions of the world, and not autonomously.

Professor Nasr is known the world over for his all-embracing expertise on Islam and Islamic studies (he has been University Professor of Islamic Studies at George Washington University since 1984), on which he has written a prodigious number of books: on Islamic science, cosmology, art, music, philosophy, religion, spirituality and Sufism, as well as on the lives of great sages such as Jalal ad-Din Rumi. Exceptionally, he is also an expert on modern physics (receiving a PhD in physics from M.I.T. in the 1950s), geology, geophysics and the history of science. His resulting integral knowledge gives him outstanding authority as it raises him above our current world of specialisation.

One of Nasr's most famous books, *Man and Nature: The Spiritual Crisis of Modern Man*, gets straight to the heart of the matter of humankind's relationship with nature. In it he points out that "It is hopeless to expect to live in harmony with that grand theophany which is virgin nature while remaining oblivious and indifferent to the Source of that theophany both beyond nature and at the centre of man's being."

If it were not for Professor Nasr, the Department that Professor Keith Critchlow founded at the Royal College of Art in 1983 (Visual Islamic and Traditional Art, now The Prince's School of Traditional Art under the patronage of HRH The Prince of Wales) would never have been initiated. The fundamental criteria on which this Department was based was inspired by Nasr's own views—that is, in brief, that the only valid reason for art to exist is if it transmits something of the Timeless, the Eternal Reality invisible beneath the outward veil of forms. Geometry, one of the four universal sciences/arts of the 'Ever true' is considered the essence of the School's teaching, since it is the foundation on which the sacred art of all the great traditions is based—particularly the aniconic art of Islam. To participate with the hand, the eye and the heart in this universal language is to participate with the Intelligence which lies at the heart of all creation.

As Nasr writes: "If we define spirituality, as I do, as that which is related to the world of the Spirit, to the Latin *spiritus*, as an objective reality with an ontological status, then spirituality can only be attained through the channels which Heaven has provided for our access to that world, channels which are contained within the various traditions of divine origin." Therefore the traditional artist/craftsman practises their craft using time-honoured inherited canons, methods and forms. These forms are the symbols which act as a window onto Heaven, leading us back to the archetypal world, 'to the Ultimate Reality beyond itself and beyond all forms'.

There continue to be vast changes in the modern world, at an ever-increasing rate, and Nasr's book, *The Heart of Islam*, throws much-needed light and understanding on these changes, and on how change can only be measured by the Unchanging. He makes clear that if the sincere seeker wishes to find the heart of Islam, the best path is through Sufism. It is truly an inspired and inspiring book and, in our view, should be required reading for all teenagers.

In these troubled times, the presence of such a one as Professor Nasr who so clearly represents the integration of knowledge and the sacred, is not only a great blessing but also a mercy. His constant and tireless efforts to elevate wisdom are ever more vital and sorely needed, demonstrating that the supreme contribution of one man has a radiating effect which, like ripples in a pool, reach far and wide. Nasr's insistence on the Oneness of God and on the principle that Unity and unification at every level of our great theophany are the ultimate goal of the true philosopher, is his most important message today. His authoritative voice contains a powerful reminder that all three Abrahamic revelations worship the same One God. As Nasr often quotes, "The pen of the scholar is mightier than the sword."

Keith Critchlow and Emma Clark

KAHLIL GIBRAN
Poet of the Soul

*"Your neighbour is your other self dwelling behind a wall.
In understanding all walls shall fall down."*

*"Faith is an oasis in the heart which will never be reached
by the caravan of thinking."*

*"Keep me away from the wisdom which does not cry,
the philosophy which does not laugh and the greatness
which does not bow before children."*

*"Advance, and never halt, for advancing is perfection.
Advance and do not fear the thorns in the path,
for they draw only corrupt blood."*

I N ONE OF HIS EARLY Arabic pieces, *A Lamentation in the Field*, Kahlil Gibran communes with various aspects of nature—in turn the breeze, some flowers, a brook, some birds—and finds each of them lamenting the polluting and deadly effects of humankind and urban life. Rather than being an isolated expression of concern for the environment, this should best be seen as part of Gibran's Rousseauistic and Romantic opposition between a natural life and an urban life. Gibran is one of the unacknowledged prophets of environmentalism. There is an episode in *The Garden of the Prophet* where one of the Prophet's would-be disciples stubs his toe on a stone and curses the stone as a dead thing. Almustafa replies, "Have you been thus long in this garden and know not that there is nothing dead here? . . . You and the stone are one. There is a difference only in heartbeats . . . Its rhythm may be another rhythm, but I say unto you that if you sound the depths of your soul and scale the heights of space, you shall hear but one melody."

In one of his poems, *My Soul Counselled Me*, Gibran wrote, "But now I know that I was formed even from the same dust of which all humans are created, that my elements are their elements, and my inner self is their inner self. My struggle is their struggle, and their pilgrimage is mine own. If they transgress, I am also the transgressor, and if they do well, then I have a share in their well-doing. If they arise, I too arise with them; if they stay behind, I also, to company them."

A great many problems on this Earth are created by the kind of arrogance that cannot see further than its own, often materialistic, interests. This was the subject of Gibran's most sustained and passionate campaign. His first books— *Nymphs of the Valley* and *Spirits Rebellious*—inveighed against a number of injustices in his native Lebanon.

One of these injustices was the arrogant materialism of the Church in north Lebanon, which seemed less concerned with saving people's souls than with lining its coffers and protecting its interests. In disgust, Gibran foreswore his Christian upbringing, but Christ remained throughout his life a potent symbol and a close friend, who often appeared to him in dreams. One of his later books, *Jesus, the Son of Man* (1928), picked up the theme that Christ came to help the poor, not to found a worldly, wealthy organisation.

Gandhi was also one of Gibran's heroes, as a perfect demonstration of the power of humility. Like Gandhi, Gibran was always a champion of the life of poverty and simplicity. In fact, in his early works, wealth was not just a hindrance, but a positive impediment to goodness.

Humility, the interconnectedness of all things, caring for other people—these are the themes which underpin Gibran's poetry. In his 1919 poem *The Procession*, Gibran pitted a world-weary older man against a free-spirited, hymn-singing younger man who is still full of the joys of the world. At one point the older man proclaims the doctrine that might is right—that if humankind can exert its will over the world, it has a right to do so. Gibran's response, through his youthful spokesman, is illuminating. Instead of just combatting this philosophy with its opposite, he points out the actual superior strength of the biosphere. Humankind is in fact as transient as autumn leaves: our time on this planet is brief, in the timescale of the planet as a whole. If the human race were to be exterminated, the biosphere would easily adapt and continue.

Gibran is saying that we should acknowledge the mightier potency of the Earth as a whole. And in the face of that, what else can one do but adopt an attitude of reverence? In his poem *Before the Throne of Beauty* Gibran imagines an apocalyptic vision of the spirit of nature and learns the crucial lesson: "When you see beauty, you desire to give, not to receive." If we could see every creature, every aspect of creation, as the true and unique entity it is, we would be seeing its beauty, and then we would want only to respect and revere it.

Frugality is another important value with which Gibran opposed the materialistic powers of his time. He best epitomised frugality in the actions of his own life. Even in the 1920s, when fame—even adulation—and a degree of wealth came his way, he continued to live in a one-room studio in New York's Greenwich Village. He called his studio 'The Hermitage', and he lived there for eighteen years, labouring through his writings and paintings to bring something of his message to the people of his day and beyond. The continuing sales of *The Prophet* and the renewed interest in his life and his other works testify to his success.

Robin Waterfield

JOANNA MACY
Empowerment Activist

"The heart that breaks open can contain the whole universe."

"Confirming an intuitive sense I've always felt for the interconnectedness of all things, this doctrine has provided me ways to understand the intricate web of co-arising that links one being with all other beings, and to apprehend the reciprocities between thought and action, self and universe."

"It is my experience that the world itself has a role to play in our liberation. Its very pressures, pains and risks can wake us up . . . release us from the bonds of ego and guide us home to our vast true nature."

"If the world is to be healed through human efforts, I am convinced it will be by ordinary people, people whose love for this life is even greater than their fear. People who can open to the web of life that called us into being."

BUDDHIST, ACTIVIST, scholar and teacher, Joanna Macy has been working around the world for the past twenty years, addressing the global environmental and spiritual crisis. In 1972, at a Quaker conference on religion and psychology, Joanna Macy had a dream. In it, she found herself in a desolate landscape. She had chosen to go there; but she realised that there was no escape from that suffocating situation. In the midst of the darkness, a voice penetrated Joanna's dream: a woman in the room was intoning "The Lord our God is One." Joanna became aware that, indeed, this single unifying presence was everywhere, even there in that ravaged place where she was trapped. The voice gave her an insight to appreciate the beauty of the place, and gave the knowledge that it was all right for her to remain there. For Joanna the world is no longer a trap.

Joanna brings to her work a powerful combination of deep feeling, intellectual clarity and personal charisma. Joanna is a visionary: her vision consists of transformational possibilities that exist in human beings.

Socially and politically active all her adult life, beginning with the American civil rights movement, Joanna Macy has thrust her efforts in many directions. She is most frequently associated these days with the Deep Ecology movement, despair work and empowerment, and more recently with the Nuclear Guardianship Project, which she initiated in 1988.

Joanna Macy was born in 1929, and grew up in New York. She was happiest during the summers she spent at her grandparents' farm in western New York State. A conversion experience at a church camp when she was sixteen led her to feel she had a vocation of service within the church.

At Wellesley College she graduated in Biblical Studies. Soon after, she found herself on a Fulbright Fellowship studying Economics, Marxism, and Nationalism in the Third World. In the sixties she went with her husband Francis and their three children to India, where Fran was an administrator in the Peace Corps. There, in the North, Joanna encountered the Tibetans. After spending a year helping them rebuild their community, she asked for instruction in meditation.

On her return to the States, Joanna enrolled in a doctoral programme in Religion (with a focus on Buddhist Studies) at Syracuse University. Here a striking conjunction of seemingly disparate elements—an ancient Eastern and a contemporary Western philosophy—spurred her to the next stage in her work; impressed by the "revolutionary beauty", as she has called it, of general systems theory, she found it profoundly complementary with the Buddha's teaching.

Each of these philosophies affirms the interconnectedness of all things, and describes causality as residing in relationships rather than in individuals or institutions. Even the self, understood in this light, is a fluid construct. Conventional notions of the self, Macy maintains, have narrowed the horizons of both our cognition and our compassion; only as we realise that we are bound inextricably within a larger whole can we begin to see the needs of others. Responsible social action, then, Macy maintains, will emerge most effectively from the realisation that the interest of one is the interest of all.

What Joanna Macy teaches derives from two sides of her nature: her unusual openness to experiences of grief and anguish, and her equally unusual intellectual discipline. Critical to her teaching is the necessity neither to deny our feelings of despair nor to allow them to impede us from action. To be a lover of the world means to Joanna not only to love "unspoiled nature", but to embrace all the rest of it. When I spoke with her of the desire many express these days to leave the problems of modern urban living and "go dancing in the woods", she looked out the window, over the Berkeley rooftops to the fires of the Richmond Oil Refineries, and said, "We may have to learn to dance in the nuclear dumps instead."

Anita Barrows

NOTES ON CONTRIBUTORS

Peter Abbs is a poet and Professor of Creative Writing at Sussex University.

Hilary Armstrong is a freelance writer living in London.

Allan Hunt Badiner is a Buddhist writer living in California.

Diane Baker is co-founder with Starhawk of the Reclaiming collective. In 1998 she co-authored, with Starhawk and Anne Hill, *Circle Round: Raising Children in Goddess Traditions.* She is also a former first officer of the Covenant of the Goddess.

Anita Barrows is a journalist living in California.

Alick Bartholomew's fascination is how nature works. The reconciliation of science and spirituality was a theme of his two publishing businesses, Turnstone Press (1971–82) and Gateway Books (1982–2001); which is how he came to write *Hidden Nature—The Startling Insights of Viktor Schauberger* and *The Schauberger Keys.* He can be reached at alick@schauberger-books.org.uk.

Roger Berthoud worked as a diarist, foreign correspondent, feature writer and leader writer on (successively) the *Evening Standard, The Times* and *The Independent.* He has written the biographies of Graham Sutherland and Henry Moore, and lives near Bath.

David Boyle is an associate of the New Economics Foundation.

James Brabazon's career has spanned stage, film and television, as writer, actor, story editor, director and producer. He has also written acclaimed biographies of Albert Schweitzer and crime novelist Dorothy L. Sayers.

Michael Brander is the biographer of Lady Eve Balfour.

Peter Bunyard was a founding editor of *The Ecologist,* and is currently Science Editor. He is a Fellow of the Linnean Society, and author of *The Breakdown of Climate: Human Choices or Global Disaster* (Floris Books). Since 1972 he has lived on a smallholding in Cornwall.

John Burnside's article on Rachel Carson is an extract from an article in *The Guardian,* 18th May 2002.

Robert Butler's most recent publication is *The Art of Darkness: Staging the Philip Pullman Trilogy* (Oberon Books). See www.robertbutler.info. He also edits the Ashden Directory (ashdendirectory.org.uk), an online magazine about environmentalism and the performing arts.

Fritjof Capra's books include *The Tao of Physics* and *The Turning Point.*

Noel Charlton has been a lifelong environmentalist and a student of Gregory Bateson's work for many years. He has worked with Schumacher College, Devon, and within the Institute for Environment, Philosophy and Public Policy, Lancaster University, England. His book *Mind, Beauty and the Sacred Earth: an Introduction to the Thought of Gregory Bateson,* is forthcoming from the State University of New York Press.

Swati Chopra writes on spirituality and is author of the book *Buddhism: On the Path to Nirvana* (Brijbasi Art Press, New Delhi, 2005). Her next book, a travelogue of the spirit based in Dharamsala (the home in exile of the Dalai Lama in India), will be published by Penguin in 2006. She is currently researching the place of gender in contemporary spirituality. Swati can be contacted through her website, www.swatichopra.com.

Emma Clark is the author of *The Art of the Islamic Garden,* published by the Crowood Press.

NOTES ON CONTRIBUTORS

Chris Clarke was Professor of Applied Mathematics (and is now a Visiting Professor) at the University of Southampton, UK. His main published research has been on cosmology, astrophysics, quantum theory and the physics of the brain, and he has recently moved into consciousness studies. His most recent book, the edited volume *Ways of Knowing: Science and Mysticism Today* (Imprint Academic) explores a pluralistic vision of the nature of reality. www.scispirit.com.

Philip Conford has been researching organic history for more than two decades and is the author of *The Origins of the Organic Movement* (2001). He is currently working on a second volume, covering the past fifty years, and is a Visiting Research Fellow in the Department of History at Reading University. Contact details: 88 St Pancras, Chichester, West Sussex PO19 7LR.

David Cook was appointed as Chief Executive of TNS International from April 2004. He is now based at the Stockholm TNS office. David is the author of the Schumacher Society Briefing *The Natural Step—Towards a Sustainable Society*, published by Green Books.

Jonathan Coope is a teacher and actor currently completing a PhD in the History of Ideas. His research explores the psychological readings of contemporary environmental crisis offered by Theodore Roszak, Charlene Spretnak and Ken Wilber. Email: jonathan.coope@britishlibrary.net. Further information on ecopsychology can be found at www.ecopsychology.org.

Keith Critchlow is a leading expert in sacred architecture and sacred geometry. He is Professor Emeritus of The Prince's School of Traditional Arts in London. His book *Islamic Patterns, an Analytical and Cosmological Approach*, with a Foreword by Seyyed Hossein Nasr, is published by Thames & Hudson.

Jim Cummings is a writer and editor who has lived in New Mexico for the past twenty years. He is the Founder of Acoustic Ecology Institute and elected first President of the American Society for Acoustic Ecology.

Shirley du Boulay was for some years a producer of religious programmes for the BBC and has written many books, including highly acclaimed biographies of Teresa of Avila, Dame Cicely Saunders, Desmond Tutu, Bede Griffiths and, most recently, of Swami Abhishiktananda. She was married to the late John Harriott and lives in Oxford.

John Einarsen is the founding editor and art director of *Kyoto Journal*, www.kyotojournal.org.

Ianto Evans teaches sustainable living in rural communities in Latin America. He is also working to revive cob building.

Harry Eyres is a poet and freelance writer. His first poetry collection, *Hotel Eliseo*, was published by Hearing Eye in 2001.

Richard Flyer is President of Northern Nevada Wound Care and Hyperbarics, and a resident of Reno, Nevada and a founder of the Conscious Community and Business Network (www.ccbnreno.org).

Stuart Franklin is a journalist-photographer represented by Magnum.

Alan Gear was Chief Executive of HDRA from 1985 until his retirement in 2003. He has had a long and prolific career as a writer, speaker and broadcaster. He has written/co-authored five books. In 2003 he was awarded the MBE for services to organic horticulture. He now runs an organic consultancy, Gear Changes Ltd, with his wife, Jackie. Email: agear@gearchanges.co.uk.

Joanna Griffiths is at St Antony's College, Oxford, where she is writing a nature history called *Ultima Thule: the Myth of the Pure North*.

Stephan Harding holds a doctorate in ecology from the University of Oxford. He is Resident Ecologist at Schumacher College in Devon, where he also co-ordinates the MSc in Holistic Science.

Kate Hartgroves is former Assistant Editor at *Resurgence* magazine. She lives in Cornwall and is training to be an English teacher.

Dr Yitzhaq Hayut-Man is an Israeli who has studied architecture, urban planning and Cognitive Cybernetics, and worked in Israel, Brazil and the USA. website www.thehope.org/index.htm, email: yrusalem@actcom.co.il.

Marjorie Hope and James Young This article is part of a chapter on the American Indians in Hope and Young's new book entitled *The New Alliance: Faith and Ecology.*

Liz Hosken co-founded and is Director of the Gaia Foundation. In 1991 Liz Hosken received the Jameson Award and, on behalf of Gaia, has received the Schumacher Award and a One World Award for media work on biodiversity-related issues. She is a fellow of the Findhorn Foundation and adviser to the Goldman Prize.

Francis Hutchinson is a feminist economist based at Bradford University.

John Irving was born in Carlisle, Cumbria and has spent all his professional life in Italy. A collaborator of *Slow Food* for over ten years, he is a regular contributor to a number of the Slow Food movement's publications and is editor of the international magazine *Slow*. www.slowfood.com.

Pico Iyer is a renowned travel writer who is author of books such as *Video Night in Kathmandu, The Lady and the Monk* and *The Global Soul*. He writes regularly for *Time* magazine and *The New Yorker*. He has known His Holiness the Dalai Lama since 1974.

Ben Jolliffe is a freelance writer who specialises in food, faith, education and modern culture. Email: benjolliffe@onetel.net.uk.

John A. Kirk is Professor of United States history at Royal Holloway, University of London. He has written extensively on Martin Luther King and the civil rights movement, including a short biography *Martin Luther King, Jr* (Pearson Longman).

Satish Kumar is Editor of *Resurgence* and Programme Director at Schumacher College.

Peter Lang is an environmental consultant and events director for *Resurgence*. He formerly worked for the Green Group in the European Parliament, and is the author of books on money and investment.

Richard Lanoy is a painter and writer. He is the author of *The Speaking Tree*, a classic book on Indian life and spirituality.

Anna Moore Lappé is the co-author of *Hope's Edge: The Next Diet for a Small Planet* and *Grub: Ideas for an Urban Organic Kitchen* (Tarcher/Penguin). She is also the founding principal with Frances Moore Lappé of the Small Planet Institute and the Small Planet Fund. She lives in Brooklyn, New York. See www.smallplanetfund/org, www.eatgrub.org, www.smallplanetinstitute.org.

Sheryl Leach, the Creator of Barney™, is an independent film producer and co-President of the Shei'rah Foundation.

Bob Lebensold is an American radio journalist specialising in social and cultural broadcasting.

David Lorimer is a writer, lecturer and editor, and Programme Director of the Scientific and Medical Network. He is the author and editor of a number of books on science and spirituality. His book about the ideas and work of the Prince of Wales, *Radical Prince*, was published in November 2003.

Mia MacDonald is an animal activist, environmentalist, women's rights activist, and international public policy analyst. www.miamacdonald.com.

George McRobie was a friend and colleague of E. F. Schumacher, and co-founder with him of the Intermediate Technology Development Group (now called Practical Action). He is the author of *Small is Possible*.

Nic Marks is Head of the Centre for Well-being at the New Economics Foundation. He is also a consultant to a project sponsored by the Government of Bhutan on how to construct indicators for assessing Gross National Happiness in Bhutan.

Fred Matser has initiated many environmental projects in The Netherlands.

Ed Mayo is Chief Executive of the National Consumer Council (NCC), which he joined in June 2003. He has worked in the non-profit and the private sector, including the New Economics Foundation (NEF).

Liz Medler works in the field of paediatric cardiac surgery. She is a regular contributor to *New Vision*.

Stephanie Mills is a long-time bioregionalist who lives on a peninsula in Lake Michigan. She wrote *In Service of the Wild* (Beacon Press 1995) and *Epicurean Simplicity* (Island Press 2002).

Maya Kumar Mitchell lives in Barcelona, where she writes, dances and teaches English. She is joint editor of *The Beauty of Craft*, another *Resurgence* anthology in this series.

John Moat is a poet, novelist, painter and columnist. For further details visit www.johnmoat.co.uk.

Andrew Mueller is an Australian-born, London-based journalist and author, currently contributing to *The Independent, The Independent on Sunday, The Guardian, Uncut, Arena* and opendemocracy.net, among others. His next book, *I Wouldn't Start From Here: Travels In The Early 21st Century*, will hopefully be available in 2007. He can be contacted at mail@andrewmueller.net.

Edmund O'Sullivan is a Professor Emeritus of the Ontario Institute for Studies in Education at the University of Toronto, and Associate Director of the Transformative Learning Centre. He has written a number of books on Transformative Learning. Email: eosullivan@oise.utoronto.ca. Website: http://tlc.oise.utoronto.ca.

John Papworth was the founder of *Resurgence*, and is the Editor of *Fourth World Review*.

Bhikhu Parekh is a Member of the House of Lords and a retired professor at Hull University.

Fred Pearce is a regular contributor to *New Scientist*.

Jason Peters is Associate Professor of English at Augustana College in Rock Island, Illinois (USA), where he teaches both British and American literature. He has written on John Donne, T. S. Eliot, Samuel Taylor Coleridge, Henry Adams, Flannery O'Connor, Wendell Berry and C. S. Lewis. His edited volume, *Wendell Berry: Life and Work*, will be published by the University Press of Kentucky in 2007.

Jordi Pigem is a writer, lecturer and ecophilosopher. He holds a PhD in Philosophy from the Universitat de Barcelona, is the author of *La Odisea de Occidente* and *El pensament de Raimon Panikkar*, and won the *Resurgence* and Scientific and Medical Network Essay Competition in 2006. He can be contacted at jordi2048@yahoo.co.uk.

Andrew Pring is a Peace Studies graduate of the University of Bradford.

William Radice is the translator of Rabindranath Tagore's poems and stories for Penguin Classics. He is also a poet in his own right, his latest book being *Green, Red, Gold: A Novel in 101 Sonnets* (Flambard Press). He is Senior Lecturer in Bengali at SOAS, University of London. More information at www.williamradice.com.

A. Rangarajan is an Indian economist who specialises in traditional cultures and Gandhian philosophy. He studied in India and in Germany.

Kate Rawles lectured in Philosophy at the University of Lancaster for nine years before going freelance in 2000. She specialises in values and sustainability, environmental ethics and animal welfare.

Meredith Sabini is irector of Depth Psychology Programmes in Berkeley, CA. She is the author of *Jung: on Nature, Technology and Modern Life*.

Keith Sagar, formerly Reader in Literature at Manchester University, is the author of several books on Lawrence and Hughes. His most recent book (with chapters on both) is *Literature and the Crime Against Nature*, Chaucer Press, 2005. Website www.keithsagar.co.uk. His collected poems are published by Arrowhead Press under the title *Mola*. www.arrowheadpress.co.uk.

Diana Schumacher is President of The Schumacher Society. Since the late 1970 she has been actively involved in worldwide movements for healing, conflict resolution and peace through economic and social development. She has served on the executive council of more than twenty-five organisations.

John Seymour was known primarily as the founder of the modern UK self-sufficiency movement. His many books include *England Revisited*, published by Dorling Kindersley.

William Irwin Thompson is the founder of the Lindisfarne Association. He is the author of fifteen books, the most recent of which is *The American Replacement of Nature* (Doubleday).

Christopher Titmuss, formerly a Buddhist monk in Thailand and India, teaches Awakening and Insight Meditation around the world. He is the founder and director of the Dharma Facilitators Programme and the Living Dharma programme. A poet and writer, he is the co-founder of Gaia House, an international retreat centre in Devon. England. He lives in Totnes, Devon.

Mark Tredinnick is the author of *The Land's Wild Music* (Trinity University Press), a book that explores the life and work of Terry Tempest Williams, along with Barry Lopez, Peter Matthiessen and James Galvin. He is an Australian essayist, poet and nature writer, and the author also of the forthcoming book *The Blue Plateau: A Landscape Memoir*. He lives in Glebe, New South Wales.

Paul Vallely is Associate Editor of *The Independent,* where he writes on social, ethical and religious issues.

Jay Walljasper was editor of *Utne* Magazine for ten years, is now editor of *Utne* Magazine books and an editor-at-large at the magazine. He also writes a series for *The Nation* magazine about positive social and political initiatives and a column on political and environmental topics for *Resurgence, Shambhala Sun*, and *Conscious Choice* magazines.

Harland Walshaw is an architectural photographer and writer.

Colin Ward was an editor of the British anarchist newspaper *Freedom* from 1947 to 1960, and the founder and editor of the monthly libertarian journal *Anarchy* from 1961 to 1970. He is the author of numerous books on the subjects of anarchism, education, architecture and town planning.

A. C. Warne is Chairman of the International Tree Foundation, the organisation founded by Richard St Barbe Baker to implement his ideas. He is an ecologist and entomologist, and has worked in nature conservation both professionally and as a volunteer, mainly in the UK but with short periods in The Ivory Coast and Bolivia.

Robin Waterfield's biography of Gibran—*Prophet: The Life and Times of Kahlil Gibran*—was published by Allen Lane in August 2006. He is also the consultant editor for Penguin's Arkana list.

Ken Webster is an associate of the Education Department of WWF. He is the author of *Can White Be Green?*

Freddie Whitefield has worked in the field of environmental policy and now lives in Cornwall renovating houses and editing.

James Young *see* **Marjorie Hope and James Young**

Paul Zeal is a psychoanalytic psychotherapist and writer. He helped to establish the UK Council for Psychotherapy, and chaired the Severnside Institute for Psychotherapy. Formerly a schoolteacher, he trained in psychoanalysis in order to work more closely with the inner worlds and their influence in love and work. He is now writing about the psychology of eco-carelessness. paul.zeal@btinternet.com.

FURTHER INFORMATION ON VISIONARIES

David Abram's best-known book is *The Spell of the Sensuous: Perception and Language in a More-Than-Human World* (Vintage).

Sri Anandamayi See www.anandamayi.org.

A. T. Ariyaratne For further information on the Sarvodaya Shramadana Movement in Sri Lanka, see www.sarvodaya.org.

Maurice Ash's *Where Division Ends* and other books are published by Green Books.

Richard St Barbe Baker See Man of the Trees, www.manofthetrees.org, and International Tree Foundation, www.internationaltreefoundation.org.

Lady Eve Balfour's *The Living Soil* is currently out of print, but the full text is available online in the Agriculture Library at www.soilandhealth.org. The Soil Association is at www.soilassociation.org.

Maude Barlow For further information see The Council of Canadians' website, www.canadians.org.

Gregory Bateson A good source of information is www.indiana.edu/~wanthro/bateson.htm.

Thomas Berry's many books include *The Great Work: Our Way into the Future* (Bell Tower).

Wendell Berry's books are published by Counterpoint Books, USA.

Vinoba Bhave's *Moved by Love* and *The Intimate and the Ultimate* are published by Green Books.

David Bohm See *The Essential David Bohm*, edited by Lee Nichol (Routledge).

Peter Brook See *Peter Brook: A Biography* by Michael Kustow. The best website for Peter Brook is www.peter-brook.net/brookFR/PB.html.

Joseph Campbell For further information see the Joseph Campbell Foundation website, www.jcf.org.

Rachel Carson There is a website devoted to the life and legacy of Rachel Carson: www.rachelcarson.org.

Prince Charles The official website of HRH Prince Charles is www.princeofwales.gov.uk.

G. K. Chesterton See www.chesterton.org.

Deepak Chopra See www.chopra.com.

Jacques Cousteau See the Cousteau Society website, www.cousteau.org.

Bob Dylan The CDs, digitally mastered early LPs and Songbooks are readily available. Also recommended are Martin Scorsese's film *No Direction Home*, an Arena Production; *Chronicles*, Dylan's own account of early musical influences and adventures, and *The Rough Guide to Bob Dylan*.

Riane Eisler is best known for her international bestseller *The Chalice and The Blade: Our History, Our Future* (Harper & Row).

Matthew Fox See the Friends of Creation Spirituality website, www.matthewfox.org.

Eric Fromm's books are readily available. Especially recommended are *The Art of Loving* and *The Anatomy of Human Destructiveness*. The Fromm Archive is held in Tubingen, Germany. E-mail: frommfunk@aol.com, archivist Dr Rainer Funk.

Masanobu Fukuoka To obtain Seedballs, see www.seedballs.com. *The One Straw Revolution* is available from www.eco-logicbooks.com.

Buckminster Fuller The Buckminster Fuller Institute serves a global network of design innovators: www.bfi.org.

Mahatma Gandhi's autobiography is entitled *The Story of My Experiments with Truth* (or *My Experiments with Truth*). There is a Gandhi website, www.mkgandhi.org.

Patrick Geddes There is a Geddes Institute at the University of Dundee's Department of Town and Regional Planning, informed by Geddes' ideas: www.trp.dundee.ac.uk/research/cpr.html.

Kahlil Gibran See www.kahlil.org for all his works, photographs, artwork, biography, and downloads.

Edward Goldsmith See www.edwardgoldsmith.org.

Jane Goodall See www.janegoodall.org.

Bede Griffiths See The Bede Griffiths Trust website, www.bedegriffiths.com.

Thich Nhat Hanh's books are published by Parallax Press, founded by Thich Nhat Hanh's community: www.parallax.org. Plum Village, Thich Nhat Hanh's main monastery and practice centre, is located about 85 km east of Bordeaux, France: www.plumvillage.org.

Mary Harris ('Mother Jones') Books about her include *Mother Jones, the Miner's Angel* by Dale Fetherling (Southern Illinois University Press), *Ronnie Gilbert on Mother Jones: Face to Face with the Most Dangerous Woman in America* (Conari Press), and *Mother Jones Speaks: Speeches and Writings of a Working-Class Fighter* (Pathfinder Press).

Robert Hart's *Forest Gardening* is published by Green Books. There are several other books about forest gardening, including Dave Jacke's two-volume *Edible Forest Gardens* (Chelsea Green).

Julia Butterfly Hill *The Legacy of Luna: The Story of a Tree, a Woman, and the Struggle to Save the Redwoods,* is published by Harper San Francisco.

Lawrence D. Hills' autobiography *Fighting like the Flowers* is published by Green Books. The Henry Doubleday Research Association (HDRA) website is www.gardenorganic.org.uk.

Albert Howard's *An Agricultural Testament* is published by Oxford University Press. This is the book that started the organic farming and gardening revolution, the result of Howard's 25 years of research at Indore in India.

Ted Hughes's website with biographical information and essays is at www.earth-moon.org.

Ivan Illich's books include *Deschooling Society, Tools for Conviviality, Energy and Equity* and *The Rivers North of the Future—The Testament of Ivan Illich* as told to David Cayley.

Carl Gustav Jung Recommended reading: *Modern Man in Search of a Soul* and *Man and His Symbols* by C. G. Jung, and *Jung and the Story of Our Time* by Laurens van der Post. Information and resources can be found at www.cgjungpage.org.

Petra Kelly See *The Life and Death of Petra Kelly* by Sara Parkin (Rivers Oram Press/Pandora) and *Thinking Green! Essays on Environmentalism, Feminism, and Nonviolence* by Petra K. Kelly (Parallax Press).

J. M. Keynes For an extensive list of resources see http://cepa.newschool.edu/het/profiles/keynes.htm.

Martin Luther King The Martin Luther King Papers Project is at Stanford University: www.stanford.edu/group/King. National Civil Rights Museum: www.civilrightsmuseum.org.

Leopold Kohr's seminal work is *The Breakdown of Nations,* reprinted by Green Books.

Jiddu Krishnamurti Contact the Krishnamurti Foundation Trust, Brockwood Park, Bramdean, Hants SO24 0LQ, UK. www.kfoundation.org.

Peter Kropotkin's *Memoirs of a Revolutionist* is published by Fredonia Books,US.

J. C. Kumarappa See *Of God and Mammon: J.C. Kumarappa's Religious Theory of Economics as a Counterpoint to the Religion of Economics* by John Dilip Chakkanatt (Intercultural Pubns, New Delhi).

Winona LaDuke *The Winona LaDuke Reader: A Collection of Essential Writings* is published by Voyageur Press.

R. D. Laing Recommended books are *The Voice of Experience, R. D. Laing: A Biography* by his son Adrian, *R. D. Laing: A Divided Self* by John Clay and *Mad to be Normal: Conversations with R. D. Laing* by Bob Mullan.

Dalai Lama See www.dalailama.com.

Frances Moore Lappé of the Small Planet Institute and Small Planet Fund: www.smallplanetfund.org and www.smallplanetinstitute.org.

D. H. Lawrence There is a D. H. Lawrence Centre at the University of Nottingham: see www.nottingham.ac.uk/mss/online/dhlawrence.

Aldo Leopold For more information see The Aldo Leopold Foundation at www.aldoleopold.org.

James Lovelock's books include *Homage to Gaia: The Life of an Independent Scientist* (Oxford University Press) and *The Revenge of Gaia* (Allen Lane).

Caroline Lucas is the Green MEP for the South West of England: www.carolinelucasmep.org.uk.

José Lutzenberger The Gaia Foundation in Brazil was created to assist amplify the work of its founder and president, José Lutzenberger. www.fgaia.org.br.

Oren Lyons More information on Oren Lyons, on indigenous peoples and the Onondaga Nation can be found at the Indigenous People's Literature website www.indigenouspeople.net.

Joanna Macy See www.joannamacy.net.

Jerry Mander's books include *Four Arguments for the Elimination of Television, Alternative Globalisation: a Better World is Possible* (with John Cavanagh), and *In the Absence of the Sacred: The Failure of Technology and the Survival of Indian Nations.*

Lynn Margulis's books include *Symbiotic Planet: A New Look at Evolution* (Basic Books), *Acquiring Genomes: A Theory of the Origins of Species* (Perseus Books Group), *The Ice Chronicles: The Quest to Understand Global Climate Change* (University of New Hampshire).

H. J. Massingham An anthology of his writings, *A Mirror of England*, is published by Green Books.

Wangari Maathai See the website of the Green Belt Movement: www.greenbeltmovement.org.

Peter Matthiessen's many books are mostly published by Random House: www.randomhouse.com.

Manfred Max-Neef's books include *From the Outside Looking In: Experiences in Barefoot Economics* (Dag Hammarskjöld Foundation), *Human Scale Development* (Apex Press) and *Real-Life Economics: Understanding Wealth Creation*, with Paul Ekins (Routledge).

Donella Meadows For further information contact The Sustainability Institute: www.sustainer.org.

Thomas Merton See The Thomas Merton Center and The International Thomas Merton Society at Belarmine University, www.merton.org.

Mary Midgley's books include *The Myths We Live By, Gaia: The Next Big Idea* and *Science and Poetry.*

Bill Mollison's *Permaculture 1* and *Permaculture 2* are available through www.eco-logicbooks.com and www.green-shopping.co.uk.

Thomas Moore is the author of many books, including *The Re-enchantment of Everyday Life, Care of the Soul, Soul Mates, Dark Nights of the Soul, Rituals of the Imagination, The Planets Within*, and *Dark Eros.*

Arne Naess *The Selected Works of Arne Naess* (Springer) is a ten-volume work. *Life's Philosophy* by Arne Naess is published by The University of Georgia Press.

Seyyed Hossein Nasr The Seyyed Hossein Nasr Foundation propagates spirituality through perennial philosophy and traditional teachings contained in the Quran: www.nasrfoundation.org.

Scott and Helen Nearing For further information go to The Good Life Center: www.goodlife.org. Several of their books are published by Chelsea Green, www.chelseagreen.com.

Raimon Panikkar Some of Raimon Panikkar's major books in English are *Invisible Harmony, A Dwelling Place for Wisdom, The Cosmotheandric Experience, The Vedic Experience, Blessed Simplicity* and *The Intrareligious Dialogue.* Contact Fundació Vivarium, E-08511 Tavertet, Catalonia (Spain).

Carlo Petrini For further information see the Slow Food website: www.slowfood.com. The Slow Food publishing house is Slow Food Editore, via Mendicità Istruita 45, 12042 Bra (Cn) Italy.

Jonathon Porritt is Programme Director of Forum for the Future and Chairman of the UK government's Sustainability Commission.

Ilya Prigogine See The Center for Complex Quantum Systems (formerly The Ilya Prigogine Center for Studies in Statistical Mechanics and Complex Systems): http://order.ph.utexas.edu.

Kathleen Raine Many of Kathleen Raine's books are still in print. The Temenos Academy can be contacted at PO Box 203, Ashford, Kent, TN25 5ZT, www.temenosacademy.org.

Peter Redgrove *The Book of Wonders: The Best of Peter Redgrove's Poetry* is edited by Jeremy Robinson.

Karl-Henrik Robèrt's *The Natural Step Story: Seeding a Quiet Revolution* is published by New Society Publishers, and the Schumacher Briefing *The Natural Step: Towards a Sustainable Society* by David Cook is published by Green Books for the Schumacher Society. Find out more about the Natural Step at www.naturalstep.org.uk.

Anita Roddick's books include the autobiographical *Body & Soul* and *Business As Unusual*, and she was editor of the popular 2001 title *Take It Personally: How To Make Conscious Choices to Change the World*. See www.AnitaRoddick.com and www.takeitpersonally.org.

Theodore Roszak's many books include *World Beware! American Triumphalism in an Age of Terror* (with Kanner & Gomes) and *Ecopsychology: Restoring the Earth, Healing the Mind* (Sierra Club Books).

Aruna Roy Further information can be obtained from the Barefoot College: www.barefootcollege.org.

Arundhati Roy's many books include *Public Power in the Age of Empire* (Seven Stories Press), *War Talk* and *Power Politics* (South End Press), *The Algebra of Infinite Justice* and *The God of Small Things* (Flamingo).

Oscar Arias Sanchez's work is continued by the Arias Foundation for Peace and Human Progress: www.arias.or.cr.

Viktor Schauberger See *Living Energies* by Viktor Schauberger and Callum Coats, and *Hidden Nature* by Alick Bartholomew.

E. F. Schumacher's major books are *Small is Beautiful: A Study of Economics as if People Mattered, A Guide for the Perplexed* and *Good Work*. *This I Believe* is a collection of 21 articles that Schumacher wrote for *Resurgence*, published by Green Books. The UK Schumacher Society is at www.schumacher.org.uk.

Albert Schweitzer For further information contact The Albert Schweitzer Institute, Trinity College, Broad Street, University of Oxford, OX1 3BH. UK. Email: info@iseps.org.uk.

Rupert Sheldrake See www.sheldrake.org.

Paul Shepard's books are published by Island Press, USA.

Vandana Shiva's many books are mostly published in the UK by Zed Books, www.zedbooks.co.uk, and in the US by South End Press, www.southend-press.org.

Sulak Sivaraksa See www.sulak-sivaraksa.org, homepage of the Sathirakoses-Nagapradeepa Foundation, a network committed to social justice with ecological vision and based on engaged spirituality and the work of Sulak Sivaraksa.

Starhawk See www.starhawk.org.

Aung San Suu Kyi See www.dassk.org.

Rabindranath Tagore The best website on Tagore is probably Visva-Bharati's www.visva-bharati.ac.in, but see also www.tagorecentre.org.uk and www.parabaas.com.

John and Nancy Todd See www.oceanarks.org.

Chogyam Trungpa See Shambhala meditation centres website at www.shambhala.org.

Desmond Tutu The Desmond Tutu Peace Foundation is at www.tutu.org.

Terry Tempest Williams See www.coyoteclan.com, a gathering place and resource for information related to the life and work of Terry Tempest Williams.

Frank Lloyd Wright The Frank Lloyd Wright Foundation is a non-profit organisation dedicated to conserving the work of Frank Lloyd Wright and advancing the principles of organic architecture: www.franklloydwright.org.

Mohammad Yunus For further information on the Microcredit Summit and Grameen Bank, write to: Results, 13 Dormer Place, Leamington Spa, Warwickshire, CV32 5AA.

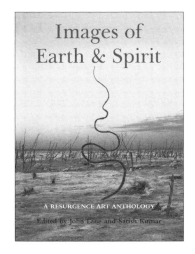
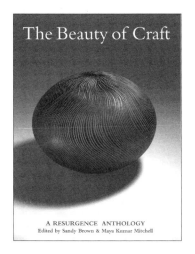

Resurgence